LONDON, REIGN OVER ME

LONDON, REIGN OVER ME

How England's Capital Built Classic Rock

Stephen Tow

ROWMAN & LITTLEFIELD
Lanham • Boulder • New York • London

Published by Rowman & Littlefield
An imprint of The Rowman & Littlefield Publishing Group, Inc.
4501 Forbes Boulevard, Suite 200, Lanham, Maryland 20706
www.rowman.com

6 Tinworth Street, London SE11 5AL

British Library Cataloguing in Publication Information Available

Library of Congress Cataloging-in-Publication Data

Name: Tow, Stephen, author.
Title: London, reign over me : how England's capital built classic rock / Stephen Tow.
Description: Lanham : Rowman & Littlefield Publishing Group, 2020. | Includes bibliographical references and index. | Summary: "London, Reign Over Me captures all of the excitement, freedom of expression, love, wild abandon, and the moment of cultural transformation that gave us classic rock. Stephen Tow draws from an array of sources, including influential London music newspapers as well as original interviews with key participants in the scene"—Provided by publisher.
Identifiers: LCCN 2019043509 (print) | LCCN 2019043510 (ebook) | ISBN 9781538127179 (cloth) | ISBN 9781538127186 (epub)
Subjects: LCSH: Rock music—England—London—1961–1970—History and criticism. | Rock musicians—England.
Classification: LCC ML3534.6.G7 T68 2020 (print) | LCC ML3534.6.G7 (ebook) | DDC 781.6609421/09046—dc23
LC record available at https://lccn.loc.gov/2019043509
LC ebook record available at https://lccn.loc.gov/2019043510

CONTENTS

FOREWORD

Bill Bruford

Those of us who stood tapping our feet to the sounds of Chris Barber and Alexis Korner at the 100 Club in London's West End in the early 1960s would surely have had no idea what was about to happen to popular music in the febrile next decade. How did we get from there to skiffle, R&B, the Blues Boom, Fairport Convention, the Floyd, and progressive rock all in such a short space of time?

From 1963—the year that, according to Professor Stephen Tow, "everything changed" and "the '60s began"—I watched and then participated in most of the developments in the London music scene. Initially I was in a safe house in Tonbridge, about 30 miles away. Occasionally my friends and I would escape and go up on the train to the Marquee Club to get a shot of R&B. When we could no longer resist, my drums and I moved into a bedsit flat at the epicentre of the explosion. The nascent British scene had several weekly music papers churning out the latest information and job offers. When you were on the front page of the *Melody Maker*, we thought, you'd made it.

Stephen argues that it is only with the benefit of hindsight that we can assess it as a particularly fruitful time for music. Musicians of any era operate within a more or less benevolent ecology. Where music appears unimportant, irrelevant, unloved, demanded for free, and the audience stays away in droves, atrophy and sclerosis descend. Where, on the other hand, there is a reasonable chance of fair payment for musical labour, freedom of thought, technological development, critical engagement, and a ready and enthusiastic audience; oh, what gems may emerge.

Such was the music ecology of London in the 1960s. We could play anything we wanted. Two gigs a week would pay for my flat and prevent starvation. The rest of the time we could practice, do our hair, and look for better gigs in *Melody Maker*—sometimes all three at once. We could appropriate the first names of American bluesmen Pink Anderson and Floyd Council for our new group, just because it sounded cool. More than people making things happen, it seemed rather as if things were happening to us, at breathtaking speed, and we'd just better be ready. I don't really remember signing a record contract; I just always had one.

Technological developments abounded, such as the advent of decent amplification, stereo recording on vinyl LPs, the appearance of "pirate" and then commercial radio. Government education policy sent a small army of creatives to art school, where they promptly became Musicians with Ideas. University and college campuses offered gigs, lots of them. You only had to fall out of bed to get one. On Monday, you joined a hardcore blues band; by Wednesday it had metamorphosed into something psychedelic, and by Saturday you were in a fully paid-up progressive rock outfit.

Alcohol played its part, as it so often has in music. The UK being less concerned with young people in bars—no ID required, unlike North America—I'd been to a lot of clubs before the age of 16, mostly trailing after Peter (later "Ginger") Baker, Jack Bruce, Graham Bond, and sometimes Johnny (later "John") McLaughlin, who played with Bruce and Baker in the Graham Bond Organisation and who I'd seen at the 100 Club, the Marquee, and elsewhere. These places were our University of Groove, where we learned to play, sweat, and hold a cigarette properly.

Stephen chronicles the changing nature of the relationship between white British acolytes and African American originators with a keen eye and a sharp ear. Reverence, awe, and paying appropriate obeisance to the real thing diminished as the British grew in confidence in their own interpretations, with a negative impact on the originators as the fans drifted away. Texan singer P. J. Proby knew the real thing, and in his view the British boys "profitably misinterpreted" the *records* of the real thing. Fifty years later, US college students wear shirts referencing the

Beatles, Floyd, and Led Zeppelin and they spend a lot of time talking about these bands. Rather than a musicological study of why they tend to find them more interesting than contemporary groups, Stephen situates them on their home turf in the beery, sweaty music scene of England more than half a century ago. His book is not gossip-oriented, nor does it get into the petty jealousies, egos, mansions, dirty managers, Bentleys, or how much coke certain rock stars did. Emphasizing instead the sheer joy of making music, of creating in a benign atmosphere of a rapidly expanding industry. The book is intended for anyone who wants to delve deeper than the typical surface rock star narrative.

Audiences were much more receptive to musical variety back then, much less programmed by genre. You could go out to a show at the Middle Earth, or wherever, in 1968 and catch the Small Faces, John Lee Hooker, the Bonzo Dog Doo-Dah Band, and Pentangle, all on the same bill. In a particularly astute observation, Stephen highlights the role of a genre called progressive folk (discussed in chapter 5), of which I knew little at the time, but from which emerged the unlikely form of Led Zeppelin. It was an age of innocence: many believed in an immutable connection between notions of integrity, quality, and record sales. "If the rest of the album is as good as this, it should be a big seller for them," said Led Zeppelin's guitarist Jimmy Page, referring to a track on the latest (1969) Fairport Convention album. That connection got lost some time after the progressives, who, while they were around, never gave way to bitterness, cynicism, or self-pity.

Stephen has seemingly extracted the views of everyone who contributed meaningfully to the scene as musician, promoter, record company person, producer, or journalist. He deftly deploys an arsenal of anecdotes to bring the reader into the heart of the music community. The focus pulls in and out, moving from small-picture close-ups of, for example, a trip to Eel Pie Island to experience the atmosphere of traditional jazz and R&B scenes, to a bigger-picture study of how we local musicians moved on from American influences to create our own uniquely British identity.

Considering the contents of the book happened mostly within a decade, it is extraordinary how active the music scene was in the short period that generated the core of what came to be known as "classic rock." This is characterised as an era more than a genre: an era that began, perhaps, with an identifiably British sound. Was that sound initially provided by Chris Barber, Alexis Korner, or the Beatles? Did the era irredeemably expire with the advent of punk, or will it struggle on until the Rolling Stones finally call it a day? These are important questions that will continue to be debated long into the night over several pints of warm beer. "Since we're half a century on now," Stephen told me, "I think we have the ability to view the '60s/early '70s era as a truly special period in music, one not likely to be repeated." As one individual with lived experience of the time, I'm not arguing with that. "My job," continued Professor Tow, "is to put London's contribution to that music in its proper place." In that, it would seem, he has undoubtedly succeeded.

INTRODUCTION

Americans. Why do we neglect our own rich musical history, notably our distinguished black artists? It took a generation of English kids, born in the rubble of World War II's aftermath, to show us what we've missed. Yet despite the best efforts of Eric Clapton, the Rolling Stones, and Led Zeppelin, most of us still don't get it.

In December 2012, Jimmy Page—along with the other surviving members of Led Zeppelin—appeared on the *Late Show with David Letterman* in New York City. During one exchange, the British-born Page recounted early influences, including legendary American bluesman Buddy Guy. "Jeff Beck and myself, we were still probably teenagers when we heard Buddy Guy," Page told Letterman. "I remember being with Jeff and playing the vinyl which was called *Folk Festival of the Blues*, where Buddy Guy's really young on it and he's playing with Muddy Waters, Sonny Boy Williamson, . . . Howlin' Wolf. But he sings two songs on it and just the whole delivery and the passion and the drama. His guitar was just out of this world."

"Now these names that you mentioned," Letterman responded. "Sonny Boy Williams?"

The 1960s ended a half century ago, but the decade remains intensely relevant. I have a 21-year-old daughter who listens to music popular among her age group: Bastille, Imagine Dragons, twenty one pilots, Coldplay, etc. But she has the Jimi Hendrix classic "Purple Haze" as her ringtone. In addition to Hendrix, she's also a big fan of Bob Dylan and Neil Young. She's exploring. She's excited about the unknown. This "old" era of music, even to her, just seems so much *better* than today's prepackaged stars.

I teach a course on rock 'n' roll history at Delaware Valley University, located near Philadelphia, where I have had a number of well-known artists chat with the students via Skype, including Jethro Tull's Ian Anderson, Yes's Steve Howe, and the Byrds' Roger McGuinn.

McGuinn gave us an impromptu performance of "Eight Miles High," while Howe serenaded us with Yes songs like "Mood for a Day" and "Clap" and threw in some Wes Montgomery and Vivaldi for good measure. The students were spellbound. Afterward, I mentioned that we had a couple of minutes left for one more question, to which one student responded, "Let's just stop here. It doesn't get any better than that."

During one of my classes, I jokingly said in my best "old man" voice that "music was so much better back then" (I don't subscribe to that theory, by the way; I think it's a total cop-out), to which a number of students replied, "But it was."

Jaded oldsters like me (I'm in my late 50s) can look back on the classic rock era and wax nostalgic. But young people's listening experience represents a new world of discovery. We now have generations (plural) that need to be exposed to this unprecedented era of musical creativity, one that will never happen again.

So where did it come from and why did it occur? That, to me, is the real story, not another book about the Rolling Stones or another overly indulgent rock star autobiography. As seems obvious now, it came from London. Well, not originally of course, but London became the incubator for the greatness of the music that began in the 1960s and spilled into the 1970s. London was the engine that drove rock music to heights never previously imagined. Because of England's capital city, the world of music profoundly and abruptly changed.

London in the 1960s needs to be placed in proper perspective. Why did a bunch of postwar British kids become obsessed with black American music and then take that inspiration to create something entirely original? Why them? Why then? Why not in America, where white baby boomers lived in a relative lap of luxury? Why in the United Kingdom, where kids played in bomb sites and grew up with food rations . . . many not tasting candy bars (aka "sweets" to Britishers) until their teenage years? Why in Britain, where the BBC would not play current music, where young people had to seek out American blues and jazz, either by listening to a faint Radio Luxembourg signal in the middle of the night or by venturing into basements of obscure London record shops to find such valued imports? The answer to these questions provides us a much fuller picture of the musical phenomenon we now call *classic rock*.

England is diverse, contradictory, and a bit eccentric. Brits are known for their stiff-upper-lip mentality, but they also embrace Monty Python. Modern British culture resulted from a disparity of traditions. As a result, Britain is a combo meal, borrowing from others to create its own wonderful cultural stew. And the music follows suit, especially rock 'n' roll.

British kids growing up after World War II were determined to find out if anything existed beyond their parents' humdrum factory lives. English baby boomers became the first generation to break out of the direct line from childhood to adulthood, to explore alternative paths of existence and expression. "Before the late '60s, no one [in Britain] would have ever talked openly about love," Emerson, Lake & Palmer's Greg Lake told me, "as being something that you should be incorporating into your everyday life, or showing to your fellow human being. Far less, looking upon it as indeed the Beatles did when they wrote the song 'All You *Need* Is Love.' And so, love was an important expression of this new awareness."

"I have a theory," Peter Frampton told me, "about why we were allowed . . . the baby boomer generation—were allowed by our parents, to do a lot more than they'd been allowed to do. Because, they were so thrilled to be alive, most of them that got home, arrived from the war. And they hadn't seen each other for so long. My parents went nearly six years without seeing each other because of the Second World War. They were so restricted when they were growing up—that when they went through a world war, and they survived, I think there was a different outlook on life and they wanted their children to experience more than they had."

Unlike their American counterparts, British boomers didn't necessarily rebel aggressively against their elders. They didn't grow their hair long, take drugs, and listen to outrageous music just to piss off their parents. For the most part, English kids understood their parents' hardships during the 1940s and realized that their elders found contentment living a quiet postwar existence free from the constant threat of the German Luftwaffe. As a result, the British youth rebellion took the form of exploration, of venturing beyond the ordinary toward a mystical world their parents could only guess at.

Initially this rebellion took the form of embracing or reinterpreting the blues. It has been said that every London band of the 1960s started as a blues cover band, and that's not terribly far off. The blues as a genre was rebellious because it was so un-English, so vital, and just plain exciting.

But here's the thing. The music got interesting when it *became* English. Around 1965, after running through the blues in their own way, British kids began to discover their own influences as well as those throughout continental Europe. After that, any rules that had previously existed were summarily broken.

In the 21st century, we talk about how things change so quickly, but it's mostly technological. Certainly there have been some significant social changes recently, but if you look at the 1960s it seems as if dramatic cultural events occurred on a monthly basis. If you had fallen asleep in London in 1962, when the city was a pretty staid town still recovering from World War II and entertained by traditional jazz bands, you wouldn't know what hit you if you woke up in 1967 and saw "Swinging London" enveloped with the colorful clothes of the Mods and Hippies and encountered wild music experiences by bands like the Pink Floyd (it was *the* Pink Floyd in those days) and the Move at a "psychedelic freak-out" show.

Let's get the elephant in the room out of the way before we go any further. This book is not about the Beatles, but none of this stuff happens without them. Hailing from Liverpool, the Beatles paved the way for everything that was to come. The London musicians I interviewed still put the Fab Four on a pedestal because, for about seven years, the Beatles led the way. So we won't neglect them in this book because, well, that would be stupid. But we will treat the Liverpool lads as a part, albeit an enormously significant one, of London's ascent during the 1960s.

By the end of the 1960s, any rules that had existed, including the requirement to have three-minute (or less) hit singles with hooks, had been obliterated. Audiences were open to almost anything. Even within London, you could go to a show at the Roundhouse Club in late 1968 and catch acts as diverse as Led Zeppelin, blues great John Lee Hooker, acoustic blues/folk combo Pentangle, and vaudeville comedy–inspired Bonzo Dog Band . . . often on the same bill!

This intense openness to *anything* allowed the artists unprecedented freedom within the studio and during live performances. Additionally, the musicianship continued to improve. Even the older generation could no longer dismiss the younger's music as childish. Drumming legend Buddy Rich complimented Yes percussionist Bill Bruford's playing in a column in London's premier weekly music newspaper *Melody Maker*. Later, Rich would become lifelong friends with Emerson, Lake & Palmer drummer Carl Palmer. Deep Purple even went so far as to give a concert of an original work backed by the London Royal Philharmonic Orchestra.

Eventually all good things come to an end (I can't tell you how much I despise that expression; it's right up there with "everything happens for a reason"), and London's dominance of music would begin to peter out around 1970. It's hard to explain why. You could just sense it. You can even feel it now when you page through the *Melody Maker* issues and notice the excitement had waned. The Beatles' breakup in April of that year elicited barely a ho-hum from the newspaper, as in "we knew this was going to happen and so what."

The end had to happen at some point, but mostly you'll enjoy the ride of the 1960s. You'll hang with the Small Faces' Ian McLagan as he goes to see his first Rolling Stones show at the Crawdaddy in 1963. You'll watch as Jimi Hendrix shows up to a Fairport Convention gig at the Speakeasy and ends up jamming with Fairport's virtuoso guitarist Richard Thompson. You'll hang with Who drummer Keith Moon, described by one of my interviewees as "certifiable," and experience the craziness.

When you're done with this book, you will appreciate what a magical time it was to be in London in the 1960s, a time when anything could happen. And it did. As Roger Daltrey put it in his recent autobiography, *Thanks a Lot Mr Kibblewhite*, "So much had been destroyed, there was only one thing that could happen. To build. We were a generation of builders." And he was right.

I

OUT OF THE GRAY AND INTO THE BLUES

"We're educators in that respect. We try and spread the word. Fortunately, people respond to it and they go exploring on their own. I hear from people all the time saying that they started off with me, and then they found out where it all came from. So, in that way, we're doing our job."—John Mayall, of John Mayall's Bluesbreakers

While John Mayall had a lot to do with creating and nurturing British blues, it didn't start with him. All of what became known as "classic rock" began with a low-key jazz trombonist named Chris Barber. Who?

Ask anyone with at least a cursory knowledge about the origins of British blues, and they will likely mention the Rolling Stones. If they're more in the know, they might offer up Mayall, who at times featured superstar guitarists Eric Clapton and Peter Green in his band. Experts on the subject typically trot out Alexis Korner as the father of British blues. But they are only partially correct. Korner certainly had a major hand in getting the English R&B scene going in the 1960s. Nevertheless, Korner really didn't get his start without Chris Barber; in fact, none of it would have really happened—not Korner, Mayall, the Stones, Yardbirds, Animals, or Led Zeppelin for that matter—without Mr. Barber.

Born in 1930, Barber spent his early teens huddling under German bombing raids. During those formative years, he heard some classical music around the house. Then one day, while fiddling with his father's radio, he picked up the US Armed Forces Network and began to listen to American jazz records for the first time. The vibrancy, the soul, and the excitement of it was like something he had never heard before. BBC Radio's musical palette consisted mainly of show tunes and light classical. This was something different, however. This was exciting, and of course, it was black.

Barber attended school a few miles away from an American air base, and he and his friends would sometimes bike over to check out the B-17s coming and going on bombing raids. They would typically lie in a ditch a few yards from the runway, and returning aircraft would pass only a few yards above their heads. Periodically, they would check the dumpster at the PX for interesting things the soldiers threw away. Once, as Barber was rummaging through the trash, he discovered a book that would change his life, and by extension, his country's: *Really the Blues* by an American Jewish immigrant named Milton "Mezz" Mezzrow. The book celebrated jazz and blues and set Barber upon a career as a jazz musician. At first, though, with his father's encouragement, he began to learn classical violin.

With London as a main target of the German Luftwaffe, Barber's school evacuated to a farm near Cambridge. He continued with his violin lessons, taking the bus from the farm into the college town. But the ride became boring, so he decided to save the bus fare and bike into town. "So I kept the [money] and rode my bicycle," Barber recalled, "and had my violin case in one hand, holding the handle bars of the bike with the other hand [while] holding the back of a truck. So I was getting taken in 30 miles an hour to Cambridge."

After arriving in town, Barber would find himself with time to kill before lessons, and he wandered into a music shop, looking for jazz records. "I thought, maybe they got some jazz records here," he remembered. "And [I] asked them. 'No idea,' [the shopkeeper responded]. 'Don't know. You'd better come around the back of the counter and have a look.' So I did. Normally, you don't get offers like that in shops. And there indeed I found records. They in fact [had] some jazz records in stock [so] I saved my . . . bus fare each week going to my lesson, and the [money] bought [jazz] record[s]."

Classical violin never really had staying power with Barber, and eventually a friend offered to sell him a trombone; he proceeded to teach himself the instrument, an instrument that would become his lifelong passion. In 1949, at age 19, he formed his first amateur jazz band. He was soon joined by a young guitar player named Alexis Korner.

Korner, then in his early 20s, became Britain's early proponent of the blues. While Barber believed jazz and blues came from the same place, Korner became a passionate advocate of the blues. Never a virtuoso player, Korner played what Barber describes as sort of an accompanying style of guitar, kind of a cross between a traditional lead and rhythm. Within a couple of years, Korner would leave Barber's band to pursue his blues passion, which Barber believed was kind of fruitless at the time. Korner would reemerge a little over a decade later, creating Blues Incorporated, which would feature Charlie Watts and Brian Jones (both later with the Rolling Stones), as well as Ginger Baker and Jack Bruce, who would eventually play with Eric Clapton in Cream.

Meanwhile, another prominent musician who would become a member of Barber's band, trumpeter Ken Colyer, felt the need to connect with the roots of jazz and made a pilgrimage to New Orleans. In 1952, lacking the funds to make a proper trip, Colyer signed on as a cook with the merchant navy and sailed toward Mobile, Alabama, then jumped ship and headed to New Orleans with little on hand but his trumpet. Colyer played with black jazzmen in that city in an age of segregation, eventually facing jail time for his undocumented status. He got deported back to England in 1953 and, given his mythical trip to the Mecca of jazz and his reputation as a good player, joined up with Barber's band on his return. By that time, Barber had turned professional, determined to make a go of it as a full-time jazz musician. Colyer seemed like the perfect fit and was initially given the opportunity to lead the band, calling themselves Ken Colyer's Jazzmen. Shortly thereafter, a young banjo player named Tony Donegan, who went by the stage name Lonnie Donegan, joined up.

Donegan's addition opened up a new dynamic within Barber's band. Influenced by early 20th-century American washboard music, the group would switch things up mid-set, going to an all-acoustic format. With Donegan on guitar and lead vocals, Colyer also on guitar, and Barber on stand-up bass, the band would begin to popularize a new style of music in Britain. Dubbed "skiffle," the music drew its name from a 1929 American record called *Hometown Skiffle*. "It's kind of a word which lends itself to the meaning somehow," said Barber. "It's kind of loose, easygoing, sort of amateurish but jolly washboard band type stuff."

Despite his abilities and impeccable credentials, Colyer the person presented quite a challenge, and soon tensions arose among Colyer, Donegan, and Barber. "He was a bit difficult to deal with," Barber recalled, "a very inarticulate person. Anybody who used a word longer than two syllables—he was suspicious." Personality differences became irreconcilable, and Colyer was forced out; Colyer then formed his own version of the Jazzmen. In the meantime, the new group sans Colyer became known as Chris Barber's Jazz Band.

In 1954, with Donegan in tow, the Barber band recorded British skiffle's signature tune: a cover of Leadbelly's "Rock Island Line" for Decca Records. Originally issued as a track on a 10-inch album, requests for the song began to explode. The label, not one to be at the forefront of popular music (later, Decca would become notorious for

Chris Barber's Jazz Band with Lonnie Donegan on banjo, 1953. Barber is at the far right. *Pictorial Press Ltd. / Alamy stock photo.*

turning down the Beatles), finally released the track as a single more than a year later. The record not only made stars of the Barber band but also turned Donegan into a national sensation. Even more significant, it created the British skiffle craze, providing a platform for an entire generation to make music.

Skiffle had an enormous impact on young people throughout the country, particularly among the least fortunate. Kids all over Britain took to the music immediately when "Rock Island Line" became a hit. Instantly, you could start your own band; you didn't need years of expensive musical training. For that matter, you needn't worry about purchasing pricey instruments. Just get a singer, a cheap secondhand acoustic guitar or banjo, a washboard for percussion (washing machines were anomalies in England then), along with your mom's sewing machine thimble to run along the grooves. For bass, English kids quickly figured out how to make one out of old home furniture. And, voila! You had a skiffle band. "The thing is with skiffle music: you could make your own instruments," said the Yardbirds' Top Topham. "Like, I had a washboard and you made a tea chest bass, if you know what that is. It's a broom pole, stuck in a tea chest . . . with a string [attached]. You actually pulled the stick back and forward and you can play a whole scale. And of course, people did. That's where I started, really."

"It could be played on homemade instruments," added the Animals' Hilton Valentine. "This was like tea chest bass, washboard, spoons, corn paper. In poorer areas, this was great for kids because they could get their hands on these things without a lot of money being spent. And it was really acoustic type of music, so there wasn't any cost on amplifiers and electric guitars and pickups and things like that. I think that's why it was very popular at the time. Plus, you know, you could stand there up in front of the railway yard, [playing] acoustic guitar and [wearing] a plastic leather jacket, and sing 'Cumberland Gap' [and] 'Rock Island Line.'"

Skiffle, for English postwar children, represented something. It was a doorway into another world. It was exciting. It was cool. But, most of all, it was fun. That's how it was for a young Roger Glover, who would later play bass for Deep Purple. He lived above a pub his parents owned in London's Earl's Court neighborhood. "I remember in bed one night hearing some music coming from the bar downstairs," Glover recalled. "And I crept down in my pajamas and opened the door leading from the private part to the pub itself. And there was a skiffle band playing. And I was just blown away with the boisterousness of it, the freedom of it—four or five guitarists or banjo players all banging away. Percussion was a washboard. And hootin' and hollerin.' And it was kind of rowdy, lovely kind of music—happy—and had so much energy, that it put all the music that I'd been listening [to] on the [BBC] to shame."

So many musicians who later became famous started out in skiffle groups, including members of the Beatles and Led Zeppelin. "I remember going to see Jimmy Page when he was 12 years old playing in a local [hall] in Tolworth," recalled *New Musical Express* features editor Keith Altham. "And I was in a skiffle group in school, like most of the other kids. And I saw Jimmy Page play at the age of 12 and I went home, put my guitar back under the stairs and never took it out again. . . . I told Jimmy that story [later]. He thought it was very funny."

For most, though, the excitement of skiffle became a passing fad . . . one that led to other avenues. Some would take the washboard-based music and move toward an English folk direction. For many, though, skiffle's coloring of their gray worlds led them to the blues.

While Donegan earned credit for inspiring a generation of young Brits to make music, a young lady named Hylda Sims had been playing skiffle in her group, the City Ramblers, prior to the "Rock Island Line" phenomenon. In 1955, Sims and her boyfriend Russell Quay began busking outside Waterloo Station. Then in early 1956, the Ramblers embarked on a trip to continental Europe, along with friend and American folk/blues singer Ramblin' Jack Elliott. "When we went on tour to [continental] Europe," Sims remembered, "Jack came with us— and he was with us in the first phase of that tour. And then we got back in '57, and skiffle [was huge]."

"We were touring in an old Canadian-built war ambulance—army ambulance," Elliott recalled. "Had only one seat in it—the driver's seat. Everybody else just sat on the floor, or on suitcases, or rolled-up sleeping bags."

Inspired by the new skiffle craze, Sims and Quay opened a club called the Skiffle Cellar in Soho in spring 1957. "We got back from our touring and skiffle had 'arrived' as it were," said Sims. "So Russell had this idea that we should open a club. So we found this premises in Soho and we opened it."

The Skiffle Cellar would host skiffle and folk acts, and it would become one of London's early preeminent folk venues. A few years later, the space would give way to Les Cousins, London's premier folk club. (More about that in chapter 3.)

Meanwhile, for Chris Barber, there was no real distinction between jazz and the blues. For him, the soul of both genres remained the same: African American music originating in southern United States. He played with Big Bill Broonzy as early as 1954. By 1955, his band had incorporated a strong blues singer, a Latvian/Irish woman named Ottilie Patterson. As a result of the new addition, the Barber band began to include blues numbers in its set. As with skiffle, it was a very natural progression for the musicians.

In 1957 and 1958, Barber decided to take it a step further and arranged to have American blues legends come to Britain. He connected with singer/guitarist Sister Rosetta Tharpe, the harmonica/guitar team of Sonny Terry and Brownie McGhee, and John Lewis and his Modern Jazz Quartet. Lewis, who became a close friend of Barber's, suggested bringing over Muddy Waters, the man responsible for creating Chicago electric blues. "'I wouldn't know how to find him,'" Barber recalled saying to Lewis. "Muddy Waters was like an obscure, weird name out in the backwoods somewhere. I thought, 'You send a postcard to the first cotton bush on the right on a southern plantation.' And John said to me, 'Don't be silly. He has a Cadillac and an agent.'"

So Barber brought over Waters, and the reaction was immediate. Some fans were a bit shocked by the addition of Waters's electric guitar, but for most young folks, the "real thing" had an enormous impact upon them. "The weird thing was," Barber remembered, "we had write-ups in the papers saying [he played too loud]—Muddy Waters was the quietest electric guitar player I ever heard play. He never played loud."

Future Rock & Roll Hall of Famer Tharpe had an indelible impact upon the audiences, dazzling the crowd with her Les Paul guitar and puzzling some with her penchant for unusual tuning. "She played her guitar like steel guitar players do: tuned to a major chord," said Barber. "But she tuned to a major chord of C. Now, all the blues players who did steel guitar playing—they tune it to E. . . . I remember, every song she sang—the end of the song, the guitar was hanging around her neck. And she played one chord on the guitar, with her hands off it, like that, throwing her arms up in the air. This lovely chord of C major's coming out. People would say to me, '[She's] cheating. She's got a tape recorder there. You can't do that with a guitar!'"

Waters and Tharpe's electric music caused shockwaves among British blues and skiffle fans. In particular, it motivated guitarist Alexis Korner and harmonica (called a *harp* by blues purists) player Cyril Davies[1] to change musical directions. Davies had been running the London Skiffle Club at a pub called the Roundhouse and, along with Korner, decided to move to an electric blues format. In 1957, they closed down and reopened the venue as the London Blues and Barrelhouse Club. Muddy Waters, Sonny Terry, Brownie McGhee, Roosevelt Sykes, Champion Jack Dupree, Memphis Slim, and others gigged at the new club and taught Korner and Davies how to play the blues.

"Somebody told me about that place," said Ramblin' Jack Elliott, who gigged there frequently. "Oh gosh, very early on in our first or second week of our being in London. And someone said, 'You gotta go to the Blues and Barrelhouse Club,' which is upstairs in the Cherrington's Round House Pub at Wardour Street, right across the street from the Windmill Theatre, where they had the only nude woman in England, onstage. But it was against the law for her to move. She had to remain stock-still like a statue, and then it was legal. Then people could pretend it was only a painting or something. But it was a real-live naked lady onstage and I never got to see it because we were so busy with our friends and fans at that Cherrington's Round House Pub, I couldn't get out of there and go across the street."

Wizz Jones, a beatnik turned folk artist, also has a deep connection to the blues. His freewheeling spirit and willingness to play anywhere inspired many a British musician, most notably the Rolling Stones' Keith Richards. Jones regularly attended shows at the Round House. "I saw everybody there," Jones remembered. "I mean, it was such a tiny room—about 20, 30, 40, maybe, at the most, people. And it was all very underground. . . . And I used to go there every week. One week I saw Big Bill Broonzy there. And then a few weeks later—maybe a few months later—I saw Muddy Waters there with his piano player Otis Spann. . . . And I remember, I went up to Muddy Waters, and I asked him—he had a big steel sleeve on his finger, using it as a slide—I asked him, 'What's that you've got on your finger?' And he said, 'That, boy, is a gudgeon pin.' And I didn't know what he was talking about. I had no idea—didn't know anything about cars. And it wasn't until years later,

Sister Rosetta Tharpe, London, 1957. *Keystone Press Agency / Keystone USA via zumapress.com.*

when I was working on an old car. I was taking the pistons off the con rods, I saw—in the manual—'remove the piston by tapping out the gudgeon pin.' It was metal sleeve—a big, heavy, steel/metal sleeve that holds the piston onto the con rod. I thought, 'Oh, that's what a gudgeon pin is.' So obviously Muddy was a keen motor engineer as well."

EEL PIE ISLAND

Aside from the Blues and Barrelhouse Club, an even more iconic venue came to being in West London, in the town of Twickenham.[2] The Eel Pie Island Club in some ways birthed what we now call classic rock.

Say you find yourself in London after a long flight from America. You're exhausted because you haven't had a wink of sleep with your seatmate elbowing you, some ill-timed coughs, and the jolting sound of overhead bins being slammed shut. So upon arrival, you decide to take the overland train from Central London west to Twickenham, around a half hour ride. You heard it was a charming place with nice pubs. You disembark, wander through the town, and decide to take a walk along the Thames. You make your way down to the river, enjoying the cool weather, relishing the fact that you're no longer sitting on a crowded airplane.

As you stroll along, you notice a footbridge to your left, which connects Twickenham to what appears to be a small island. You ask a passerby, "What's on the other side of that bridge?" "That's Eel Pie Island," the local says. "Hmmm," you think to yourself, "that sounds interesting and very English. Let's cross over and have a look-see." So you wander over, and as you approach the other side, you notice a bulletin board that says "Eel Pie Island Association" at the top, with some announcements for goings-on around the island. You proceed on, walking along a path winding its way through some lovely greenery, with attractive homes on either side. Nice, but unremarkable. You say hello to a woman as she takes out her garbage. "That was quite pleasant," you think to yourself. "I suppose I'll head back to London now and see if I can manage to keep myself awake for the next five hours."

As you catch the train back to the city, you have no idea that you just stumbled across a significant piece of rock music history. Fifty years ago, at the site of that woman's home, there was a hotel that housed a club. Within that club, much of England's musical legacy was created.

For British teenagers growing up in the aftermath of World War II, the Eel Pie Island Club was more than just a Saturday night hangout. It was an oasis from the grim reality of postwar life. During the venue's heyday in the late 1950s and early 1960s, young music fans would make their way down to Twickenham and head across the river to the island. Up until 1957, when a small footbridge was constructed, you had to find creative ways to cross the Thames. Some folks swam over, while others paid for a boat ride. "There used to be a chain barge—you pulled on the chain and the barge went over," remembered Ray Everitt, then a young music fan. "And it cost a few pennies. [Since] I didn't swim, I used to take [my friends'] clothes over and thereby they didn't have to pay for the barge, which was probably a couple of beers in those days. I'd stand on the other side and run away with the clothes and then look at all the young girls [emerging from the bank] naked, or in their knickers."

The footbridge represented an improvement over the barge, but it still created some logistical issues for the musicians. "Yeah, [it was] a little wooden rickety bridge," recalled the Animals' John Steel. "You had to carry all your equipment across this bloody water. It was hardly more than a plank. . . . We had to carry everything: the drum kit, the amps, and keyboards, and everything across there."

"You couldn't get the van over there to unload," added fellow Animal Hilton Valentine, "you had to put [your equipment] on trolleys, then push it over this footbridge, and set up. And do the same [thing] coming back."

As patrons crossed over the river, they would notice that dress was casual, in contrast to the formal wardrobe their parents forced upon them. Eel Pie Island was not a place where people dressed to the nines, as a young fan named David Snelling would quickly find out. "Walking by the riverside [on one occasion], coming up to the bridge, there were five guys going over [it]," Snelling recalled. "Never seen anything like it. They looked like something out of the Stone Age, perhaps . . . because they were the Rolling Stones."

> And let me tell you what I was wearing. I was wearing a Tyrolean hat—green felt, with little cow bells stuck all over it . . . a white shirt, a striped tie with horizontal stripes, a two-piece suit from Bentalls in Kingston, with a tiny checked pattern and suede brogues. And I thought I was really cool. And then I saw these five guys on the bridge—something snapped inside. [I thought], "Snelling, what are you doing? You'll never pull a chick like this"—as had proved to be

the case. So after that, I abandoned the sense of trim haircut and
stripy tie . . . and moved into the casual, comfortable look.

The casual, comfortable look extended to the relationship between the
musicians and fans. Unlike later, when bands like the Stones became
international superstars, fans could chat it up before or after sets with
the players. Frequent club attendee Mike Murphy recalled such a conversation he had with Keith Richards about whether Chuck Berry constituted R&B or rock 'n' roll. "I always regarded Chuck Berry as a rock
and roller. And I was having this discussion with Keith," said Murphy,
"and he said, 'Well, yeah, but what about a song like 'Wee Wee Hours,'
which is one of Chuck Berry's blues songs. My argument was it wasn't
really so typical of Chuck Berry. . . . These kind[s] of conversations at
the time were really important. And of course, in those days, the Stones
really hadn't gone into orbit, so they were quite accessible."

Through word of mouth, kids began to discover this hidden gem
amid the gloom of postwar England. The older generation viewed Eel
Pie Island as a den of iniquity, and many parents forbade their children
from going, which of course meant they had to check it out. Music fans
would make their way across the bridge and pay a small sum to a little
old woman collecting fees in a sort of sentry box. "We would get ready
to go to the island—all week," recalled Jan Roberts, another regular
visitor. "At school, we'd be practicing our moves, and practicing our
dance routine. And on Saturday, I'd meet my mate Bev, and we would
walk down towards Richmond and then get the bus to Twickenham. . . .
We'd go over the bridge onto the island. And we loved paying our
money to that—I remember, a little wizened old lady, with cut-off
gloves where her fingers poked out the end [and she would greet us
with] 'Hello, dearie,' and she'd stamp your wrist."

"And you'd give [her] four pence," Snelling added, "and [she would
say], 'Thank you very much, dearie.' . . . And then you'd see this hotel,
like something out of Tennessee Williams, broken down catwalk to the
place, right by the river. The smell of mud, and river water, and sweat
and beer—all sorts of exotic smells come wafting from it. And you can
hear music [in the distance]."

After arriving on the island, patrons would pass some odd bungalows
as they made their way to the hotel. They would be careful to step over
folks camping out, maybe catching a hint of marijuana as they traversed

the island. The hotel itself was once a grand building, but by the 1950s it had begun to crumble. As music fans began to wander inside, they'd notice the facility had seen better days, with peeling paint and holes in the ceiling. Patrons paid a small fee to enter the club and then walked into the large main room, with pillars on either side providing a border to narrow alcoves. On the left, they'd see young men and women conversing. On the right was the bar, where customers would have to navigate through a kind of rugby scrum to purchase bottles of the obligatory Newcastle Amber. Fans could now make out the band members playing on the opposite end of the main room with a mass of dancers reveling directly in front of them. "And that [dance] floor," said Roberts, "it was a spring-loaded floor—you could absolutely fly. . . . Going into the pub, and getting your beer, there [were] footprints all over the ceiling. I thought, 'This is really weird.'"

"The bands' dressing room, meanwhile, was a strange kind of hutch, or doll's house, suspended above the stage," wrote Rod Stewart, a frequent visitor and performer, in his autobiography *Rod*, "with little curtained windows through which the performers could look down on the audience. The stage was accessed via a narrow staircase in the corner. Many were the singers who attempted a dramatic entrance down those steps and finished on their arse in the audience."

"That's where I first saw [Rod Stewart], funny enough," said the Small Faces' Ian McLagan. "And the two of us were dating the same girl at around the same time—years later, we discovered, because of a particular item she had in her brassier: a safety pin holding it together. [Laughs.] Anyway, I didn't get any, and he didn't get any. I spent all night trying to undo that damn thing."

Once the music started, the crowd was treated to an unprecedented array of mostly local talent including the Rolling Stones; the Yardbirds (with Eric Clapton); Rod Stewart (then known as "Rod the Mod"); David Bowie (then David Jones); the Tridents (with Jeff Beck); British blues and jazz pioneers like Alexis Korner, Cyril Davies, Long John Baldry, Graham Bond, John Mayall, Chris Barber, and Ken Colyer; and American blues legends Howlin' Wolf, Champion Jack Dupree, John Lee Hooker, Memphis Slim, and Buddy Guy.

"I saw Memphis Slim there," McLagan remembered. "I saw Graham Bond and his band, Georgie Fame there, Art Wood—Ronnie Wood's

[Rolling Stones] brother's band. I saw every band there including the Stones. And I booked the Stones there for an art school dance—twice.

"[Cyril Davies had] a great band. [They were] like Muddy Waters and his band had descended into West London. Because Cyril Davies played like Little Walter—he was a good harp [harmonica] player—[although] nobody's as good as Little Walter. And the band would just—Nicky Hopkins was playing [like] Otis Spann, like nobody else could. Cyril didn't have much of a voice. But halfway through the show, his other singer, Long John Baldry—he was six foot seven—would come up onstage. Cyril would take a break, go to the bar, and Baldry would sing for half a dozen songs with three voluptuous African or West Indian women with big tits, called the Velvettes."

The bohemian atmosphere, the forbidden fruit, the musical excitement . . . all of that combined to make Eel Pie Island not only a respite from grim postwar life but also a doorway into another world, a world of brilliant color, a highway to a land of endless possibility.

And life in postwar England could indeed be grim. Britain, with the help of its American and Soviet allies, had technically won the war, but it had suffered greatly. Much of the destruction came from the relentless bombing by the German Luftwaffe. "I can remember one time. . . . I was a little toddler [during the war]," recalled the Animals' John Steel, who was born in 1941. "My mother was standing, ironing clothes on an ironing board and the air raid siren went off. And she just carried on ironing and she told me to go under the table, the dining table."

Spencer Davis, who later formed the Spencer Davis Group, grew up in Swansea, Wales, which, like London, was a major target of German bombing. He recalled witnessing the action as a small child. "I was looking at the pretty lights," said Davis, "i.e., the flares that were being dropped by the Luftwaffe before they demolished the City Centre of Swansea. My mother ran from behind me and grabbed me—I'm five years old and I'm watching a city being demolished.

"Both of our houses were bombed. But each time we managed not to be there. [In one instance,] a bomb went down the chimney. Finished that house off."

Mike Cotton, who later formed the Mike Cotton Sound, was a small child during the Nazi blitz of 1940–1941. "I remember being wheeled by one of my uncles, who was in the navy on leave, wheeling me down the road and we had to make a rush for it because the sirens all went—

the warning siren. And you'd dive for the nearest cover. And I couldn't have been more than 18 months old when that happened. But I can remember it as plain as day," Cotton recalled.

Arthur Brown, who later invented shock rock with the Crazy World of Arthur Brown, recalled surviving a bombing in his hometown of Whitby, Yorkshire: "My grandma's hotel, which overlooked the bay in Whitby, was reduced—by bombing—reduced to dust. And we were pronounced dead in the newspaper—the *Whitby Gazette*. So we've already risen from the dead."

German attacks during the war left England, particularly the London area, littered with gaping holes in the landscape for years to come. "We used to go and play on a bombsite," the Yardbirds' Jim McCarty recalled. "We were surrounded by bombsites that were created by the war. And there was one just up the road. We used to go down and play, maybe play tennis, or chuck a ball against the wall or something. And it was actually an old pub that—I heard the story—it got wiped out one night. It was full. It was a Saturday night. It was full of people and it was bombed—direct hit and everyone was killed.

"A site like that would be a whole block. And there'd be some remnants of what was there—some buildings. The rest of it would all be grown over with bushes and flowers and things."

"Where I lived, which was above my grandfather's shop in Hayes, in Middlesex," said fellow Yardbird Top Topham, "a V-2—which was a [German] rocket—had actually landed in the back garden. . . . The crater, you could stand two trolley buses in it—those big, red London buses. I mean, it was pretty frightening stuff, actually."

London in the 21st century is a sparkling, high-priced, clean, bustling metropolis. But after the Second World War, besides consisting of rubble amid bomb craters, the city was gritty and filthy. Coal fires, mostly from home heating during the colder months, drenched England's capital in an impenetrable, fog-like smoke. "I remember," said McCarty, "quite often the school would be closed because there was a fog—and they were real thick fogs—you couldn't see. It was like one of those Jekyll and Hyde movies. [Later] I remember driving my car in it—in the fog—going about two miles an hour 'cause you just couldn't see anything."

"The smell—everything was black," recalled Ian McLagan. "I remember walking through a section of the West End—walked down this terrible street. We were looking for a bus. And all the buildings were so black from smoke. It got in your lungs. It got in your clothes . . . the Houses of Parliament were black. And they found that actually it was beautiful pink stone underneath all that crap."

"We lived in a semi-detached [*duplex* in America] house which had no electricity upstairs and no heating," Yes's Rick Wakeman wrote me, "except [for] a small coal fire downstairs. It was freezing in the winter. . . . I can remember breaking the ice off of the window in my bedroom—on the inside!"

"[My parents and I] used to sit and have Sunday lunch together," said Snelling. "I can still remember one Sunday lunch. A bottle of homemade bourbon on the table, made with elderberries. Outside, thick smog, with the smell of soot in the air. And a miserable little piece of roast beef, with some mushy vegetables."

THE BLUES

Much more than jazz, the blues touched an entire generation of postwar English kids. The Brits called it "R&B," or rhythm & blues, but we in the United States refer to it as just "blues." That is, those of us who know about it.

Ask a group of Americans if they've heard of the Rolling Stones, Led Zeppelin, or Eric Clapton, and 99 out of 100 hands will go up. But ask them about Muddy Waters, Sister Rosetta Tharpe, Sonny Terry, Brownie McGhee, Sonny Boy Williamson, Big Bill Broonzy, Otis Spann, and you'll be greeted with mostly blank stares. And that is unfortunate, because none of the stuff that England made famous would have happened without these folks and many other African American legends.

But the British kids did know about them.

Even though American teenagers had access to commercial radio, that outlet, like much of the South, remained segregated. In other words, white people were fed white music by white artists, and black people heard black music played on African American stations. In England, though, because of a lack of music radio (other than the staid BBC), kids so inclined had no barriers to discover music they fancied.

Further, black American musicians coming to the United Kingdom found they were treated with reverence, for the most part. Paradoxically, that made some of them feel uncomfortable . . . playing in front of white folks celebrating their art. That just didn't happen back home. African American blues legends even found themselves guests at British households. For some, it was the first time they ever had a meal with a white person. The Yardbirds' Top Topham noticed this phenomenon when he went to a blues festival in the early 1960s. "You had Muddy Waters, Big Joe Williams, Willie Dixon, Otis Spann, Matt Murphy, Victoria Spivey, Lonnie Johnson, Sonny Boy Williamson," he recalled. "I mean, that's just a few of them. But actually, I stood [close to] those guys and watched them play when I was 15. I mean, you could tell by the way like Big Joe Williams was dressed—they had no money. You could see they were very poor. I mean, we were poor as well. I mean I was as poor as them, actually. But you could see that the fact they were so close to white people was something very strange for them. Very strange, indeed. They were nervous. You could see it."

"[British audiences] certainly did have a great deal of respect and admiration for the [black] musicians," added Ramblin' Jack Elliott, an American guitar player who played with and socialized with greats like Big Bill Broonzy and Muddy Waters.

There was just something about the blues that fired up these young people growing up in London proper, in its suburbs, in Manchester, in Liverpool, in Newcastle, in St. Albans, in Portsmouth . . . in all of England. But what was driving that? Although they led a rather austere life prior to the 1960s, British kids certainly didn't experience the extreme poverty and racial hatred that fueled the artistry of the blues. What then?

"I have always had a theory about [World War II] and its effect on our generation and music," the Moody Blues' Mike Pinder wrote me. "I think the reason we were attracted to the American blues and soul music was that, like black musicians, our generation had experienced war and the deprivation that war brings. We understood the basis for the blues and identified with it. . . . For the youth of America, it was a long way off. For the youth of Britain, it was at our doorstep."

"I think it was exciting," added the Yardbirds' McCarty. "It was an exciting sort of music. It was emotive music . . . it was like something we never really heard before."

"Well, my own opinion was the fact we had no heritage in music from the heart, from the soul . . . you had no music that moved you," said Topham. "I mean, the first time I put on 'Smokestack Lightnin'' by Howlin' Wolf—it changed my life, I think, 'cause it was hypnotic, magically hypnotic, somehow."

"I have a friend who had a couple of Jimmy Reed records," recalled the Small Faces' McLagan. "I bought [a] Muddy Waters record, and like-minded people just sort of clung together and—the next thing you know I'm actually watching Muddy Waters play live, with Otis Spann on piano, Freddie Below, and Willie Dixon, Matt Guitar Murphy. And I'm thinking, 'My whole life just changed.' Well, I mean there was nothing, nothing like that in England, or in Europe."

The Animals' John Steel recalled his first exposure to live American blues in the early 1960s. Steel and fellow Animal Eric Burdon decided to make the trek from their hometown of Newcastle, near the Scottish border, to see blues legends play in Manchester. "Eric and me and a couple of other guys—it was called the American Blues/Folk Tour, I think it was. The nearest it came to Newcastle was Manchester, Manchester Free Trade Hall. . . . And that was Sonny Terry, Brownie McGhee. Willie Dixon, with his trio, was the sort of the tour house band, if you like. And [Dixon's band had] a guy called Shakey Jake [who] played harmonica [and] T. Bone Walker—I mean, friggin' hell, that was the first time we really saw electric blues giants [and] it was basically the Chess [Records] house band. And Eric and me and two other guys persuaded a friend who had a car—this was a big rarity in those days. So all five of us jammed into this tiny-little four-seater car and drove to Manchester. Took about five hours."

And, as with skiffle, standard 12-bar blues was easy to play. "Blues, part of the reason it appealed to so many British and European musicians was it was a simple framework," said Jethro Tull's Ian Anderson, "to absorb, and to use as a jumping off ground to play more complex music. So, it became a simple framework that allowed the beginnings of improvisation. It was repetitive, so if you didn't get it [right] in the first verse, you could try again in the second."

"It's the magic of the form," added Bill Bruford, virtuoso drummer for Yes and King Crimson. "The form is really great. It's really simple. If you don't know what a 12-bar blues—Do you play an instrument?" he asks me. "I play guitar," I respond. "So you know what a 12-bar blues is.

And if you didn't, I could tell you by the time you left here. It's that simple. Every time you want to play a song together with some unknown people, you play blues. It's easy."

The ease, the excitement, the power, and sheer exuberance of the blues fired up an entire generation. The music's authenticity and raw sensuality began to provide color to an otherwise gray world. That being said, British baby boomers view their formative years from much a different lens than their American counterparts.

In contrast to postwar England, the United States basked in the glow of its newfound superpower status. In the years following World War II, America enjoyed an economic and military dominance it would never achieve again. Returning veterans, buoyed by the passage of the GI Bill, went to college for free. Millions of Americans had access to higher education for the first time. President Franklin Roosevelt's landmark legislation helped create a modern, affluent middle class . . . well, at least a white middle class.

By the 1950s, flush with high-paying, secure jobs, white America fled the urban centers, venturing to these new things called "suburbs." Having themselves grown up during the Great Depression, World War II veterans were determined to give their children everything they didn't have, and now they had the means to do so. Furthermore, encouraged by child-rearing guru Benjamin Spock, American baby boomers were being taught to challenge their parents. Unfortunately for the older generation, though, their kids took them up on it. By the 1960s, US boomers began to purposely offend their elders at every turn . . . in the way they wore their hair, in their open sexuality and drug use, and certainly in their choice of music. By that decade, the rebellion known as the Generation Gap came into its own, with the baby boomer mantra "the more offensive, the better."

For their English counterparts, the rebellion against their parents took on a much more subdued tone. Unlike the Americans, they grew up in a comparatively poor country that rationed food well into the 1950s. In fact, you couldn't even get your hands on candy (or "sweets" as the British refer to it) until 1953. They played in bombsites and inhaled the smoke from coal fires. They watched their parents struggle to eke out a meager living. Yet, despite all that, British kids did not have a burning desire to "stick it" to their elders. For many, even those who later became quite wealthy, they don't recall those times as borne from suffering. Some, in fact, remember their youth quite fondly. "We used to go and get fish and chips every Friday, miles from [where I lived]. So we had a kind of—I'd think of it as quite idyllic," Yes guitarist Steve Howe remembered.

"All in all, I wouldn't have changed my childhood for anything else," Yes keyboard player Rick Wakeman wrote me. "I never felt deprived. There was always food on the table. I had clean clothes and we had our fortnight's [two-week] holiday in Devon every year. We did day trips for picnics, Dad took me to football [soccer] matches, and, as there were no computers, we made our own entertainment. How great was that? We actually had it good—us kids back then."

Furthermore, British kids had to go much further than their American counterparts to obtain their cherished music. Unlike in the United States, where commercial radio proliferated, the United Kingdom had no such outlets over the airwaves. The BBC would not play blues or rock 'n' roll, only what many term *safe* elevator music for the middle classes. So, if you wanted to hear the music you liked, your choices were limited. You had Radio Luxembourg, which on occasion would play jazz and blues. Unfortunately, reception was so bad that often you could only tune in to the station in the middle of the night. "We listened to Radio Luxembourg a lot," said the Zombies' Rod Argent. "And the thing was—because it was on AM, the signal just was fading in and out all the time. . . . And because you were listening to it at night, it had this sort of romantic, magical quality to it."

"Radio Luxembourg was notoriously difficult to keep on station," Keith Richards wrote in his autobiography *Life*. "I had a little aerial and walked around the room, holding the radio up to my ear and twisting the aerial. Trying to keep it down because I'd wake Mum and Dad up. If I could get the signal right, I could take the radio under the blankets."

Other than Radio Luxembourg's limited reception and quality, the other option was to obtain the records themselves . . . and that was no easy task. Blues and rock 'n' roll records would filter in from port cities such as Liverpool and make their way to select London record shops. Those in the know figured out where and how to get this exotic music, and by the late 1950s, young people in and around London began to coalesce around this secretive blues society.

This musical exploration, borne out of necessity, also opened up some doors not available to white American baby boomers. In America, white kids heard white stars such as Elvis, Bill Haley, Jerry Lee Lewis, and Eddie Cochran . . . and a handful of black artists like Little Richard and Chuck Berry, but that was about it. The 1950s—the golden age of Chicago blues, which generated some of the best music made by Muddy Waters, Willie Dixon, Elmore James, Sonny Boy Williamson, Howlin' Wolf, and many others—remained unavailable and unknown to young white Americans in the suburbs. It was those artists that British kids did have access to, and then only after some serious investigation on their part, which made this musical discovery even more exciting and mysterious.

For English kids, the best music emanated out of America. Britain did have its pop stars—notably Tommy Steele, Cliff Richard, and the Shadows—but they didn't seem to hold a candle to the power and authenticity coming from American artists. "We British guys were very much enthralled [by] the United States," said Bruford. "We imported records. . . . I was at a boarding school, so you'd get [American records] in the mail, at breakfast, to great excitement. So I learned jazz that way, and of course blues as well. We saw the English guys [as] pretty much a pale imitation."

This feeling of British inferiority, reinforced by the idea of America overtaking the United Kingdom as the preeminent Western world power, pervaded the music as well. That lack of artistic confidence, or perhaps better put, that feeling of being second best, would completely turn on its ear by the mid-1960s. But, for now, these English kids grabbed everything and anything they could coming from the United States.

ART SCHOOL CULTURE

On the surface, Britain and America seemed to have much in common. America sprang from the same Western European tradition as England, using pieces of Enlightenment philosophy and Judeo-Christian thought to break off and create a new country in the 18th century. Nevertheless, much separates the two cultures besides the Atlantic Ocean. It's become clichéd now, but the standard saying "two countries separated by a common language" rings true. Other than dialectical and accentual differences, however, the emphasis on commerce, or perhaps the role of commerce in a person's life, differs dramatically depending on which side of the Atlantic you sit.

Go to London and visit some of the seminal sites of British music— the Crawdaddy (where the Rolling Stones and Yardbirds got their starts), Eel Pie Island (as mentioned previously), the Marquee (where everyone from the Stones, to the Moody Blues, to Jimi Hendrix played)—and you'll find a pub, a rugby athletic club, private homes, a bank, and apartments. The only indication that something happened at any of these venues might be a small circular blue plaque that would tell you Jimi Hendrix played there or Paul McCartney met Linda Eastman there, or a photo of a young Mick Jagger. At the Richmond Athletic Association, for example, where the Yardbirds played, you can walk into a small nondescript bar area and ask where the club was . . . and you'll get mostly blank stares. "But didn't Eric Clapton play right *there*?" More blank stares.

In America, we would go in a completely opposite direction. If the Crawdaddy had started up here, we would have created an interactive museum, complete with a studio, where you could make your own record and pretend to be Clapton, Jagger, or Keith Richards. The museum would sell everything from T-shirts to CDs and shot glasses, emblazoned with the band and club name on it. That notion, that drive to extract commerce from any and all angles, does not exist in England. "[America is] really entrepreneurial," said Jan Roberts, a regular at the Eel Pie Island Club. "We pretend to be refined and above such things, but we're just incompetent" [laughs].

That entrepreneurial drive is in some ways unique to the United States. Americans pride themselves on creating that better mousetrap. And certainly we have it down. There is, of course, a price to be paid for such passionate single-mindedness. In the United States, a person's position in life is entirely defined by the trappings of wealth. Your occupation, the size of your house, the neighborhood in which you live, the car you drive, the clothes you wear, the school your kids attend, your choice of vacation spot . . . all of that utterly and completely defines your place in American society. Artists and musicians—unless they can make a living out of it—are not worth a damn here.

While returning American servicemen attended college for free under President Roosevelt's GI Bill, England was experiencing something similar, with a unique British twist. Young people finishing grammar school (aka high school) in the 1950s generally had two choices: work in a factory like your father or go to art school for free. For a lot of kids who would end up creating the classic rock era, art school sounded a whole lot better, even if they had no intention or desire to become artists. Why not spend a couple of years making sketches and hanging out at pubs with your friends before entering that dreaded working world? Additionally, art schools did not present stringent entrance requirements, in contrast to academic colleges and universities. "Suddenly there was this option open to us and it kind of just seemed like a little magic window," the Animals' John Steel recalled. "I more or less got in without so much as having to produce a portfolio. And then I just spent three and a half years having a whale of a time. A lot of that time was spent going to the movies in the afternoon. Me and [fellow Animal] Eric [Burdon] did a lot of that."

"My dad dragged me around to art school. I walked in, they sat me down," said Barrie Wentzell, later a photographer with *Melody Maker*. "I didn't have to show [them] any work in there. But then I looked around and found a lot of the other characters I'd seen from school who didn't really fit into the system. . . . The art school was an incredible, important place because, not only I, but Lennon, Clapton, Jeff Beck, Townshend, and many other characters I ran into later also went to art school."

The list of artists who emerged from Britain's art schools is staggering. In addition to Lennon, Clapton, Beck, and Townshend, the art school community produced Keith Richards and Ronnie Wood of the Rolling Stones, Freddie Mercury (Queen), Ray Davies (Kinks), Sandy Denny (Fairport Convention), Keith Relf (Yardbirds), Dick Taylor (Pretty Things), Ian McLagan (Small Faces), and many others.

For some, art school presented an opportunity to develop serious creation, but many spent their time socializing with others who also looked to escape their parents' dreary industrial lives. For these like-minded souls, the art college interlude allowed them to bounce ideas off each other and to compare musical thoughts. The time became an incubation period that eventually led to the creation of their own serious art.

Furthermore, the art colleges helped foster a new teenage demographic, which had not previously existed in England. You were a child, and then you were an adult, with a job in the factories or the fields. But by the late 1950s and early 1960s, a whole generation of teenagers suddenly appeared on the scene, beyond childhood but not quite adults. "Before the war, people seemed to go from childhood straight to adulthood—from short pants to long," said Eel Pie Island Club founder Arthur Chisnall, as quoted in the book *Eel Pie Island* by Dan Van Der Vat and Michele Whitby.

Innovators like Chisnall emerged within this post–World War II culture. He would use the Eel Pie Island venue as an outlet for this new emerging teenage class. These teenagers lacked a culture of their own, and Chisnall helped create one, as art school kids and others would congregate at his club and enjoy dancing to traditional Dixieland (referred to as "trad") jazz, which peaked in popularity in the late 1950s. The club, and others of its kind, allowed for yet more interaction between teenagers in and around London.

By that time, as kids began to emerge from England's art schools, another key venue opened up on Oxford Street in London's Soho neighborhood: the Marquee. Founded by Chris Barber and his friend Harold Pendleton, the new club capitalized on the trad jazz boom, billing itself as "The London Jazz Centre." "[The first floor] was a cinema which had a basement which was not being used," said Barber. "So [Harold] arranged to rent that downstairs place of the cinema. We called it the Marquee because it had a stage in it, [with] a marquee awning over top of it."

The Marquee, at this location and later when it moved to nearby Wardour Street, would host nearly every band you can think of that comprises what we now know as classic rock: the Rolling Stones, the Yardbirds, Manfred Mann, the Who, the Moody Blues, the Jimi Hendrix Experience, Cream, Pink Floyd, and countless others. But for now, in the late 1950s, the Marquee became a symbol of the rising jazz movement—mostly traditional, but some modern—as exemplified by the Ronnie Scott club, also located in Soho.

Trad jazz dominated the London music scene for the next few years, but as the 1950s gave way to the 1960s, the blues—incubated with the help of Chris Barber and nurtured by Britain's baby boomers—began to slowly rear its head in London's club scene. And the new movement, referred to by the young Brits as "rhythm & blues" or "R&B," would once again get its jump start by Alexis Korner and Cyril Davies.

Davies had made quite a name for himself as a fine harp player. A working-class bloke employed in auto repair, the rather rounded, balding, and middle-aged figure didn't seem to embody the blues. But he did, becoming arguably the finest harp player in England. "He used to come in the [Marshall] shop," remembered co-owner Terry Marshall, "and I used to get all of his harps for him. . . . And he used to come in and his hands were black and scarred. And you looked at him and you thought, 'There's no way he's a musician' when I first met him. [But] you put a harmonica near his lips and he was in a different world. He was incredible. Total surprise to anybody who saw him visually and looked at his hands. You wouldn't believe what could come out of that guy. But he was exceptional."

Having been kicked out of the Blues and Barrelhouse Club for playing electric music, Korner and Davies had trouble finding appropriate venues since most of the jazz venues had little interest in Chicago-style blues. Once again, Barber stepped in. Recognizing the rising current of the blues, in 1961 Barber invited the pair into his jazz band, where they would do blues sets. "For about six months—every concert we played, we had a set with them," Barber recalled, "with Ottilie Patterson singing of course. We had a blues singer and a good guitar player and harp player."

After the stint in the Barber band, Korner and Davies desired to go blues full time but still required a venue to host their music. So they found a place called the Ealing Jazz Club with the help of Art Wood, brother of the Rolling Stones' Ronnie Wood. Located in the basement under a pub, the pair added supporting musicians and created Britain's first true electric blues band: Blues Incorporated. Its Ealing debut, in March 1962, featured a jazz drummer named Charlie Watts. Word got around about the new band and club. "Everybody used to go there," said frequent attendee Paul Jones, who later fronted Manfred Mann. "When I say everybody, I'm talking about Mick Jagger, Keith Richard[s], Brian Jones [and] guys who later turned out to be the Animals, or the Spencer Davis Group, or whatever.

"There were lots and lots of us young kids sort of lined up in front of the bandstand, desperately hoping that we would be the next person that Alexis Korner would beckon onto the stage so that we could give the long-suffering audience the benefits of our versions of 'I'm Going to Kansas City.' [Laughs.]"

The Ealing Club was literally a dump, in every sense of the word. "It was known as the 'Moist Hoist,'" said Jones, "because the condensation—once it got full of people—all the breath, and the sweat . . . would all kind of condense, and run down the walls. But actually, the really difficult thing was that it would drip off the ceiling [including] onto the drum skins. So the drums became unplayable. So they actually suspended on a rope—like a sail—a canvas sheet . . . so that the moisture dripping off the ceiling didn't drop on the stage and didn't drop on the drummer's drum skins."

Crowds grew, and the Ealing Club began to overflow. Searching for a larger venue, Korner again crossed paths with Barber, who offered him a Thursday night residency at the Marquee. "A group like that—mostly singing involved, every number—they need a support band, 'cause they can't just sing all night," said Barber. "It's too hard on their voices. So, somebody recommended they get the Rolling Stones as the support band. . . . After two weeks, Cyril Davies, harp player with Alexis Korner, said, 'Get those bastards out. They're terrible—that shit they're playing. I don't want that. They're just like pop music.' So, Harold Pendleton, my partner, did what he had to do. When you've got a main band there, they get to choose a support band. And they chose not to have that one. So Harold had to go tell the Stones, 'I'm sorry. As of this week, you're sacked.' And Keith Richards never forgave Harold for that. And every time he saw him since then, he hit him. I mean, through the years—40, 50 years [afterward]."

THE ROLLING STONES

The Rolling Stones were not the first Brits to play the blues, or let's say, pull off playing the blues. Barber had been there before them. Korner and Davies, too. In fact, the Stones' ability to re-create black music is subject to interpretation. Some fans believed they were nearly as good as the originals. Others, like Davies, saw them as poseurs playing pop music. Nevertheless, the Stones became the first of their generation, of Britain's baby boomers, to embrace the genre. It was almost like punk rock. You went down to see them and saw they were just like you—except the Stones were up onstage doing it.

The genesis of the Rolling Stones rests with a blues-obsessed triumvirate: Mick Jagger, Keith Richards, and Brian Jones. Jagger and Richards had known each other as kids growing up in postwar London, then moved apart, and eventually reunited in 1961. By that time, Jagger was attending the London School of Economics and Richards studied at Sidcup Art College. They compared notes about music and found they had nearly identical tastes . . . poring over such artists as Jimmy Reed, Memphis Slim, John Lee Hooker, Muddy Waters, and Bo Diddley.

At that point, as the 1960s began to emerge, Mick and Keith identified themselves as rhythm & blues aficionados—R&B. R&B was a distinct genre from rock 'n' roll; rock 'n' roll meant all things 1950s— Elvis, Chuck Berry, and Eddie Cochran—which was stuff your older brothers listened to. R&B was hip and now. Funny thing, though . . . Jagger and Richards both loved 1950s music. They didn't realize until much later—as with many of their peers—that it all kind of constituted rock 'n' roll. Nonetheless, the genesis of the Stones did emerge from what they called R&B and from a desire to make that kind of music and reinterpret the art their Chicago heroes had created.

Jagger and Richards began to frequent the Ealing Jazz Club, located near the Ealing Tube station. They would venture over on Saturday nights to see Blues Incorporated, which at the time included harp player Cyril Davies and drummer Charlie Watts. Korner, who had a keen interest in promoting R&B, invited the pair to play with them, and they did. And that's where they came across a young, talented, but already hardened guitarist named Brian Jones.

Jones, who at the time went by the stage name Elmo Lewis, fashioned himself a young Elmore James and played slide guitar—then a novelty in England. "I came to London at the instigation of Alexis Korner," Jones told Richard Green in the May 29, 1964, issue of *New Musical Express*. "He started the whole thing off and should be at the top now. Unfortunately, he's not. He introduced me to Mick and Keith at a club in West London and it's really true that he is responsible for the birth of the Rolling Stones in as much as he introduced us. I originally met Alexis when he came to Cheltenham with Chris Barber. We struck up a friendship because we liked the same things."

Impressed with Jones's playing, Jagger and Richards joined up with him, and the genesis of the Rolling Stones had begun. Through Jones, Jagger and Richards were introduced to keyboard player Ian Stewart.

They added bassist Dick Taylor (later with the Pretty Things), a friend of Richards at Sidcup. Their next task was to find a drummer.

The emerging band's first choice was Watts, a talented jazz percussionist from Korner's band. But he turned out to be too expensive. So they temporarily found Mick Avory, who would later go on to play for the Kinks. Nonetheless, the new band got its first break, filling in for Blues Incorporated at the Marquee when Korner and Co. were booked to do a BBC broadcast. Jones phoned up *Jazz News*, which publicized London gigs. The reporter asked for a name of the band. Scrambling, Jones tapped into a Muddy Waters tune called "Rollin' Stone." "Rolling Stones," he said.

The band's first six months remained inauspicious. Gigs were few, with little money to be had. Jagger, Richards, and Jones roomed together in a disgusting London flat. In July, the Stones (replacing Avory with drummer Tony Chapman, although Keith Richards insists it was Avory in *Life*) made their debut at the Marquee in Soho, supporting Cyril Davies's band, which had broken off from Blues Incorporated by that point. The accounts of these early Marquee gigs differ.

According to Richards and eventual manager Giorgio Gomelsky, the Stones outshone Davies's group, and the harp player's resentment led to the band's ouster from the Marquee. Chris Barber, however, recalls that Davies merely didn't like the Stones, believing them to be too pop, and too rock 'n' roll, and thus wanted them out. So, club co-owner Harold Pendleton did the nasty deed, and the Stones found themselves hunting for shows.

Things began to pick up, though, later in 1963, when the Stones found their rhythm section.

Much has been made of the Stones' front men, but the key to that band's success lay in the back court. In early 1963, they found bassist Bill Wyman, who initially became a Stone because he possessed his own bass amp. "They [the rest of the Stones] didn't like me," Wyman told Richard Green in the May 1, 1964, issue of *New Musical Express*, "but I had a good amplifier, and they were badly in need of amplifiers at that time so they kept me on."

Then came the coveted drummer, Charlie Watts, and the Stones became the Stones. This new rhythm section would provide the critical groove and backbeat that would come to define the band. At the time, the Stones also featured keyboard player Ian Stewart. "I joined before

Charlie or Bill," Stewart told Richard Green in the September 4, 1964, issue of *New Musical Express*, "and when we wanted a new drummer, I suggested Charlie to Brian."

Gomelsky, a large bearded figure from the old Soviet Union, saw an opportunity with the band and, after the Marquee incident, decided to find a new venue. He found one at a hotel across from the Richmond train station, about a 30-minute ride from London. "I decided to find me a place as far as possible from Soho," Gomelsky stated in an interview with blogger Joly MacFie.

The only evening available at the Richmond spot was Sunday, which was the worst possible night as the pubs closed an hour earlier than the rest of the week. The rather well-to-do suburb did not seem like an obvious spot, either. It had no real blues tradition or even much of a club scene. The only link to relevance was Kingston Art College, about a 20-minute bus ride away. Art schools tended to attract musicians, who might want to check out the Stones. As it turns out, Eric Clapton, the Yardbirds' Keith Relf, and Fairport Convention's Sandy Denny attended Kingston.

Gomelsky's plan was to have the band play a weekly residency at the Station Hotel to build an audience. He put up a big sign outside the hotel that read "Rhythm & Blues This Evening." The Stones would do a 45-minute set, followed by a 45-minute break, and then another 45-minute set. Gomelsky encouraged the band to groove out to get the audience dancing—especially so after people had the opportunity to have a few drinks during the interlude. And slowly, his plan began to work.

A young music fan named Mike Murphy was one of the first to come down to the new club. "One Sunday afternoon, we were in Richmond," Murphy recalled, "wondering what we could do with ourselves and we saw a notice outside a pub saying, 'Rhythm & Blues, This Evening, at 7 O'Clock.' We didn't know what rhythm & blues was at all. We heard of the blues, but the combination of 'rhythm & blues' was something new to us."

The musical act that night was called Dave Hunt's R&B Band, which failed to impress Murphy and his friends. "But then, a couple of Sundays later," he said, "the Dave Hunt Rhythm & Blues Band stopped appearing and the guy who ran the place, Giorgio Gomelsky, said, 'We've got a new band coming, and we want you all to come along and give them your support. They're called the Rolling Stones.' So we came along and then I think the first night they were there, there were about 30–35 people, no more. And, wow. We'd never heard anything like this before, sort of harmonica—wailing harmonica—very, very rhythmic playing. They relied very much in those early days on the repertoire of Bo Diddley and Chuck Berry—basically the two of them, with other people thrown in: Jimmy Reed, Slim Harpo, stuff like that. But it was really magic."

For Murphy, an original member of the club, and his friends, the Stones became an introduction to American blues. "I didn't know who [the blues artists] were until I heard the Stones," said Murphy. "And the Stones would introduce a number, 'Now, this is a Jimmy Reed number. This is a Slim Harpo number. This is a Howlin' Wolf number.' And I'm saying, 'Who are these guys?' So, in the interval . . . I'd go up and [ask the band], 'Where can I get their records?' And the most helpful of all was Brian Jones, who told me the place where they got them from . . . through a shop in London that was called Imhoff's.

"And then gradually more and more people used to come on Sunday nights and queues started to form."

> "And by the looks of the Station Hotel, Richmond, flourish is merely an understatement considering that three months ago only fifty people turned up to see the group. Now club promoter bearded Giorgio Gomelsky has to close the doors at an early hour—over four hundred R&B fans crowd the hall."—Norman Jopling, *Record Mirror*, May 11, 1963

Sometime in 1963, likely late spring, 18-year-old Ian McLagan (later with the Small Faces and Faces), who also toured with the Rolling Stones in the 1970s, just had to go see this new rhythm & blues band everyone was talking about. McLagan prepared himself by spending the previous night sleeping on a park bench near the venue. He headed to over to the hotel that evening. "And we got there at maybe six o'clock, or seven o'clock," McLagan remembered, "and there was a *line*. People were lining up to go in."

Having never seen the Stones before, McLagan was not sure what to expect. As he waited in the long line, he heard this grinding 12-bar blues blasting out into the chilly air. "And I'm really excited now," he said, "'Cause I am imagining I'm seeing a blues band, right? Well, what do blues bands look like? They're black. And they're from Chicago, or from the South."

The raw, thumping beat and bass line slowly became louder as McLagan inched closer and closer toward the door. The excitement continued to build as the volume increased. Finally, the young music fan and his friends entered the venue. They looked up at the stage, expecting to see a group of middle-aged African American men wailing on the blues. Instead, they witnessed Mick Jagger and his compatriots playing on a rather tiny stage. "[I] walk in," said McLagan, "and it's . . . *white* guys. [Laughs.]"

To continue to get the word out about the Stones, Gomelsky phoned the local newspaper, the *Richmond/Twickenham Times*, hoping to get someone to come down and check out his band. Eventually, he found a young reporter named Barry May who showed interest in R&B and would write an expansive feature on the Stones. As May was putting together his piece, he phoned Gomelsky, asking for the name of his club. "A local paper did a write-up on us and asked us what we called the club," Gomelsky told Ian Dove in the July 3, 1964, issue of *New Musical Express*. "Up to then we'd never had a name. Without thinking almost, [I] said 'Crawdaddy' because this was a number the Stones played, a Bo Diddley number and very popular."

With the Stones' residence at the now-christened Crawdaddy Club, attendance began to grow by leaps and bounds. Within a few months, the 300-capacity room in the Station Hotel became insufficient, and Gomelsky found a larger space down the street at the Richmond Athletic Association. The new venue could accommodate around 800 patrons.

The Stones represented more than just an emergence of one band. They represented the beginnings of a new sound and a turning point in British culture. By 1963, the band's Crawdaddy residency began to spread to other clubs throughout London. The advent of rhythm & blues began to challenge what Keith Richards refers to in *Life* as the "Dixieland mafia." In addition to the Crawdaddy and Eel Pie Island venues, trad jazz clubs like the Marquee, Ken Colyer, and Ronnie Scott Clubs began to feature regular rhythm & blues nights with the Stones, Alexis Korner's Blues Incorporated, and newer acts like the Cyril Davies All-Stars (who had by then split off from Korner's band), John Mayall's Bluesbreakers, and the Graham Bond Quartet. Even some of the jazz artists began to recognize the coming musical shift. In an April

1963 interview with *Melody Maker*'s Ray Coleman, trad jazz musician Alex Welsh commented, "Trad—I'm glad it's on the way out . . . so much inferior music is being served up under the general heading of trad. It had to come. Trad has been thrashed to death."

Of course by that time, a band from up north called the Beatles had become nationally popular with two number 1 hits: "Please Please Me" and "From Me to You." Although the Liverpudlians had little to do with London's R&B scene, the Beatles' entry onto the national stage represented a breakthrough for the younger generation of musicians, just like the Stones had in London. By 1963, the tipping point for new music had been reached. "We realized," said Mike Murphy, "that this [was] the beginning of something really, really big."

2

R&B BOOM!

"R&B is, in fact, the London sound."—Bob Dawbarn, *Melody Maker*, April 18, 1964

It was 1963, and everything changed. In fact, you could argue the 1960s began that year with the emergence of the Beatles, the death of John F. Kennedy, and the basis for the coming British invasion of America.

In London, as the year dawned, clearly change was afoot, and a major part of that had to do with the new beat groups coming out of Liverpool, especially the Beatles. The Beatles sounded nothing like the Rolling Stones of course, but they did tap into a similar musical aesthetic—their fascination with American blues and rock 'n' roll. But they were totally original and made it a point to be so from the get-go. It started with John Lennon talking about the lack of echo the band used onstage, and it went from there. The Beatles made it a point not to sound like popular British pop acts at the time like Cliff Richard and the Shadows.

"Don't copy—and keep it simple! The Beatles tell Jerry Dawson."
—*Melody Maker* headline, February 23, 1963

The heart of that originality lay of course in the Lennon-McCartney songwriting genius, which we now take for granted. But back then artists rarely wrote their own material. Typically, the producer would buy songs considered appropriate for the band and tell them who's going to play on the record, often inserting behind-the-scenes session

musicians. EMI producer George Martin had such a plan for the Beat-
les when he bought a song for them called "How Do You Do It?"
Martin admitted it wasn't a great piece of songwriting, but it fit the
Beatles well. He told them if they wanted a number 1 hit, there it was.

After recording "How Do You Do It?" the Beatles decided against
releasing it, not wanting to "be seen with that song" as Paul McCartney
put it. Instead they recorded an original, the Roy Orbison–influenced
"Please Please Me," and promptly tore up the rule book. In March
1963, "Please Please Me" surged to number one one the *Melody Maker*
top 50 chart, proving to all that a group could write and record its own
smash hit.

A young keyboard player named Rod Argent, then living in St. Albans, a town roughly an hour north of London, clearly remembers the
moment he first heard it. He had already started a band, but the Beatles
would inspire him to take things to the next level. He would form the
Zombies and move to London within a year. "I [first] heard, on Radio
Luxembourg, 'Please Please Me,'" Argent recalled. "And I remember
staying up most of the night hoping they would play it again.

"And the Beatles hit with the force of a pile-driver. They really did.
It was so exciting and much more honest. The production was terrific,
the George Martin production was very sort of straight-ahead and gritty
and honest . . . and it came completely from the enthusiasm of the
band. And they were a *group*, so unlike a lot of the other hit records we
listened to; *they* were playing the drums and the bass and the guitars.
So you had that honesty coming through."

"They were too good," said Greg Lake, later in King Crimson and
Emerson, Lake & Palmer. "You couldn't even believe how good they
were. They were fantastic. They were unbelievably good. It's hard to
explain, but the only way you can [explain] it is to listen to their music—
loud. Imagine a band up there playing it, because they sounded like the
records.

"When you analyze [Ringo Starr's] drum parts in the Beatles," continued Lake, who later toured with the Beatles' percussionist, "it's fascinating to analyze them, because they're all perfect. There's not a single
beat that's extraneous or gratuitous. Not one beat. Not one tambourine
click—nothing. Everything's got a purpose. . . . And I would say it was
true of all of them. They all had this incredible economy where everything meant something. . . . I went to see them live a couple of times in

the early days and they were overwhelming, and brought audience[s] to tears, literally."

Texas singer P. J. Proby, who would come to England in spring 1964 to appear on a television special called *Around the Beatles*, was not impressed initially. "I thought they were the worst group I'd ever heard in my life. As far as singing groups were concerned, I was used to the Ames Brothers and the Four Preps—those beautiful, beautiful, singing groups in America. The Four Seasons and everything.

"I told John Lennon," said Proby, who later became friends with the Beatles legend, "I said, 'John, I tell ya. Y'all are the worst group I've ever heard in my life. Y'all don't hold a finger to the beautiful singers that sing 'Shangri La' and everything like the Ames Brothers and the Four Lads and everything. I'll tell ya something else, too. I'd give y'all a year at the top and then I'm gonna take over.' And John turned to me and said [Proby imitating Lennon's thick Liverpudlian accent], '*Well, P. J., if anybody does it, I hope it's youuu.*'"

By that August, though, even Proby's assessment began to change as he saw the tide turning from the lush orchestral sounds of Phil Spector to the tight raw arrangements of the young rock groups. "Top quality singers come from America," Proby told Valerie Ward in the August 22, 1964, issue of *Record Mirror*, "but we couldn't hold a candle to groups like the Beatles or Stones."

Much has been made of a supposed rivalry between the Beatles and Rolling Stones; some of that did exist in fact, and certainly fans had their allegiances. Nevertheless, at least in the early days, there was no conflict as the Stones struggled to get beyond the local club circuit.

In September 1963, the Stones made a major jump in popularity, beginning a tour in the United Kingdom with the Everly Brothers and Bo Diddley, but their output paled in comparison to the Beatles. Other than a minor hit, a cover of Chuck Berry's "Come On," the Stones had little to go on and no original material. Sensing the problem, Stones manager Andrew Loog Oldham, who had taken over from Giorgio Gomelsky, approached John Lennon and Paul McCartney that September in London. The pair offered up a new song for the Stones called "I Wanna Be Your Man," and London's R&B kings made it into a hit. "We were a mutual-admiration society," Keith Richards wrote in his autobiography, *Life*. "Mick and I admired their harmonies and their songwriting capabilities; they envied us our freedom of movement and our image. . . . The thing is, with the Beatles and us, it was a very friendly relationship."

The Beatles even came down to Stones gigs at the Crawdaddy, and they enjoyed them immensely. "I don't suppose they [came] down just to see us," Stones drummer Charlie Watts told Chris Roberts in the June 29, 1963, issue of *Melody Maker*. "They can't like our faces. They must like the music."

> "One group that thinks a lot of the Rollin' Stones are The Beatles. When they came down to London the other week, they were knocked out by the group's singing. They stayed all evening at the Station Hotel, listening to the group pound away."—Norman Jopling, *Record Mirror*, May 11, 1963

It wasn't unusual to run into the Fab Four in those days and find yourself hanging out with them. Peter Noone, who arrived in London in 1964 with his band Herman's Hermits, unexpectedly crossed paths with John Lennon. At the time, the underaged Noone and his band were enjoying a number 1 hit with "I'm into Something Good." "I'd go to the Ad Lib Club in Leicester[1] Square," Noone recalled, "and I'd meet John Lennon in the lift going up. And he knew I wasn't 18. . . . So I'd sit down and there was like a Playboy kind of bunny waitress. And she didn't ask me my age, but she said there's a two-drink minimum. So John Lennon said, 'I'll have two Bacardis and he'll have two cokes.'"

For the Stones, though manager Oldham consciously recognized the importance of image and marketing his band, clearly he didn't want to manage a Beatles II. So, along with the Stones' natural inclination, Oldham helped differentiate his band as the "Bad Boys of R&B" as opposed to the squeaky-clean image of the Beatles and the other beat groups. "[The Stones'] image is perfect," columnist Ray Coleman wrote in the February 8, 1964, issue of *Melody Maker*, "five dishevelled [*sic*] rebels who have already made a firm imprint on the hit parade, who have gained a huge following among young people, who never wear stage uniforms, and who just don't care."[2]

"We had a set of uniforms once," Richards told Coleman, "but everyone kept losing his suit, so we decided to call it a day and go on as we liked."

Despite the cordial relationship between the Beatles and Stones, most fans within London did pick an allegiance. Similar to the grunge rivalry of 30 years later between Nirvana and Pearl Jam, you were either a Beatles or a Stones fan, but probably not both. In London, especially, fans usually favored their hometown heroes over their Liverpool counterparts. "You were in one camp or the other," recalled Stones fan and Crawdaddy Club member Mike Murphy. "And we hated the Beatles' stuff . . . the Beatles, well they [wore] those Pierre Cardin suits and everybody used to laugh at them. [We thought,] 'Our guys are much rawer—raw music, we're the real thing.'"

Meanwhile, outside of London, the beat phenomenon spread throughout the United Kingdom. In Liverpool, Manchester, Sheffield, and Birmingham, the upbeat sounds of bands like the Beatles, the Searchers, the Hollies, and Gerry and the Pacemakers began to dominate. This wasn't the case in London. "London, strangely, is getting late on this," the June 8, 1963, issue of *Melody Maker* exclaimed, "the biggest beat boom since Bill Haley started rocking around the clock."

That's because London distinguished itself as England's R&B capital, and it wasn't going to change . . . at least for a while. As the Stones would move on to tour the United Kingdom that fall, the local R&B crown would fall to a new band: the Yardbirds.

THE YARDBIRDS

The Stones and the Yardbirds knew each other well since the R&B scene was so small in the early days. Both bands listened to and played similar blues covers, many of which were derived from the 78 collection of Yardbirds' guitarist Top Topham's father. "We used to go and see [the Stones at the Crawdaddy]," Yardbirds drummer Jim McCarty recalled. "And . . . I think that sort of music we found to be different. You know, it was different from Elvis, although sometimes they overlapped [with Chicago blues]—that sort of music overlapped. Jimmy Reed and Howlin' Wolf and all that stuff. It was totally unusual and original.

"In fact the Stones sort of took most of their repertoire, first of all, from about 10 albums. We sort of got the same albums, but we did different covers. We made sure we didn't do the same songs as they did."

The Yardbirds were a somewhat eclectic mix of art and grammar school (equivalent to US high school) kids. Singer/harmonica player

Keith Relf became friends with Topham and rhythm guitarist Chris Dreja at Kingston Art School near Richmond, while McCarty and bassist Paul Samwell-Smith knew each other through grammar school. The Yardbirds' genesis occurred when Topham and Dreja, who had been playing together by that point, walked into a pub near the art school one Friday evening in 1963. "It was in Norbiton, outside of Kingston," Topham recalled. "There used to be a pub there—a huge pub. It used to have a guy playing boogie-woogie downstairs on a piano. You had sort of an Irish band in the public bar. You'd go upstairs and it was a trad band. That was a Friday night . . . basically, I saw Keith, Paul, and another guy playing guitar there. We actually didn't think they were very good."

Topham, Dreja, and a friend occasionally would play gigs at the pub, and despite their musical differences, someone suggested the two groups combine forces with Relf taking on singing and harmonica duties, Topham on lead guitar, Dreja on rhythm, Samwell-Smith on bass, and McCarty on drums. "We had this rehearsal in Putney," said Topham. "I'd never met Jim before that day, but Paul was there with Keith. And Jim turned up . . . and there was Chris and I. And I think the first track we played was something like [Jimmy Reed's] 'Bright Lights' or 'Baby What's Wrong,' . . . we did some Jimmy Reed stuff because they were easy to do. And we sort of looked at each other afterwards. We couldn't believe how good it was!"

The new band played its first gigs at Eel Pie Island, supporting Cyril Davies's All-Stars. Despite his reputation as a curmudgeon, Davies was duly impressed with the Yardbirds, especially in the passion that these young musicians displayed for the blues. Those gigs led to others, and eventually the band crossed paths with Giorgio Gomelsky, who was looking for a new band to manage after Oldham had signed the Rolling Stones away from him. Gomelsky quickly gave the Yardbirds a weekly booking at his new Crawdaddy location, the Richmond Athletic Club.

Because the Stones and Yardbirds knew each other, and because they both played blues covers, and now with the Yardbirds taking over the Stones' residency at the Crawdaddy, the comparisons became inevitable. Quickly, though, the Yardbirds began to find their own voice. Initially sticking to the script of the songs they covered, the Yardbirds began to expand what they could do within a song and created more intricate rhythmic structures brought to the fore by Samwell-Smith.

While the Stones could create a groove and a backbeat like no one's business, the Yardbirds added an element of sheer exuberance, of wild edge-of-your-seat borderline insanity. Beginning with Relf's manic harp playing, through the dual guitars, bass, and drums, the Yardbirds began to dramatically reinterpret blues classics from such stalwarts as Sonny Boy Williamson and Howlin' Wolf. They also began to add another element that hadn't been present within American rock 'n' roll: improvisation. Finding themselves without enough material to fill an entire evening, the Yardbirds began to stretch out their songs. In other words, they improvised out of necessity. "Sometimes we'd have to play like three hours or something. We wouldn't have enough material, so we'd jam around," said McCarty. "I used to like the improvisation. When it worked well, it was great. It was a great gig when we all clicked."

"Our stuff—it had a place where you could improvise," said Topham. "So therefore, you could build up excitement, which you hear in the Yardbirds with these sort of crescendos and things that went on in numbers. It drove people crazy, when you played. They kinda went ape-shit."

"We wanted to make it consciously more exciting," McCarty continued. "So we put in all those sort of big buildups in the bass and drums and everyone joining in. We'd play a song for quite a long time like that. It was just an idea to make it a bit different and also to make it more exciting, to get the crowd going. And they did! They went crazy at the Crawdaddy Club. They used to jump onto each other's backs and swing on beams and everything. They'd go mad."

In the accepted version of rock history, the Yardbirds get the credit as *the* first band to improvise, as in, "The Stones played their songs as written. The Yardbirds expanded upon that, creating the notion of the rock jam." That statement would be nice and neat if it were in fact true. For one, the Stones themselves improvised prior to the Yardbirds' days. Mike Murphy, an original Crawdaddy Club member, remembered: "The final song by the Stones, both at the Station Hotel and later at the Athletic Clubhouse, was nearly always Chuck Berry's 'Bye Bye Johnny.' People would climb on the shoulders of those already dancing, wave their arms in the air and join in with the chorus. With this song, and several others that got people dancing, when the band saw that the crowd was really worked up, they would improvise in the sense that

Brian or Keith would extend their solos more than normal, or Mick would strut his stuff, all with the aim of making the number last longer."

Further, other bands that came from a jazz background, notably Manfred Mann, Georgie Fame & the Blue Flames, and the Animals, improvised prior to or contemporaneously with the Yardbirds. So the notion of the Yardbirds owning that credit seems overstated. Perhaps that band's penchant for employing famous guitarists (Eric Clapton [see below], Jeff Beck, and Jimmy Page) contributed to the tale. "I think what the Yardbirds would say was that they went in for the extended guitar solo," said the Blue Flames' Colin Green, "which if you call that improvisation, it's great. But it's the sort of the start of the guitar hero thing, which I suppose didn't really exist before them. And it certainly wasn't a Blue Flames thing. [If there] was a solo, there was a solo—whoever took it . . . took it. It wasn't the guitar player [taking precedence over] the sax player or the trumpet player."

"[Improvisation] was the essence of what [Manfred Mann, the band] were doing," recalled the band's namesake and keyboardist, Manfred Mann. "Mike Vickers, the saxophone player, he was improvising; I was the keyboard player, I was improvising; Paul [Jones] was doing harmonica solos, he was improvising."

Regardless of the credit or lack thereof, 16-year-old Topham's days in the Yardbirds quickly became numbered. His parents would strongly disapprove of his band activities, forcing him to leave and return to his art studies. "We seemed to be playing on a circuit around London, playing a lot of late-night gigs," said McCarty, "and all-nighters and things like that. And it was difficult for Top. He was the youngest in the band, and he was like seriously studying art. And his parents were quite strict with him and they didn't really approve of him, you know, giving up his studies. So he had to give up the group. And that's when we enlisted Eric. And Eric had been at the same art school—Kingston Art School—as the other guys. He'd already had a bit of a reputation as a sort of guitar player. He played in a couple of bands already. And he was very happy to come and join us."

The addition of Eric Clapton changed the dynamic within the band. Like any group he would ever be in, Clapton would become the focus as the virtuoso guitar player. Furthermore, he would expand upon the band's improvisational tendencies. "What singled us out from most other bands was the way we were experimenting with band dynamics,"

Clapton wrote in *Clapton: The Autobiography*, "a direction we were taken in by Paul Samwell-Smith. We became quite well known for the way in which we improvised, for example, taking the frame of a blues standard, like Bo Diddley's 'I'm a Man,' and embellishing it by jamming in the middle, usually with a staccato bass line, which would get louder and louder, rising to a crescendo before coming back down again to the body of the song."

After having lost out on managing the Stones, Gomelsky seized on the opportunity to lead the Yardbirds forward, and he got them signed to Columbia Records in early 1964.

For music fans in London, experiencing the emerging greatness of bands like the Stones and Yardbirds became commonplace by 1964. Tony Norman, later a music journalist with *New Musical Express*, recalled such an experience in 1964, when he and a friend were looking for something to do on a Saturday night. "[My friend] saw in the [*Melody Maker*] that the Yardbirds were playing at the Marquee," Norman said. "And so we caught the Tube into Tottenham Court Road. Walked into Soho. There was a short queue, maybe no more than 40 people ahead of us in the queue. We paid about a dollar in [American] money at time, about 7 and 6 UK. And just walked into this club and saw the Yardbirds with Eric Clapton. . . . a wonderful, wonderful band with one of the greatest guitarists the world had ever seen. And that was London in the '60s."

As the Yardbirds began to dominate the London club scene, Gomelsky became aware of another R&B outpost in England, in a town called Newcastle. Located near the Scottish border in northeast England, Newcastle was the home of a new rising R&B band with a jazzy slant called the Alan Price Rhythm & Blues Combo, who later became the Animals.

THE ANIMALS

The Animals' origins resulted from an art school friendship between R&B enthusiasts Eric Burdon and John Steel. "We met in the first year in the first class," Steel recalled, "and we hit it off straightaway with a kind of common interest in jazz and rock 'n' roll and movies and books—all American."

Unlike their London contemporaries, Burdon and Steel absorbed everything they could, from traditional jazz to modern jazz and all kinds of blues. That became a melting pot they would incorporate into their music. The pair formed a band called the Kansas City Five, featuring Burdon on lead vocals, Steel on drums, and keyboardist Alan Price. Adding bassist Bryan "Chas" Chandler and lead guitarist Hilton Valentine, the KC 5 morphed into the Alan Price R&B combo by 1963.

The new band's sound mirrored their London contemporaries to some extent, but the five-piece band came from much bleaker territory than their musical cousins to the south. Newcastle in those days was a dreary mining and shipbuilding town, much grittier and grubbier than London. And the music reflected that. "Chas Chandler, he actually was a year or two older than Eric and me. He really was in the factory," said Steel. "He became a sort of shop foreman type. He spent all his teenage years doing that. When we finally got to the point where we could say, 'Let's go for it and head for London,' he was sorely pleased to say, 'The hell with this,' and dropped his tools and [got] out of there."

"'We Gotta Get out of This Place' is a good phrase for . . . Newcastle," added Valentine.

In the meantime, the band continued to enhance its reputation as a live act in its hometown, playing its raw version of R&B in pubs around Newcastle. Their ability to play jazz-inspired time signatures while improvising distinguished them from others around town. Furthermore, Burdon's deep, soulful vocals would come to define the emerging band's sound. Soon, the Alan Price R&B Combo found itself with regular residencies. "Mike Jeffery, who became [our] manager . . . his first venture was a room above a pub in the center of Newcastle, which he called the Newcastle University Jazz Club," said Steel. "It was nothing to do with Newcastle University. Mike was a student there, but this was just private enterprise. He just kind of rented this room above a pub."

Jeffery soon opened a space called the Club A'Gogo and made the Alan Price R&B Combo its resident band. And word got around. In late 1963, the Graham Bond Quartet from London visited the club. Bond had originally played in Blues Incorporated but split off to play Hammond organ in his own band along with a brilliant bassist/percussion pairing of Jack Bruce and Ginger Baker; Bruce and Baker would later play with Clapton in Cream. Bond was impressed with the house band, sat in on jam sessions, and hooked Jeffery up with Giorgio Gomelsky, the Yardbirds' manager. Jeffery and Gomelsky desired to spread the exposure of both of their bands, working out a deal whereby the Yardbirds would come up and play Newcastle, with the Alan Price Rhythm & Blues Combo traveling to London to take the Yardbirds' spots at the Crawdaddy, Eel Pie Island, and other venues in and around London. Steel remembers Jeffery informing the band about a name change after he returned from London in December 1963. "'And, by the way, you've got a new name [Jeffery told us]. You're gonna be called the Animals,'" Steel said while bursting out in laughter. "It was great. We actually [wanted to] get rid of that clunky name—the Alan Price Rhythm & Blues Combo. . . . And Graham [Bond] had said, 'You wanna drop that and get something a bit—look at the Beatles—do something like that.' And he suggested 'the Animals' [to Jeffery]."

The Newcastle natives made an immediate impression upon London while playing Eel Pie Island in January 1964. John Steel read from his diary:

> January 12, 1964. Sunday. We played the Olympia Ballroom—an afternoon session. And then we played Eel Pie Island that night for the first time. . . . That's when Peter Grant [a promoter who would later manage Led Zeppelin] and [producer] Mickie Most turned up. We could see them in the crowd. . . . They talked to Mike Jeffery and [they came] to check us out.

The Animals quickly signed to EMI/Columbia and, within a few months, found themselves in a studio recording the now classic "House of the Rising Sun," which came to represent the increasingly free-spirited rebellious nature of the times. The band had been performing "Rising Sun" and found it knocking the audiences out. The plan was to plug the track on a new hip TV show called *Ready Steady Go!*

The origins of the song go back perhaps 100 years, with no credited composer. The best known take belonged to American folk legend Woody Guthrie, but it was Bob Dylan's version on his 1962 debut album that most inspired the Animals to record it. The Newcastle natives, though, would make it *their* song, much like Jimi Hendrix would later do with Dylan's "All along the Watchtower."

Dylan's "Rising Sun" was a solo performance featuring his now familiar rhythmic guitar strumming accompanied by his nasal vocal style. The Animals would take the traditional ballad in a whole new direction, though, beginning with how the notes were played on the guitar. Instead of strumming the chords like Dylan, guitarist Hilton Valentine played them in sequence (called an arpeggio). He would do it in a specific rhythm: Da da-da-da da da da. Valentine came up with the arpeggio idea while listening to the opening of a 1957 song by Paul Anka called "Diana." "I don't know. It just felt right to do that arpeggio thing," said Valentine. "And funny enough, Alan Price [laughs], when he heard me playing that, he said, 'Can't you play something different? That is so corny.' . . . to which I replied to him, 'You play your keyboard. [I'll] play my guitar.'"

The word *epic* has become so overused these days that we've become desensitized to it, but the Animals' version of "Rising Sun" is, in fact, *epic* in every sense of the word. Beginning with one verse of Valentine's arpeggio, Burdon begins in his deep baritone, "There is a house in New Orleans they call the Rising Sun," then he ups the ante, belting out in his powerful, soulful upper range, "And it's been the ruin of many a poor boy, and God I know I'm one." Burdon, then only 23 years old, sounds like a man twice his age, a man who has experienced the depth and breadth of a hard life. Steel's subtle cymbal playing combined with Price's organ overlay add to the mystery and magic of "Rising Sun," making Dylan's version pale in comparison. Steel read a letter he wrote to his girlfriend a couple of days after the session:

> We had a recording session this week. One side was . . . Ray Charles' "Talkin' 'bout You." The other side is "Rising Sun." It's going to be plugged as an A record—both sides. "Rising Sun" sounds great. We did it in one take.

There was only one problem, however. After recording "Rising Sun," the band realized it clocked in at more than four minutes, a then unheard of length for a single. "Mickie [Most, the producer] just said, 'Come on and listen to this.' And he said, 'I think we've got a hit here,'" Steel recalled. "And that's when David Siddle, the engineer, turned from the desk and he said, 'You've got a problem 'cause it's [more than] four minutes [long.]' Mickie just said, 'The hell with that. We're in the vinyl age now.' And that stood [out] in my mind. I never forgot that. That was really ballsy, you know, because it was unheard of to have anything more than two and-a-half, three minutes in a single."

"The Animals have been given a 'four minute warning' by Britain's TV companies. They have been turned down by major TV shows because their single, 'House of the Rising Sun,' is considered too long at four minutes."—*Melody Maker*, June 27, 1964

But the Animals and their management persisted, refusing to edit down the single, performing the song live on a hit TV show called *Ready Steady Go!* And their efforts paid off. Within a week, "Rising Sun" would top the *Melody Maker* chart, and then became a US number 1 hit—the first by a British band since the Beatles. The Animals' defiance would begin to represent the crumbling of the old order.

The notion of experimentation/breaking the rules pervaded throughout London in 1964. A working-class group of ex-skifflers called the Ravens changed their name to the Kinks and found themselves experimenting with a new guitar sound, working on a single called "You Really Got Me." Guitarist Dave Davies was playing around with an Elpico loudspeaker, using it as kind of a pre-amp to try to come up with a fuzzy sound, but whatever he attempted didn't satisfy him. "[So] I messed around with it and I got [a] razor blade and I slit the cone with a razor blade. And I plugged it in and that's where I got that raunchy guitar sound from," said Davies. "I was hoping this funny little amp would do something new. But when I plugged it in, it was the same as everything else. I got a bit frustrated with it, a bit angry with it. So I was kind of gonna destroy it. But I ended up creating a new tone." The Kinks also stumbled onto something else: feedback.

"On stage and in the recording studio, the Kinks are perfecting their own ideas for sounds, one of which is using 'feedback' from a guitar amplifier—a constant or increasing hum obtained by holding the guitar in front of the amplifier's loudspeaker."—Chris Roberts, *Melody Maker*, August 22, 1964

"The guitar I had was very microphonic, and it was semi-acoustic, although it was an electric," said Davies. "It was a Harmony Meteor. And so, the part-hollowed body was very microphonic to the pickups. And you get feedback very easily. If you would tune to your amp, it would start to oscillate and the drone would [get] bigger and bigger. So it was kind of something that was hard to control, and especially when I had my new guitar sound. . . . But it was cool as well, 'cause you could use it as an effect. It could swell up and you could dampen it . . . with your fingers. So you could use it musically—like noise, but it was like effective noise. It helped enhance the music."

Live, the lurching finale of "You Really Got Me" sometimes left audiences stunned. "We've changed the ending on 'You Really Got Me,'" Davies told Cordell Marks in the August 28, 1964, issue of *New Musical Express*. "It used to have a very abrupt ending. So abrupt, in fact, that when we'd finish playing it, the audience just sat there silently. We had to yell at them, 'Come on, you lot, clap!'"

The Kinks and the Who are not the only folks claiming ownership of feedback. The Yardbirds lay claim to that as well.

> "Jim McCarty, drums: 'The Who and ourselves are the only groups doing anything new. I think that's far better than reviving these old numbers like Peter and Gordon have. We all dislike that kind of thing.' Jeff Beck,[3] guitar: 'I was experimenting with echo effects and feedback years ago. Now it's become the thing. The Who's effects are drawing the crowds. I think they incorporate their own sound with some of the Beach Boys' style, and they are very good.' Keith Relf, vocals: 'I also believe that the Who have been inspired by us. We were always seeing them in our audience at one time either at the Marquee or the Crawdaddy.'"—Keith Altham, *New Musical Express*, July 9, 1965

Another band's recording debut also exemplified the creative defiance then emerging in London. In 1964, the Zombies released their first single, "She's Not There." To the 21st-century listener, the track sounds like a pretty love song. But to the discerning ear, and certainly back then, "She's Not There" stretched the boundaries of what a pop song could be.

Composed by keyboard player Rod Argent, the single experimented with minor keys and modal scales not previously used in pop music. Argent wrote it while he was listening heavily to jazz great Miles Davis. In particular, he became fascinated with Davis's use of modal scales, which was unheard of in pop music. "I never studied it. But it was so ingrained in me . . . some of that came out in the record of 'She's Not There,'" said Argent. "And I remember years later talking to [jazz guitarist] Pat Metheny. And [he] said, 'Man, that was the record that made me think I had a way ahead in fusing rock and jazz.' Now, he may have been particularly kind when he said that, but he certainly said it to me. And he said, 'All that modal stuff you were playing.' And I thought, 'Modal stuff? I wasn't playing any modal stuff.' But then I went back to the record . . . where I was just thinking of A Minor Seventh to D, as a chord sequence—the way I actually played it, I played a little modal scale over that, to fit in with those chords. And I didn't even think about it. . . . But because I was listening to so much of the stuff that Miles Davis was doing at that time, that came out in the mix."

OTHER R&B BANDS

Within the R&B scene, bands displayed a plethora of styles and skill levels. On the upper end of the sophistication scale sat Zoot Money's Big Roll Band, Georgie Fame & the Blue Flames, and Manfred Mann. Those bands, coming from a jazz background, offered up a higher level of technical musicianship than, say, your Stones and Yardbirds.

Zoot Money's group, which at one point included future Police guitarist Andy Summers, probably provided the most varied instrumentation, including flutes, keyboards, and horns. "People who were Rolling Stones fans would come along and say, 'Why have you got a squiggly trumpet?'" Money recalled. "They meant a saxophone. . . . I'd say, 'Because we prefer it and we don't like the Rolling Stones anyway.' [That] was a lie, but you have to say something to keep them off your back."

On the other end of the spectrum sat the Pretty Things, who have been described as a more "raw" version of the Rolling Stones.

When someone uses the word *raw*, what exactly does it mean? Perhaps the word can be related to the Seattle grunge era of the late 1980s (which is when grunge actually existed in Seattle). At the time, grunge meant "going for it"—getting the feeling out without worrying about getting the song "right," or worrying about technical proficiency. If singers forgot a verse, for example, they might just scream or leap into the audience. The Pretty Things offered a similar aesthetic. "One of the reasons we were more raw was [because] our musical technique was not as polished, basically not as good as a lot of other bands," said Pretty Things guitarist Dick Taylor. "A lot of people liked it for the fact that, again, it was kind of—maybe it makes it more accessible, maybe a bit more exciting. I mean, I [later] produced the first Hawkwind album. The reason I really, really liked Hawkwind when I went to see them was they again were so raw. And I saw something in that which is kind of a bit like the early Pretty Things."

The Pretty Things didn't just sound raw, they looked the part as well, with singer Phil May featuring long hair as early as 1964—roughly three years ahead of current trends—and even outpacing the Beatles in that department. The look and sound made parents very afraid. Singer P. J. Proby, who would become a major teen sex symbol in mid-1960s London, recalls the beginnings of extra-long locks. "Me and Phil started it," said Proby. "I mean, I had the pony tail, but a lot of times I didn't wear it in a ponytail, I wore it down like in a page boy, kind of like a girl would wear . . . even the day that I met Phil May [in 1964], his hair was down to his waist, already. So he was the first one that ever wore it that long. And then I started wearing it that long."

"[The Pretty Things] were rougher than the Stones," observed Peter Frape, who later managed drummer John Alder (aka Twink). "If you didn't want your child to marry a Stone, you certainly didn't want them to marry a Pretty Thing."

Then there was the Spencer Davis Group, who created quite a stir in Birmingham before emigrating to London in 1964. The energy of this young band captured and infused London's vibrant R&B scene. But what distinguished the SDG from its contemporaries? "I must be honest and say [the other bands] didn't have a Steve Winwood," said Davis, who played guitar. "And we did."

> "A warning to R&B groups. Watch out for Birmingham's Spencer Davis group. Their gimmick? Sixteen-year-old Steve Wingwood [sic], who plays guitar, piano, organ and harmonica. He also sings better than most bluesmen in the Southern States."—M. Simcox of Birmingham, Melody Maker mailbag, June 27, 1964

"What we brought to the table [in addition to Winwood]," said Davis, "was—we were authentic. And I was so authentic I was playing 11-bar and 13-bar blues, 'cause that's what the old blues guys did."

CAN WHITE BOYS PLAY THE BLUES?

> "It's *their* [my italics] music. I feel just a little embarrassed when people say I can 'blow Wilson Pickett off the stage'—no matter how hard you try you can never sing the blues like a coloured person. That's their life they are singing about."—Steve Winwood to Keith Altham, *New Musical Express*, February 11, 1966

By 1964, a host of American blues legends, most notably Champion Jack Dupree, John Lee Hooker, and Howlin' Wolf, returned to play with the new crop of London R&B bands. And then there was the inimitable singer/harp player Sonny Boy Williamson.

Born in Mississippi somewhere around the turn of the century—no one knows for sure—Williamson became a giant of the Chicago blues scene by the 1950s. Then he became the ultimate link between the pre–World War II acoustic blues of Robert Johnson, urban electric blues, and the British Invasion. By the time he ventured to England, he was already in his 60s, a hardened and somewhat bitter man, a wild character with a devilish sense of humor, and one with little tolerance for precocious young musicians. Eric Clapton found that out when Williamson guested as a front man with the Yardbirds. "His real name was Rice Miller," he wrote in *Clapton: The Autobiography*. "So when we were first introduced to him at the Crawdaddy, I couldn't wait to show off, and tried to impress him with my knowledge, asking him, 'Isn't your real name Rice Miller?' At which point he slowly pulled out a small penknife and glared at me. It went downhill from there."

Sonny Boy was perhaps the ultimate blues character—a hard man and a hard read. His harp would sometimes disappear in his mouth as he laid out short, rhythmic bursts of raunchy melody. He would show up to gigs wearing a two-tone suit and carrying a briefcase filled with his trademark harmonicas and his favorite whiskey: Johnnie Walker Red. He'd had extra pockets sewn into his jacket to hold extra bottles. Sonny Boy was daring, unpredictable, and sometimes unreliable, but he was always a top-notch player.

It must have been rather strange for both band and audience to watch British kids in their early 20s backing a much older African American legend. People's reactions to Sonny Boy's presence differed depending on their perspective. According to English jazz great Chris Barber, Sonny Boy and his ilk were less than impressed with their young protégés. "What Sonny Boy Williamson did, when he got with some of the amateur blues bands who had come up—obviously, a backing group for Sonny Boy—the Yardbirds did it, and the Animals," Barber recalled. "Just beginners, they were. And all of them—Sonny Boy would stop in the middle of a number and say, 'Wait a minute! Why can't you play the blues?!'" [laughs].

> "Sonny Boy Williamson was right when he said British blues groups need to 'cool it' to achieve a good blues sound."—Chris Roberts, *Melody Maker*, August 8, 1964

"They [American bluesmen] were quite hard on a lot of people, I think," recalled Manfred Mann's Mike Hugg. "You really had to be on your toes. They didn't take any prisoners. If you didn't come up to scratch, they let you know it in no uneasy fashion."

Singer P. J. Proby, an American who grew up on a Texas farm worked by black sharecroppers, doesn't believe the British artists matched up to the originals. "I'd learned everything off the real thing and they had learned theirs off the real thing's *records*," said Proby, "the phrasing I look for, [how the original artist] did the phrasing. Even to this day, none of [the British artists] phrase right. Like [the Brits] say, 'I'm gonna.' They don't realize that colored people say 'I'm gwanna.' I'm going back to the colored people that I was raised with who had never even heard of school hardly. . . . A lot of the words, you wouldn't be able to understand, because colored people don't vocalize it that way. It's like Bo Diddley doing 'Hush Your Mouth.' He didn't say, '*hush* your mouth,' he said, '*herschi* mouth.' [He starts singing] 'Ohhhh, herschi mouth. Herschi mouth.' So when Mick Jagger did it, he'd go, [starts singing again] 'Ohhhh, hush your mouth.' And he should be saying 'herschi mouth,' like a Hershey bar."

R&B bands like the Yardbirds don't necessarily share that sentiment. By 1964, they had added a much more raucous, high-volume, borderline out-of-control element to the blues. Effectively, they had ceased being slavishly loyal to the old records and begun to bring in their own personalities to their playing. "We did quite a few gigs with [Williamson] and did a recording with him," said the Yardbirds' Jim McCarty. "And this is when we were playing at the Crawdaddy Club. I think he really didn't go down that well with us. I think [our fans hadn't] really heard about him. They were all into us."

The Animals recall a more equal relationship. Drummer John Steel remembered his band as being seasoned and fearless from years of playing Newcastle's pub scene. Further, their jazz backgrounds gave them an ability to change things up on the fly. "Sonny Boy was evil, you know," said Steel. "We backed him a couple of times, and he had this evil trick of—he'd call out the key and stomp the time and off you'd go in that key. And then suddenly he'd start playing harmonica in a completely different key. You had to just do a quick about-turn. And we could do that. At the drop of a hat, we could turn it 'round and be in the right key within a half a bar. It was good fun. He was an interesting character, that guy."

Spencer Davis recalled an encounter with Sonny Boy when Eric Clapton decided to sit in with the band. "He found out we were playing at the Twisted Wheel and wanted to sit in with us. So Steve's [Winwood] busy playing the keyboard. Clapton's next to me. And Sonny Boy's in front of us and we're gonna play behind him. And Clapton said to me, 'What key?' And Sonny Boy heard Clapton and he said, 'A.' And I quietly nudged Clapton and said, 'He means E.'"

"I was playing at the Crawdaddy Club one night, and the Marquee people had brought over Sonny Boy," said jazz/blues organist Brian Auger, who later played in the Steam Packet with Rod Stewart. "And all of a sudden, up steps this guy onstage. We're playing away and he pulls out from his inside pocket—he's got this bowler hat on and this kind of frock coat with tails and he looked kind of like an English gentleman gone crazy. And he started to play the most insane harmonica stuff."

Auger, who led the Brian Auger Trinity, remembered another unexpected Sonny Boy appearance at the Marquee. "I'm in the middle of wailing away [during an organ solo]," Auger recalled, "and all of [a] sudden there's a kind of chuckle from behind my ear. And at my side—I look up—as I'm blazing through this solo, and it's Sonny Boy. He opens his frock coat and he's got this pocket that he's had put inside, and in it he's got a bottle of Johnnie Walker stashed. Which he pulls out, takes a swig of onstage and he offers it to me while I'm in the middle of this frantic solo. 'No, not quite now,' [I said]. 'No, thanks, Sonny Boy.' And he joined in the rest of the concert."

Mike Cotton, who led the bluesy Stax-influenced Mike Cotton Sound, recalled a gig in London's Holborn neighborhood where Sonny Boy was absorbing a major ribbing from legendary harp player Little

Walter. "Sonny Boy was so angry," Cotton said. "He stood up, and he got this great big knife out and he grabbed hold of Little Walter and he said, 'Little Walter, you carry on like that, it's gonna be your funeral and my trial.'"

Williamson's apparent poor health, not the least of which came from excessive whiskey intake, came to the attention of Auger. So in 1965, just before Williamson was to head back to the United States, Auger booked a studio session featuring the blues legend. "He was drinking a lot of booze before he got out of bed every day," said Auger. "So I thought, once he got on that plane, we weren't gonna see him again. And so, I persuaded my manager to actually book some time. I assembled my [band], which was Micky Waller on drums, who went to the Faces eventually; Rick Brown [on bass]; and [sax players] Joe Harriott [and] Alan Skidmore. . . . And I loved those guys, man. They were a lot of fun. And basically, that was it. There were no arrangements. And nobody knew what was gonna be played. So we got to the studio and basically made up this album. We got in about 9 o'clock in the morning, and Sonny Boy had to leave at around about 1 o'clock to get to Heathrow and get on the plane. . . . There was no rehearsal. No nothing. So I said, 'Well, what do you wanna play, Sonny?' So he got a harp out, and he blew on it—he went 'Bam bam bam bam bah-dum.' That's it. So I said, 'Did you get that?' to the guys. . . . We worked out what the key was. 'Okay, here we go then. Let's just jam it, you know.' So we jammed through this album like that. And they kind of rushed him away and managed to get him on the plane and that really was it. That was the last time we saw Sonny Boy."

Wasn't Jimmy Page on that session?

"Jimmy Page was on that session, yeah," said Auger. "Jimmy was very important actually, man, because he was doing a lot of sessions for blues bands and things at the time." (Note: The record *Don't Send Me No Flowers* finally saw the light of day in 1968.)

The presence of American bluesmen like Williamson, Howlin' Wolf, John Lee Hooker, and others seemed to intensify a debate that raged throughout London in 1964: Just what exactly constitutes true R&B? These exchanges in *Melody Maker* debate the issue:

"I can assure you we're an R&B group."—Mick Jagger, February 29, 1964

"We are not original R&B, but if you are referring to R&B as it's understood in Britain, then yes, we're R&B."—Allan Clarke (Hollies), February 29, 1964

"The desecration of real rhythm and blues is unforgivable, but to have it finally mutilated by Brian Poole, the Hollies, and the rest of that lot is an insult."—Bill Grey (mailbag), March 14, 1964

"I get niggled about all this talk of desecration of real rhythm-and-blues. We don't claim to play real R&B."—Mick Jagger, March 21, 1964

"R&B's a bit of a giggle. It's hard to say what R&B is. So many people say Chuck Berry is R&B, then he says he is rock and roll, so where do you go from there?"—Keith Richards, May 8, 1964 (from *New Musical Express*)

"The Rolling Stones do a splendid job of country blues in the Bo Diddley style. I quite like them. Manfred Mann is playing a sophisticated form of blues, but it's still an authentic style of R&B. But Long John Baldry and his Hoochie Coochie Men come closest to the sound of authentic R&B, like Muddy Waters. In my opinion, this is the most genuine rhythm-and-blues group in Britain."—Chris Barber, May 9, 1964

"I'd like to make it clear that we are a blues band and as such we dissociate ourselves from the current R&B scene."—Long John Baldry, May 30, 1964

"I call it blues, just blues. That's all it is."—Sonny Boy Williamson, January 11, 1964

The commitment to creating rhythm & blues remained central throughout 1964, as led by one Long John Baldry. Originally a member of Cyril Davies's band, Baldry took over the lead when Davies passed away from leukemia in January. Strikingly handsome and lean, and standing six foot seven, Baldry commanded the stage with his powerful presence and voice. "Baldry was a huge name at the time . . . his friends were kind of amazing: the Stones, the Beatles, Elton John," said Auger, who later played in the Steam Packet with him. "[They] would be sitting in the front row at some of the gigs that we did and they're all fans of

Baldry. And Baldry was considered the best kind of blues singer that we produced. . . . It took me maybe about a month, or six weeks, looking at him being surrounded by all these beautiful ladies every night . . . and never going home with them, to realize he was actually gay. He was a very cool guy, also an incredibly kind person, and a real person. And one of the best people I met in the music business, [and] who wasn't an egotistical lunatic."

After Davies's death, Baldry changed the name of his group to Long John Baldry and the Hoochie Coochie Men in deference to Muddy Waters. Waters himself appreciated the gesture. "All those bands patterned after me: The Rolling Stones, the Hoochie Coochie Men, that makes me feel good," Waters stated in the May 9, 1964, issue of *Melody Maker*. "I feel responsible for something of what's happening here. Those kids doing all my songs over here, that's big for me. Of course, I ought to get some money but . . . tell them to send me a bottle of whiskey."

In addition to Baldry's group, a new crop of bands began to appear on the scene, determined to continue to define British R&B, including Zoot Money's Big Roll Band and Georgie Fame & the Blue Flames, both adding to the R&B pool championed by pioneers like Alexis Korner and Graham Bond. As the R&B scene continued to heat up, more outlets for the new music abounded. Since the BBC continued to refuse its support for the genre, two new radio stations began to broadcast from the North Sea: Radio Caroline and Radio Atlanta. Known as "the pirates," these stations would wake up millions in Britain to popular music, providing more options than just a weak-signaled Radio Luxembourg.

Initiated by young entrepreneur Ronan O'Rahilly, who had helped get the Animals gigs in London at his Scene club in Soho, Radio Caroline was born out of frustration with the status quo. Thwarted by the BBC and Radio Luxembourg's slow or nonexistent support of young people's music, O'Rahilly decided to go out on his own. He learned that American and Dutch radio ships legally transmitted signals in international waters. So he headed to America to obtain financing for his offshore venture, whose purpose was to broadcast new music the BBC wouldn't play. While in the United States, O'Rahilly came across a *Life* magazine photo showing a young Caroline Kennedy playing in the

White House, which disturbed government officials, and the name came to him: Radio Caroline.

Sailing in the North Sea, Radio Caroline would begin broadcasting to England on Easter Sunday 1964 with the simple announcement: "This is Radio Caroline on 199, your all-day music station" and then played the Rolling Stones' "Not Fade Away." Shortly thereafter, Radio Atlanta and Radio London would join the cast of pirates in the North Sea, and suddenly young Brits had the same access to the music as their American cousins. "What we were doing was fighting against the forces of the Establishment [BBC]—the British government," said Keith Skues, a DJ with Radio Caroline. "And we were providing a service, I think, for the very first time, which made music available any time of day or night."

Conditions on board ship were cramped and primitive. DJs worked two weeks on board, then took a week's vacation (or "holiday," as the Brits refer to it) on land. Despite these difficult working conditions, or perhaps because of them, Radio Caroline DJs developed a special bond with their listeners, a bond that could not be duplicated by the BBC. Skues, who later worked for the BBC's Radio One, explains: "[I wanted] to talk to the audience," he says. "I didn't want to talk *at* them. The BBC tended to talk at you, whereas offshore radio was that much more informal. [Listeners] would write. They would send presents to you. [I would] casually mention [on air], 'Oh, it's my birthday next week.' People would send you scarves, gloves, teddy bears, whatever. The listeners were just incredible. I've never—ever since then—experienced anything like it."

In December, Caroline was joined by another pirate station—Radio London—which was owned by an American company. London was much more sophisticated than Caroline, with a larger ship and commercials that featured jingles, which the Who later parodied on their 1967 album *The Who Sell Out*. "They had jingles, which we in Britain had never heard before," says Skues, who would spend some time at London after leaving Caroline in 1966. "And they just knocked me sideways. I thought, 'Wow! Fantastic. Singing jingles about the radio station and about the DJs.'"

Pirate DJs, unlike their BBC counterparts, had the freedom to play what they liked. And for Skues, that meant a wide variety of pop music, blues, and R&B that state-run radio refused to broadcast. By year end,

DJ Simon Dee broadcasting from Radio Caroline, circa 1964. *Trinity Mirror / Mirror Pix / Alamy stock photo.*

Caroline, despite its shoestring operation, had made a serious dent in the BBC's listening audience. A *Melody Maker* poll taken in December 1964 asked readers to name the one station he or she would pick if only one were available. The poll ranked Radio Luxembourg first at 36 percent, followed by the BBC at 33 percent, and Caroline at 31 percent. By 1966, Caroline and Radio London would dominate the British radio audience, resulting in the BBC closing down offshore broadcasters the following year.

Adding to the additional radio exposure, British television finally came to the fore with a groundbreaking show called *Ready Steady Go!*

Produced by a private company geared specifically toward a hip, young audience, *Ready Steady Go!* debuted in late 1963. By 1964, *RSG!* became the rallying call for teenagers every Friday night with the accompanying slogan, "The Weekend Starts Here!" New music beamed into English homes with appearances by the Beatles, Stones, Kinks, Animals, and Manfred Mann.

The show supported a new subculture of young kids that began to surface around this time. Bored with the usual prospects, these sort of descendants of the 1950s beatniks began to create their own image, and the high-energy *RSG!* represented their kind and their lifestyle: living

Rolling Stones on *Ready Steady Go!* August 1963. *Pictorial Press Ltd. / Alamy stock photo.*

for the weekend, partying all week, dancing like crazy, and doing so until you literally dropped. You took speed for the assist, did your hair quite carefully, backcombing it to create as much height as possible, attended to your well-manicured outfits, and probably drove a Vespa scooter to the clubs every night. "That program became immensely important," commented Manfred Mann's Paul Jones, whose "5-4-3-2-1" opened the show, "right across youth culture: how you did your hair, what clothes you wore, what make-up the girls had . . . how you danced—very important—how you danced. Everything that young people did came from *Ready Steady Go!*"

"We were asked to do a theme tune for [*Ready Steady Go!*]," said Mann. "And, so '5-4-3-2-1' is the countdown to the beginning of the TV show."

"Young journalists, now, talk about '5-4-3-2-1' as if it was just a simple pop record," said Jones. "Back in the day [however], people used to say, 'What is *that*?' because it seemed kind of strange to them. And of course, one of the reasons it seemed strange to them is it's just a blues—it's just a blues with a couple of extra bits." The program began to help define the emerging Mod movement.

> "[*Ready Steady Go!*] is the TV stronghold of mods, the frighteningly clean, sharply-dress[ed] arbiters of tomorrow's tastes in practically everything. They consider themselves a cut above anyone who does not conform to their cult in clothes, dances and behaviour. Their attitude smacks of social prejudice instilled in too-young minds."— Chris Roberts, *Melody Maker*, January 25, 1964

The Mods, short for "Modernist," became an outgrowth of the beatnik coffeehouse scene of the 1950s. While the beatniks favored jazz and social issues, the younger generation liked R&B and partying all night.

Arguments abound as to the original Mod band. The Stones played to Mods. So did the Yardbirds. "I particularly wasn't really that interested in image and getting the right clothes," said the Yardbirds' Jim McCarty. "But . . . Clapton—he was very conscious about how he looked. He went through a [phase] where he had to buy Ivy League, the Ivy League clothes that he saw on *77 Sunset Strip* or something like that, you know, [the] sort of early '60s American look. He had his hair cut really short. He had sort of [a] crew cut to look like Steve McQueen. But he was really conscious about that."

"Market for Mods. Adler's on King's Road, Chelsea: Twin Tab Double Cuff Shirts at lowest prices from 29/6 upwards."—advertisement for Mod clothing, *Melody Maker*, February 29, 1964

Perhaps the ultimate Mod, though, was a young singer who regularly attended shows at Eel Pie Island. He would methodically work on his appearance, backcombing his hair just so. And of course, he was a hit with the ladies. One day in early 1964, after a night of drinking and dancing at the Island, this young man found himself alone at the Twickenham train station, wrapped up in a blanket against the cold, playing a harmonica. He turned around, noticing a tall figure standing over him. It was Long John Baldry. Cyril Davies had just passed away, and Baldry had taken the reins of the band. He needed a backing singer and asked the lonely harmonica player if he would join. A bit bewildered, since he wasn't sure Baldry had heard him sing, the young gentleman said he had to ask his mum for permission first. Baldry would eventually visit his house and, being the presentable Englishman that he was, managed to convince the parents that their son should join his band, the Hoochie Coochie Men. And so he did. His name was Rod Stewart.

Fashionable Londoners on Carnaby Street, circa 1967. DJ Tony Blackburn (Radio Caroline, Radio London) is second from right. *Chronicle / Alamy stock photo.*

As gangs want to do, clashes can inevitably result. For the Mods, a rival group emerged out of the ashes of the 1950s: the Rockers. Riding motorbikes, wearing drainpipe jeans and leather jackets, sporting greasy hair and a general appearance of an auto mechanic who has spent all day under a chassis, this group initially became known as the Teddy Boys. As the R&B scene heated up in London in the 1960s, the Teddy Boys became known as the Rockers, despising the new music and the associated Mods. Generally a bit older than the Mods, Rockers hated R&B, Motown, Stax, and anything else the younger gang was into. Instead, they clung to their 1950s idols: Chuck Berry, Gene Vincent, and Elvis.

"And the night before the [Stones' first] album was issued, the Stones were in the middle of a mod versus rocker battle. It happened at Rochdale, Lancashire, where the group was due to open the new CubiKlub R&B centre. . . . But the doors were closed because the

Long John Baldry (singing), Rod Stewart (standing, far right) performing at the 1965 Jazz and Blues Festival, London. *Heritage Image Partnership Ltd. / Alamy stock photo.*

street outside had been cleared by police when about 3,000 rockers tried to storm this mod stronghold."—*Melody Maker*, April 25, 1964

Mods and Rockers generally detested one another, and much has been made of clashes between the groups, as displayed in the Who album and film *Quadrophenia*. Nevertheless, the dustups appear to be over-stated, with the notable exception of rioting that occurred in Brighton and other beach resorts in May 1964, in which around 1,000 Mods and Rockers went at it, resulting in a number of beatings and roughly 75 arrests.

In the meantime, as 1964 faded into 1965, the city's R&B scene began to reach a crossroads. While plenty of gigs existed throughout the region for those playing the blues, bands who wanted to jump to the next level had to make the inevitable choice between art and com-merce. You could play R&B to your heart's content, like the John May-alls, the Graham Bonds, and the Alexis Korners. Or you could angle for the pop market, find a larger audience, and . . . uh, eat. The Stones, for example, who began their careers playing Jimmy Reed and Chuck Ber-ry covers, began to write pop songs like "As Tears Go By" and found themselves touring the United Kingdom with Berry and Bo Diddley and then heading to the United States in the 1964 English invasion.

Manfred Mann's "5-4-3-2-1" had a positive effect on that band's career. The Yardbirds faced a similar dilemma, one that would exem-plify the commercial evolution of London's music scene.

A young songwriter named Graham Gouldman had written a pop tune called "For Your Love." Initially his manager considered offering it to the Beatles, but figuring that the band had things covered in the songwriting department, he sold it to the Yardbirds, who needed a hit to move beyond London's club circuit. The song would represent a com-plete turnabout for a band that had made its name playing Chicago blues, led by a gifted guitarist. Of the five players, all were on board with the band's directional change, except for one: that guitarist. "Eric [Clapton] had always been very, very loyal to the blues," says the Yard-birds' McCarty. "He'd been very intensely blues orientated, and very dedicated to it, much more than we were. . . . And I think his take on it was that—apart from certain political things within the band that he didn't really get along with—he found that we were going too commer-cial for him. 'For Your Love' was something we all liked, but he didn't."

Despite the obvious pop direction of "For Your Love," the song itself was quite unconventional within that realm, featuring a time signature change and unusual instrumentation. "[The Yardbirds] called me and said, 'Would you play on our single?'" recalled keyboard player and friend Brian Auger, "and I said, 'Sure. Where are you recording?' And they were recording opposite the BBC [on] Upper Regent Street. So I went there to this tiny studio. I was playing organ at the time and I expected to play organ on this single when I got to this studio. . . . And Paul Samwell-Smith stepped forward and said, 'Right. Let's play you the tune.' [So they] played the tune. And I said, 'Fine. What do you want me to do?' [And Paul said,] 'I want you to do an intro and I want you to . . . get a kind of rhythmic vamp going right through.' 'Fine. OK.' I looked around and said, 'Well, wait a minute. Where's the organ?' And they said, 'No, there's no organ in the studio.' And I then looked further and I said, 'Well, where's the piano, then?' And they said, 'No, no, Bri. There's no piano. There's only *this*.' *This* was this shape in the corner with a cover over it. And ripping off the cover, I discovered a double-tier harpsichord [laughs]. So, I thought that they dragged me all the way from Richmond, all the way up to town—'cause we were constantly playing pranks on one another, anyway. [I said,] 'Ok, you got me guys. That's really hilarious.' And Paul said, 'No, no, we're serious, man.'"

Auger had never played a harpsichord before but decided to give it a try. "So I messed about with it," he continued, "and I said, 'Well, I'll tell you what I can do. I can do a kind of rolling arpeggio thing over the chords—that we're playing over—as an intro. And when we get in, I'll just kind of make some kind of rhythmic vamp.' Which we did. So we cut this tune in about two hours and I remember walking back towards the Tube to go home, thinking to myself, 'These guys are completely nuts. Who the hell is gonna buy a pop single with harpsichord on it?' And, boy was I wrong. [Laughs.]"

"For Your Love" became a top 10 hit in the United Kingdom and the United States, pushing the Yardbirds into the realm beyond the London club scene.

"Eric Clapton, lead guitarist with the Yardbirds, has left the group because he says: 'They are going too commercial.' He has been replaced by Jeff Beck and leader Keith Relf told the MM: 'It's very sad because we are all friends. There was no bad feeling at all, but Eric did not get on well with the business. He does not like commercialisation. Eric did not like our new record, 'For Your Love.' He should have been featured, but he did not want to sing or anything and he only did that boogie bit in the middle. Jeff Beck, who is very, very good, was recommended to us by session man Jimmy Page, who is the guv'nor."—*Melody Maker*, March 13, 1965

"I've been involved singing with groups since I was only 15," Graham Gouldman told Peter Jones in the July 9, 1966, issue of *Record Mirror*. "I wrote 'For Your Love' for one of my groups, presented it to a certain record company—and they thought it was a worthless load of rubbish. Took a long time before the Yardbirds did it, but it was eventually proved to be OK."

As 1965 dawned, those making R&B music in London realized they could head in one of two possible directions: either they could stay faithful to their blues roots, such as Clapton, Mayall, Bond, and Korner wanted to do and thus remain a viable club act only; or they could make hit records and abandon those roots. "It was a very interesting scene," observed Manfred Mann's Mike Hugg. "There were lots of interesting lineups with very odd people in them playing quite alternative stuff. But eventually, of course, it leveled out as the business side of the music scene realized there was something happening there. When they got involved, they leveled it out into a more commercial option."

So things could have easily died, or at least returned to the bland pop music Britain had been churning out prior to the Beatles and the Rolling Stones. Fortunately, London would not let that happen as a new band made it its mission to (quite literally) destroy everything in its path. That would be the Who.

3

IT WAS JUST BLOODY WEDNESDAY

"Once you talk about these days, you sort of imagine it was all taking place in black and white some long time ago. Strangely enough, everything was still in color then. And we were all normal people walking on normal ground. It was just bloody Wednesday."—Manfred Mann

It was 1965, and England had arrived. At least it knew where it had been. The question was, then, where to go from here? R&B had put London on the international music map, but those seeking commercial success made that difficult decision on whether or not to eat: the Yardbirds with "For Your Love," Manfred Mann with "5-4-3-2-1," the Moody Blues with "Go Now" all played blues in the clubs but bought or wrote their own pop songs that became extremely successful. But was London going to degenerate into a shallow reservoir of frivolous pop songs?

Hardly. The Beatles, with their financial resources, talent, and knack for leading the pack, would assure England would remain looking creatively forward.

But what of London? Where would things head, post "For Your Love"? That answer would begin to reveal itself in 1965 and 1966 as England transitioned from R&B to the more experimental and defiantly British sounds of heavy, distorted blues, folk/rock, and progressive rock. This transitional period would become an essential time for London and all of England, a critical period where, for the first time, the United Kingdom would begin to develop its own identity apart from America.

Brits would begin to sever the tether to their former colonies and would no longer become subservient to America's music.

In the meantime, the United Kingdom, which had been in the shadow of the United States since World War II, achieved a newfound confidence by the mid-1960s. No longer did all the best music emanate from the United States. Now, essential music was coming from Britain. And it wasn't even close.

In 1965, America's biggest challenge to the dominance of the Beatles and Rolling Stones came from California, in a proto-psychedelic band called the Byrds. The Byrds had achieved success in England when their cover of Bob Dylan's "Mr. Tambourine Man" topped the *Melody Maker* chart in July. That success would be short-lived, however, as the Beatles' "Help!" would knock the Byrds off that spot upon its debut at the end of that month. In August, the Californians came to the United Kingdom to a less-than-enthusiastic response.

> "[The Byrds] left a trail of hot, tired, bored and disappointed fans, who waited hours to see them give a performance described as 'very, very dull.'"—*Melody Maker*, August 14, 1965

> "Following on their No. 1 hit, 'Mr. Tambourine Man,' the group arrived in this country with a publicity theme along the lines of 'America's answer to the Beatles.' On Saturday's performance, it was a pretty pathetic reply! After tuning up for a full five minutes behind the curtain, they were treated to a traditional slow handclap by the impatient audience. Then their first two numbers were completely drowned by over-amplification."—Keith Altham, *New Musical Express*, August 20, 1965

Further, the Byrds' tepid response in London underscored a new feeling of superiority in England.

"The likeness between the Byrds and many British groups is quite amazing," fan Jane Heaton wrote to the *Melody Maker* mailbag in the July 24, 1965, issue. "Studying their pictures I can see traces of Yardbirds, Peter and Gordon, Beatles and Rolling Stones. Even their names, Jim, David and Chris, sound English. I thought all American boys were called Clyde Weissman the Third, or Mervyn Schwartz the First, or something."

"I've never met an American who just came out on stage and per-formed," the Animals' Eric Burdon told Georgie Fame in the February 19, 1966, issue of *Record Mirror*. "When they go out there, everything has to be written down—the whole sequence from the ad lib lines, the patter, the timing and the number of steps they take. They write it all down on a bit of paper. They won't go on [stage] cold if they can help it, and do what an English artiste does who gets on stage and just goes."

The Beatles and then the Stones paved the way for an entirely new ethos in rock 'n' roll. To succeed, commercially or otherwise, musicians must write their own songs. The Animals, who had achieved commer-cial success with covers such as "House of the Rising Sun," "Don't Let Me Be Misunderstood," and "We Gotta Get out of This Place," found the well drying up by 1965 with a lack of original material. "This is where the Animals kind of lost the edge," said drummer John Steel, "in the sense that the Beatles and the Rolling Stones, particularly, formed a very powerful songwriting team. And that's what took them to a differ-ent level. . . . Basically, there was never a good songwriting setup in the Animals. That's where we sort of stumbled and fell."

And then there was the Who.

In 1965, the Who inherited the London mantle left in the wake of the popularity of bands like the Rolling Stones and Yardbirds, who had moved on to become national and international stars.

The Who would become their own genre, forging their own story, their own history, and that history would effectively represent all of rock 'n' roll. During their life span, the Who spun out R&B, Mod-inspired anthems, psychedelia, prog, and even punk rock. The Who would know no boundaries.

Mutating out of a Roger Daltrey–led group called the Detours, the Who made their London debut in late 1964. The band's creative spark germinated from the duo of singer Daltrey and lead/rhythm guitarist Pete Townshend. Dynamic bass player John Entwistle had recom-mended that Townshend join the Detours. Original drummer Doug Sandom departed in 1964, to be replaced by frenetic percussionist Keith Moon, who hailed from a surf-rock band called the Beachcomb-ers, and thus the lineup was complete.

The dynamic of four alpha males coming from differing backgrounds created an instant tension that would fuel nearly a decade of unprece-dented creativity. Pete Meaden initially managed the Who, and two new faces, who would alter the face of rock music, discovered the band at a gig at London's Railway Hotel: Kit Lambert and Chris Stamp. The pair quickly ousted Meaden and began carefully crafting an image that would appeal to a growing Mod audience. Dressing sharply with short cropped hairstyles, by 1965 the Who emerged as the champion of the Mods.

> "The Who: Maximum R&B: all enquiries PAD 5344."—ad from *Melody Maker*, November 7, 1964

Townshend quickly made a name for himself with his now-clichéd guitar-smashing routine. Funny, nowadays it has become so commonplace that most of us just shrug when we see it. A recent video, which went viral on YouTube, showed a middle school bass player violently smashing his instrument during a lunchtime gig. What did the teacher say after this "shocking" display? "OK, make sure to pack your belongings and get to your next class on time." In 1965, however, such a sight did astonish audiences.

The Who, Piccadilly Circus, London, 1964. *Trackingimages.com / Alamy stock photo.*

According to Terry Marshall, cofounder of the Marshall Amplification Company, Townshend's guitar destruction began quite by accident. At one gig with a small stage, he raised his guitar overhead, and it hit the ceiling and damaged the instrument. Frustrated, Townshend destroyed his guitar, sending the crowd into a frenzy. Who manager Kit Lambert saw an opportunity and seized it, having the guitarist regularly incorporating destruction into his act.

Daltrey had a slightly different take. "[The guitar smashing] started when Pete slipped on stage and broke his guitar," Daltrey told Norman Jopling in the September 17, 1966, issue of *Record Mirror*. "The reaction was terrific! No really, he started it when he used to play about with amplifiers and pull them and everything for the feedback sounds. It just developed. It makes us feel much better to do it. The rest of our act is for the audience. But the smashing up bit is for us."

Keith Altham, then a young music journalist, found out what the buzz was all about when he went to cover the band for the first time at a Marquee gig. "And I walked in, just in time to see their blitzkrieg, the smashing routine and the last three or four numbers," Altham remembered. "And they were so loud. And I thought, 'Jesus Christ. This is gonna deafen me.' And I started to make my way out after the dust was settling on the stage from the smashing of the guitar. And as I sort of fled out the door, I was grabbed by the arm by this little dapper character who proved to be Kit Lambert, who I'd never met. [Lambert said,] 'I'll send you back to interview the boys now,' 'No,' [I said,] 'actually, what I'd like to do, Kit, is go home and please don't tell them where I live.'

"I was supposed to interview Keith Moon. . . . And he rushed out of the dressing room at one point. 'I've gotta go, gotta go. Sorry, can't stay—can't stay. [Roger's] threatened to kill me.' I said, 'Why's he threatened to kill you, Keith?' ''cause I told him he can't sing for shit.'"

Altham found out about the band's confrontational style later when he attempted an interview over lunch. "Only a few weeks earlier I had made the mistake of offering my hand to Pete Townshend in the [*Ready Steady Go!*] canteen," Altham wrote in the October 7, 1966, issue of *New Musical Express*, "and he had reciprocated by throwing a piece of sandwich at my face, explaining he had done so because I seemed the most unimportant character at the table. This kind of attitude did not exactly cement good relations I felt—why did he do it? [So

I asked Keith Moon, and he replied:] 'Perhaps he thought you were hungry?'"

An 18-year-old music fan named Mike Rivers would experience Moon's notorious petulance when he scored backstage passes at the Marquee. "I was . . . with a girlfriend . . . and I was very polite. There was [Moon] sitting there waiting to go on," said Rivers. "[I said] 'Good evening.' Keith Moon looked up at me and said, 'Who the fuck are you? Fuck off!' I felt like dying.

"And then we saw the gig [from] backstage. Great band. Then at the end of the show they started breaking up their instruments. And I thought, 'What the hell is going on here?' I thought they were just a bunch of morons to do that. It was very interesting to see . . . the reaction of the audience at the front. And they were standing there with their mouths open, 'cause most of them hadn't seen this before."

Instrument destruction didn't just come from the hand of axman Townshend. Roger Daltrey would regularly swing his mics during performances and frequently damage them. "He used to walk in [to the Marshall amplification store]," recalled Terry Marshall. "And it was like [he was] holding a bunch of carrots if you like, like about 10 carrots on the stem. He walked in with all these broken microphones. And I used to have a deal with Shure mikes. They used to send me all their replacement heads and I could actually replace a head in a Shure mike faster than anybody at Shure, 'cause I was doing [it] more than anybody. I was buying 10 or 15 replacement heads at a time for Roger."

Daltrey quickly became adept at using his microphone for self-defense if necessary. "I remember going to see the Who and Chuck Berry one night at the Royal Albert Hall," recalled Keith Altham. "The front rows were populated by Edwardian Teddy Boys and Rockers who'd come to see Chuck Berry. And the further back you went, the majority of people were there to see the Who. Then the Who came onstage, the Rockers and the Teddy Boys let them have it: heckling, and shouting, and cackling, 'Bring back Chuck! We want Chuck!' One of them made the mistake of hurling pennies at Roger Daltrey, who immediately hurled his microphone out into the audience and caught this huge Ted in the forehead. And he was carried out unconscious."

Perhaps the best symbolic representation of the early Who comes not from their initial hit single "I Can't Explain" (released in January 1965) but from their second, "Anyway, Anyhow, Anywhere" (May

1965), the first song to really capture the Who's live act on tape . . . from Moon's cascading drums, to Townshend's massive feedback, to Entwistle's frenetic bass lines, to Daltrey's macho lead vocals. The finale even features a Stax-like vocal style from the singer:

> I can go anyway, I want to.
> I can live anyhow, I want.
> I can go anywhere, for something new.
> Anyway, anyhow, anywhere I choose.

That opening line essentially represents not only the defiance of one band but also of the Mods and the post–World War II generation of British kids. The Who symbolized the unbridled creativity their parents could not imagine. Feeling fortunate to survive four years of relentless German bombing, England's World War II generation was content merely to live in peace. The Who, meanwhile, both told and reflected the angst of the postwar generation . . . as in, "maybe there's something more."

Despite this outwardly rebellious stance, the reality is that these kids explored their newfound freedom in a much more subtle and sophisticated way than their American cousins. Instead of erupting with the in-your-face attitude of 1960s American boomers, fans of the Who quietly explored their new creative expression, from fashion, to hairstyles, to parties, and of course, to the music they chose to listen to.

Offstage, Moon was as entertaining as he was on it . . . and that could go either way. *Melody Maker* photographer Barrie Wentzell remembered drinking one night in a London pub with him. "I mean, [Moon] could drink anybody under the table. A huge American challenged [him], 'You [Brits] can't drink.' So Keith said, 'All right.' A couple of bottles of brandy, each. The American started chugging away. Keith hadn't started. And the guy gets up and starts throwing up. Keith downs it all in one. And then orders a pint of lager."

"I remember going to a party at Keith Moon's when he got the house in Chelsea," Wentzell continued. "He was carrying a load of drinks along and the floor disappeared 'cause it was a sunken floor and [the drinks] fell on top of Townshend and a few other people. Spilled drinks all over the place. Everybody laughed, and it broke the ice of the party and carried on from there."

Constantly evolving and pushing forward, the Who—and Townshend in particular—desired to move beyond their little act of sheer volume and what they called "auto-destruction." The Who began to lay the basis for a more sophisticated version of rock . . . something that would be championed later by the Beatles and the progressive rock movement. Townshend called it "pop art." "We play pop-art with standard group equipment. I get jet-plane sounds, Morse code signals, howling wind effects," Townshend told Nick Jones in the July 3, 1965, issue of *Melody Maker*.

In a lot of ways, the Who represented a more significant turning point than the Rolling Stones' role in the earlier R&B boom. The Stones essentially introduced blues to young British kids, who then used it as a vehicle to explore beyond the humdrum world of their parents. But the Who were onto something else. What *identity* can we create beyond something derived from America? What European influences can we insert into the equation? How can we become more *English*?

> "They are four mods from Shepherds Bush, London. And their popularity is gathering strength in exactly the same way the Animals experienced two years ago. . . . Mods identified themselves with the Who because the Who identified themselves with them. Pop music is often allied to social trends and fashions. This was how it was in the Who's early days. Pete Townshend wore a suede jacket, Roger Daltrey hipster trousers. Mods playing mod music. 'We think,' [says Townshend,] 'the mod thing is dying. We don't plan to go down with it, which is why we've become individualists.'"—*Melody Maker*, June 5, 1965

PEAK OF THE MODS

While the Who ruled the roost in Mod-land, another band showed up as a serious rival in that department: the Small Faces. Like the Who, the Small Faces represented the next generation of London bands, post-Stones and post-Yardbirds.

The genesis for the Small Faces came from the pairing of drummer Kenney Jones with bassist Ronnie Lane. Jones, who would later go on to perform with the Faces and the Who, initially wanted to play banjo after hearing Lonnie Donegan's "Rock Island Line." The budding musician had his eye on a banjo that sat in the window of an East End pawn shop. So he saved up his money for months and headed down with a friend to purchase the instrument. "By the time we got there, it had gone," Jones recalled. "So we went in to the shop and said, 'Where's the banjo? We want it.' And [the shopkeeper] said, 'The guy's picked it up. He's paid his money, and it's gone.'

"So we left the shop, and I was heartbroken and very sad, and my friend said to me, 'You're really upset about this, aren't you?' I said, 'Yeah.' He said, 'Well, look. A friend of mine's got a drum kit. Shall I get him to bring it over this afternoon?' I said, 'Yeah. That'd be great.' Anything to cheer me up. So we went back to my house, and his friend brought around a drum kit, which consisted of one bass drum, no foot pedal, a snare drum with no stand, and two sticks—of which one of them was broken in half. And my dad was a bit of a carpenter. So what we did was we [took] glue [from] my dad's workshop and we tried to glue this stick together. And there was no superglue in those days. So we were waiting there for what seemed like an eternity to try to get the

Small Faces, London, 1966. *Pictorial Press Ltd. / Alamy stock photo.*

stick to glue together. And it never happened. So I ended up banging this drum . . . on one and a half drum sticks. And that's how my introduction to drums came about."

After teaching himself how to play drums for a few months, 14-year-old Jones began to venture down to a local pub called the British Prince. Every Friday night, he would watch a jazz band play. He and the band's drummer exchanged awkward glances but would eventually become friendly. "And on one Friday I went there," Jones remembered, "and he said, 'We've now got a special guest. And he's gonna get up and play some drums.' And I thought, 'Oh, great. Another drummer. Let me see who that is.' And he introduced *me*. And I went, 'What do I do now?' My legs went to jelly and I found myself sitting on the drum stool. And I looked at the rest of the band, and they were like giants. And I sat down on the drum stool, and the other three members of the jazz band just looked down at me. [Again], they were like giants. I kept looking up. Everything went to slow motion. They counted this song out, '1-2, a 1-2-3-4.' And it sounded like, 'Oooonneee, Twoooooo . . .' It sounded like that. . . . That was it. That was my moment. I knew that's what I wanted to do.

"Then the barman came up to me and said, 'That was great. Really enjoyed that. Are you in a band?' I said, 'No. I'm forming my own band now [called the Pioneers].' He said, 'Well, one of my brothers just bought a guitar. And he's learning how to play it. Shall I bring him down next week?' I said, 'Yeah, that'd be great.' And so, the next Friday, I waited there and the door opens. In walks Ronnie Lane. He looked like one of the Beatles before the Beatles. He had a suit on—a gray suit, a starched collar, which was too big for him, and a tie. And every time he looked to the left or the right, his tie would stay right in the middle. And I started laughing right away. And that's how I met Ronnie Lane."

By 1965, Jones's band had adopted a Mod persona and the name the Small Faces.[1] A *face* meant a prominent Mod, and *small* referred to the diminutive statures of the band members, which by November included keyboardist Ian McLagan and singer/guitarist Steve Marriott. Marriott's height challenge did not impede his stature as a front man. His powerful, soulful vocals influenced a generation of rock singers, including, according to Jones, future Led Zeppelin front man Robert Plant. "Robert Plant used to hang around with the Small Faces," Jones recalled. "Because he was a massive fan of Steve Marriott and the Small

Faces. Because Robert was six-foot-something tall and we were half-pint size, we never liked him hanging around the dressing room so much. He was so tall. But he was such a lovely guy."

The Small Faces' Mod leanings extended to the fashion, of course, which was a huge part of the subculture. Like the Yardbirds' Eric Clapton before them, the Small Faces became fashion trendsetters. "Once I joined Small Faces," said McLagan, "it wasn't like, 'Oh, now I've got to become a Mod.' I couldn't wait to get to the stores."

Given that the country had moved beyond the postwar period by 1965, young people began to find readily available employment and corresponding money in their pockets. They now had the means to discard the bleak colors of their youth. "We grew up in black and white, or gray—everyone was wearing that," said Jones. "The minute I saw something bright—I mean, I saw a red caravelle jumper [sweater] in Aldgate's [a Tube stop outside London]. And I saw it in a shop. I stood there and went, 'Man!' Every shop, in the window, had gray clothes, except this one, bright, red caravelle jumper. And I thought, 'Gotta have that.' So I went back and saved up some money to buy it—I think it was two pounds, ten shillings. And I bought it. I wore this bright, red jumper. And I found some white Levis on sale. And I got some colorful socks. I didn't know that I was creating—or we were creating a culture, just a different change of fashion called 'Mod.' And that's exactly how it happened. We were making things up. Because then we started to be famous and be on television, whatever we wore, the fans were wearing it the next day. And the shops were selling it."

In their early days, upon signing with Decca under manager Don Arden, the Small Faces were all about obtaining hits, and they did so with a pop number called 'Sha-La-La-La-Lee," which went to number 1 in March 1966. The group quickly became frustrated, however, as the creative energies of Marriott (who came from a theater background) and Lane needed an outlet. "The whole point of recording a commercial record," Marriott stated in the February 12, 1966, issue of *Melody Maker*, "is to try and get our name really established. If we can score two or three big hits, then we'll start making the kind of records we want to. One day we hope to be doing right weird, far-out stuff."

The Small Faces' exploration into the musical beyond would have to wait until the following year, when the band would ditch Arden and Decca and sign with Andrew Loog Oldham's Immediate Records label.

Other than the Who and Small Faces, another band would quietly emerge within the Mod culture: the Eyes. Although this band had a relatively short life and minimal impact beyond London, the Eyes had a 1966 hit that arguably best encapsulates mid-1960s London and the Mod lifestyle: "I'm Rowed Out."

The track showed up on the B side of a hit called "When the Night Falls." "I'm Rowed Out" begins with four fuzzy chords followed by a frenetic Keith Moon–like drum intro. Then vocalist Terry Nolder intones, "You've got a gray suede coat and a soul like fire." Bassist Barry Allchin, who wrote the song, explained further: "The studios were at Marble Arch and we went there one night and did it. It was basically a recording of a live show as we were all miked up and [we] recorded on a four-track machine (mono of course!). There were seven takes in total and no overdubs. Three guitars, drums, and a harmonica and a gong. The lyrics were loosely based on a girl I knew. She had a fiery temperament. (A soul like fire.) *Rowed out* was a local teenage term meaning 'I can't take much more of this.'"

Fortunately for London, it wasn't just the new Mod bands making musical breakthroughs during those pivotal years of 1965 and 1966. The Yardbirds, under the stewardship of Jeff Beck, led a rediscovery of European musical roots. "Still I'm Sad," a Yardbirds hit that rose to number 2 in October 1965, symbolized this break from America. The song opens with a medieval-inspired Gregorian chant, something that had been previously unheard of in rock 'n' roll . . . certainly not in anything coming from America. "We used to listen to a lot of different music—a lot of jazz, a lot of classical music," said Yardbirds' drummer Jim McCarty. "Like the Gregorian chant [in] 'Still I'm Sad.' And sometimes it worked in there and sometimes it didn't. There were lots of little subtle influences coming in."

> "The Yardbirds are now Britain's most experimental group. While other groups talk about trying to be 'different,' the Yardbirds are quietly doing it. . . . [I]t was Paul [Samwell-Smith, bass] and drummer Jim McCarty who wrote the most interesting side of their double-hit, 'Still I'm Sad,' based on a 13th century Gregorian chant."— *Melody Maker*, October 16, 1965

Experimentation wasn't just limited to music and fashion. In 1965, Manfred Mann became the first Western band to cross the Iron Curtain. For those who have grown up after the demise of the Soviet Union, such an action may not seem particularly risky. Westerners routinely visit the Czech Republic, Eastern Germany, and throughout Eastern Europe. In the 1960s, however, with Soviet Red Army troops controlling half the continent, such travel became more than problematic: it could become deadly. Within the Eastern Bloc, free expression became anathema and illegal; it could result in death or sentencing to torture and slave labor camps known as the Gulag. Even listening to the Beatles could result in a ticket to the Gulag.

It was within these parameters that Manfred Mann decided to embark on an adventure to communist Czechoslovakia. "We stayed in a hotel where the elevators were locked," the band's namesake Manfred Mann recalled. "In order to get in the elevator, you needed a key. And only the staff had the key, because it was the 'worker's paradise.' So the staff could go up and down, but the guests had to walk up [the stairs]. As I tell the story now, it almost sounds like I'm making it up. But it really did happen—in Bratislava, that's what happened. You had to walk up six flights of stairs carrying your own bag. No one would help you. Because there was no tradition of service—[the] hotel wasn't in competition with another hotel. 'We've all got a job here. It's easier for us. You can't go in and mess up our elevator.' That was the sort of atmosphere."

The gigs themselves were frightening, with audiences kept under strict supervision by the police. "Everyone was terrified . . . if anybody stood up—just stood up in the seat—they were hauled out by the security police," Mann continued. "One guy—young bloke—got up, and was hauled out by the police. He was pissing himself with fear as he was pulled out of the hall. It was horrible."

The search for identity, that push into the beyond, continued throughout 1965 and 1966. It was all about creating new sounds, using any and all technology available at the time. Two new bands—the Move and the Creation—had the audacity to use a violin bow on an electric guitar. Taken through amplification and distortion, the result was an eerie, otherworldly sound; most people attribute the sound to Led Zeppelin, but it existed three to four years before they formed.

In July 1965, the Rolling Stones' "(I Can't Get No) Satisfaction" topped the *Melody Maker* chart and in essence helped redefine the art of recording and what constitutes a "song." Guitarist Keith Richards (then known as Keith Richard) created a distorted guitar sound that mimicked a saxophone.

> "To fuzz or not to fuzz is the question facing Britain's young guitarists. Since Keith Richard produced that teeth-grating, rusty sound on 'Satisfaction,' groups all over the country have ransacked music stores for tone benders to give them a hit sound. Purists may raise their hands in horror at the whole concept of deliberate distortion, but it is well to remember that in the early days of jazz, audiences laughed when trumpeters 'distorted' their playing with mutes."— *Melody Maker*, February 26, 1966

"I didn't think much of it ['Satisfaction'] when we first recorded it in Chicago about two months ago," Keith Richards told *New Musical Express'* Keith Altham in the September 3, 1965, issue. "We had a harmonica on then and it was considered to be a good B side or maybe an LP track. A week later we recorded it again in Los Angeles. This time everything went right. Charlie put down a different tempo and with addition of a fuzz box on my guitar which takes off all the treble we achieved a very interesting sound."

"Satisfaction," of course, offended the older generation, especially those in America who heard Mick Jagger sing, "I can't get no girlie action"; mishearing what he actually intoned: "I can't get no girl reaction."

The Yardbirds' Jeff Beck continued the trend by combining a tone-bending fuzz box with a bottleneck guitar to create a violin-like sound.

And in 1965, British bands began to experiment with Eastern influences, which would pave the way for psychedelia. The Beatles get the credit for injecting the sitar into rock 'n' roll with the release of "Norwegian Wood" in December. The Kinks, however, introduced the *sound* of the sitar five months earlier with a song called "See My Friends." Dave Davies used his guitar to mimic a sitar. "As we did with everything in the studio—in those days they didn't have synthesizers or computers or anything," said Davies. "When you [got] a sound in your head, you sort of experimented with the guitar—tuned the strings down [so] it sounded a bit like it. But after 'See My Friends,' it seemed that everybody bought a sitar all of a sudden. [And] we didn't even use one on it. Curious."

Davies gives credit to legendary British folk singer Davey Graham for exposing London to non-Western music. "He went all over the world," said Davies. "He learned about Moroccan music and Indian music. And he would play those kind of influences channeled through his own music. And he was a big innovator. Some of his early music was kind of like sitarish, and twangy, and D-tuned, and stuff like that. I don't think he ever really gained the credit that he really deserved . . . and me and Ray [Davies] were huge, huge fans."

The Who's Pete Townshend complimented the Kinks in this *Melody Maker* piece a year later:

"For me modern lyrics really started with Ray Davies' 'See My Friend' [*sic*]. The words of the song were meaningless but the sound of the words are what sold the song."—Pete Townshend, as told to Nick Jones, *Melody Maker*, October 15, 1966

Like the Who, the Kinks were known for their share of hijinks. Later touring with Chicken Shack, a band that included future Fleetwood Mac member Christine Perfect-McVie, Dave Davies and drummer Mick Avory soon became fast friends with CS's lead guitarist, Stan Webb. "Mick Avory got a hold of a yellow [pantomime horse] with big, black spots," Webb recalled, "[and] he had a local pub around the corner from his place in Bayswater. He just said, 'Stan, let's dress up in this and go 'round the pub.' And it was in August. It was bloody hot. I said, 'Mick, we'll fry in this thing.' [He said,] 'It's only 'round the corner.' So I got in the back of it and me legs down the back legs [and he said], 'When we get in the pub, don't forget to work the wires so the eyelashes go up and down.'

"So we walked in and Mick's got his hands up on the bar. Can you imagine? People in the pub looking up and seeing a horse with its hooves on the bar, black and yellow horse with its bloody great giant eyelashes going up and down and a voice coming from its mouth.

"[But] when the people saw it was Mick, they just carried on reading their papers."

In another instance, Webb and Avory got into trouble after exiting a theater onto Charing Cross Road. "There were a couple of coaches [buses] parked outside [the theater], which they could [do] then," Webb said. "And we stood by this coach and I noticed that the keys were in it, but the driver wasn't there. So the three of us got in this bloody coach and I drove it up Charing Cross Road. This is like a coach you see now, with 40 passengers or whatever it is and I drove the bloody thing up Charing Cross Road absolutely drunk as a lord, with Mick Avory walking down the [aisle] saying, 'Any more fares, please?' And we [went through a couple] traffic lights, and I thought, 'You idiot.' I turned the engine off, put the handbrake on. The three of us jumped out and just casually walked away, and of course blocked all the traffic in one lane 'cause they couldn't get 'round it. So to this day I will never know what happened when the driver came back [and] saw his coach was missing, finally finding out it's by some traffic lights, at the top of Charing Cross Road with the keys in it."

Musically, though, the Kinks' contribution of the sitar sound, along with Beatles' actual use of the instrument on "Norwegian Wood," caused the sitar to quickly become ubiquitous throughout London.

In 1966, the Rolling Stones would release one of the all-time classic sitar-based rock songs, "Paint It, Black," and were quickly criticized for copying the Beatles. "As we had the sitars, we thought we'd try them out in the studio," Keith Richards told Richard Green in the May 21,

The Kinks at a pub enjoying a beer, 1964. *Trinity Mirror / Mirror Pix / Alamy stock photo.*

1966, issue of *Record Mirror*. "To get the right sound on this song, we found the sitar fitted perfectly. We tried a guitar but you can't bend it enough. Don't ask me what the comma is in the title, that's Decca. I suppose they could have put 'black' in brackets."

BEGINNINGS OF PROGRESSIVE ROCK

The Who's adventure beyond the realm of R&B and Mod-inspired pop songs came out of accidental necessity. In 1966, the band was working on a new record called *A Quick One*. The Who needed to fill around 10 minutes, and manager Kit Lambert suggested Townshend write a mini-opera to take up the time. Lambert's influence upon Townshend was enormous in those days; he introduced Townshend to all sorts of European operating and symphonic influences. The confluence of these two personalities would move rock 'n' roll beyond America and into uncharted territory and into something today we refer to as progressive rock.

Townshend had no idea how to write a 10-minute piece of music, believing pop songs to properly exist under three minutes in length, so Lambert suggested he string together a few pop ditties into one whole. The result was a nine-minute opus called "A Quick One While He's Away," which essentially not only laid the basis for progressive rock but also in fact the concept album, an idea that the Beatles would be given credit for the following spring with the release of *Sgt. Pepper's Lonely Hearts Club Band*.

Townshend's first attempt at extended greatness was admittedly crude; the story line basically consisted of a girlfriend longing for a displaced lover, then having an affair, and finally confessing her infidelity to her lover and receiving forgiveness. Nonetheless, the level of sophistication in constructing such a piece of music within the rock realm had never been attempted before. In addition, this composition required a high level of musicianship to pull off, not the least in the vocal category.

Beginning with a beautiful Daltrey/Townshend low/high harmonic a cappella section called "Her Man's Gone," the piece heats up with a fiery electric abandon and an ascending guitar riff with "The Crying Town." Then comes "We Have a Remedy," which features an operatic harmony between the pair, as they sing, "fa la la la lah, fa la-la-la-lah." The song then abruptly segues into "Ivor the Engine Driver," who is more than willing to satisfy the main character's needs. Speculation is that Ivor also represents a real-life protagonist in Townshend's life who sexually molested him as a child. The "Ivor" section draws straight from American country and western stylings, which continues throughout the next piece and again features the pair harmonizing in "Soon Be Home." Finally, the song lurches into "You Are Forgiven," representing the ultimate reuniting between the lovers with ultimate forgiveness.

A great version of this mini-opera comes from the Who's live performance on the Rolling Stones' 1968 television special, *Rock 'n' Roll Circus*. The broadcast was not released contemporaneously; rumor had it the headliners felt upstaged.

> "Pete's musical achievement—a sort of miniature pop opera, with a cute story about a girl who cries so much she becomes a big drag to all the neighbours, crying all day because her boyfriend is a year late showing up. . . . There are several sections, including a country and western bit and some 18th-century music. It's fun, and new departure for any pop group."—Chris Welch, *Melody Maker*, December 10, 1966

"A Quick One While He's Away" told a story, an admittedly rudimentary one, but it did take the listener along on a journey; this journey—the storytelling—comes directly from folk music. As London began to venture beyond American-inspired R&B, its musicians tapped into a folk ethos, one that derived not from America but from centuries-old English, Welsh, Scottish, and Irish traditions.

FOLK CLUB SCENE

While London was hopping with the success of the Rolling Stones and the Beatles from Liverpool, the United Kingdom was quietly developing a network of folk clubs that ran parallel to the larger rock scene in London. This community mirrored the American coffeehouses of Greenwich Village, albeit with a uniquely British flavor.

Visitors, some nonmusicians even, were encouraged to get up and sing or play to welcoming audiences. Sympathetic supporters throughout the country offered up cheap lodging for traveling folk players, and it soon became possible to make a modest living traveling the country playing these small clubs.

Unlike rock/R&B venues like the Marquee or Eel Pie Island that offered a raucous good time, the small folk clubs provided more of a quiet sense of community. Folk venues existed as rooms above or in back of pubs with no sound system or PA to speak of; many hadn't even a stage. You showed up to watch the musicians perform acoustic music, and if the opportunity presented itself, you might take a turn onstage yourself.

Many of the folk performers, like their R&B counterparts, came from the same Lonnie Donegan skiffle-inspired stream. Instead of moving from there into the blues, however, folk musicians often identified themselves with the left-wing causes their American counterparts championed. Blues/R&B tended to be politically neutral, but folk rallied behind such organizations as Ban the Bomb and the Campaign for Nuclear Disarmament, as well as the general ideals of socialism/communism. "I started going on marches—antinuclear marches," said Jacqui McShee, later vocalist with the Pentangle. "And it was because of that—people used to sing. And because my sister and I used to sing—they said, 'You two have got great voices. You could lead the singing.' And that's how I started singing."

Folk venues popped up all over Britain, and the musicians coming through would soon become legends in England and throughout the world: Martin Carthy, Ewan MacColl, Peggy Seeger, Bert Jansch, John Renbourn, Sandy Denny, Davey Graham, and even Americans like Bob Dylan, Paul Simon, and Ramblin' Jack Elliott would show up and play. For those in attendance, the spartan surroundings and sense of community made this truly underground network special. J. P. Bean, author of *Singing from the Floor: A History of British Folk Clubs*, began going to folk shows in 1966. "It was just the atmosphere that drove you to folk clubs in those days," Bean said. "It was like Christmas Eve."

This underground network of small folk clubs would eventually infiltrate the larger rock scene in unexpected mystical ways. Without these folk venues, Robert Plant would likely have never had flashes in Wales of ancient Celtic wars, which would inspire him and Jimmy Page to write "The Battle of Evermore," featuring Fairport Convention singer Sandy Denny. Without the folk club influence, Traffic would likely have never resurrected a 500-year-old treasure called "John Barleycorn Must Die."

And it all started with inappropriate laughter from American musician Peggy Seeger. Seeger, half sister to folk icon Pete Seeger and married to MacColl, first arrived in England in 1956 at the height of the skiffle boom. Unlike her English contemporaries, however, Seeger was unimpressed with young Brits attempting to play American roots music. "It was humorous, what they were doing," said Seeger. "I mean, it was very funny. To hear Leadbelly sung with Cockney vowels is hilarious."

Seeger's mocking view of English skiffle would come to a head at her folk club in London, likely in 1960. As she sat in the audience, a young local kid began singing Leadbelly's "Rock Island Line," famously covered in England by Lonnie Donegan and Chris Barber's band. "Leadbelly visited our house. I was brought up on Leadbelly and the dignity of his singing," said Seeger. "And I just burst into hysterical laughter 'cause it was so funny, this Cockney. And they had to take me out. I was helpless with laughter."

As a result of Seeger's insolence, a meeting was called at the club involving fellow musicians and audience members. Seeger continued: "And so a member of the audience, who was French, said, 'Well I don't like it when you sing French songs, Peggy.' So I was stunned, and I turned to Ewan and I said, 'Ewan, I wish you'd stop singing [American songs].'

"Then we instituted a policy at our club that you had to sing onstage; didn't matter what you sang while you were ironing or in the shower or whatever—but onstage, in our club, you sang the songs of the culture you grew up in."

This dramatic shift in Seeger and MacColl's performance policy had an enduring impact on the English folk club community. It essentially forced visiting musicians to discover their own local traditions, whether it be Welsh, Irish, or Midlands English. This seemingly unnecessarily restrictive policy would bleed into the rock community, yet not overtly. But as the 1960s lurched along, rock musicians would begin to incorporate their own roots music with bands like Traffic and Led Zeppelin— not to mention Jethro Tull, Fairport Convention, and the Pentangle— and even with prog rock bands like Yes.

Seeger's inappropriate laughter at that show would create a ripple effect that would make British rock more valid, more mystical, and

Ewan MacColl and Peggy Seeger performing in London, circa 1960. *Heritage Image Partnership Ltd. / Alamy stock photo.*

more English, and in a sense, it would help fuel the powerful era we now call classic rock.

Of course, not everyone was on board with MacColl and Seeger's policy. MacColl's strict enforcement combined with his prickly personality drew the ire of many. "He was so far up his own ass," said country blues and non–Jethro Tull musician Ian A. Anderson. "I mean, he was a really unpleasant man."

"There were some inconsistencies about MacColl," added J. P. Bean, "not least that he was born in Manchester [and, later,] adopted a Scottish persona and name. And the first record he brought out was [American] Tennessee Ernie Ford's 'Sixteen Tons.'

"Putting all that aside, [since] people began to sing songs from their own heritage—yeah, it was a good thing."

This local music policy also created a division in the folk world, instituted by those who chose to expand their performance palettes. Al Stewart, who would have mainstream success in the 1970s with the albums *Year of the Cat* and *Time Passages*, would help lead a nontraditionalist faction. Stewart was initially a blues fan from Scotland, then heard Bob Dylan for the first time and switched over to acoustic.

"Eventually, it just was a matter of economics," Stewart recalled. "I couldn't afford to have an acoustic guitar *and* an electric guitar. So I had to make a choice whether I wanted to be a folkie or whether I wanted to play the [electric] guitar. The choice was pretty much made for me by Jimi Hendrix, because when I saw him, I realized that if I practiced for the next thousand years I couldn't do any of that stuff."

While the folk and rock circuits remained physically separate, they commingled somewhat in a key London club called Les Cousins (technically pronounced in French as "Lay Coozah," but most patrons used the English pronunciation and often referred to the venue as just "the Cousins"). "We had no idea it was supposed to be French," Anderson recalled. "We thought it was run by this local 'Les Cousins.' A few years later, I discovered it was [named after] a French movie."

Opening in 1964 in London's Soho neighborhood, the venue would provide a format different than provincial folk clubs, which tended to close up around 10 p.m. In contrast, on weekends, the Cousins would open its doors late and would remain active until the early daylight hours.

Les Cousins would quickly become *the* preeminent folk club. Located in a Soho basement, the space had previously been Hylda Sims's Skiffle Cellar before that club lost its lease. Unlike venues outside of London, the Cousins would actually feature a stage and a small PA. "It seemed like a kind of secret society," said Anderson. "You'd go up Greek Street in Soho and you'd go down this long staircase and you entered another world. All these people were fascinating. They were all a bit kind of *other*. And you wanted to be part of that straightaway."

Les Cousins attracted musicians and fans from all over the country who would often sleep on the floor wherever they could find space. Some would perform in the early evening at a club in the provinces and then hitchhike to London to play the all-nighter at the Cousins. The new club attracted a younger audience since it did not serve alcohol, and the minimum age was 14, versus 18 for a pub. "Quite often, whoever was playing on the evening gig in the Bristol Troubadour might be doing the all-nighter in the Cousins," said Anderson. "And it was like a three-hour drive, maximum, at that time of night on a Saturday night. And so, the Troubadour would finish at 11 and we'd jump in a car and we'd be in London half past one, two in the morning, which was fine for somebody who's doing the all-nighter."

The Cousins became an inviting alternative for young people looking to hang out. You could get in fairly cheaply and have a free place to stay for the night. Then if you scored a gig, you would get in for free. Often, though, performers had to locate a newspaper to find out if they were playing that night. In Anderson's case, he would catch the Tube to the Tottenham Court Road station, pick up a *Melody Maker* at the nearest newsstand, and scan the "Folk Forum" section. "You literally found out whether you were doing the Saturday night gig by looking in the *Melody Maker* [laughs]. These days, you'd look on the internet, obviously. But back then, the *Melody Maker* was the internet," he said.

Al Stewart heard about the buzz at the Cousins and became encouraged to try it out. "I was playing rock 'n' roll until I went up to London in early '65," said Stewart. "In London, I heard Bert Jansch. And that was a shock to the system. I'd never heard anyone play the guitar like that . . . got to see firsthand how you put together contemporary folk songs [and] I heard a lot of those early Paul Simon songs through the wall while he was writing them."

Stewart soon became the resident compère (*emcee* in the American lexicon) at Les Cousins. "They had all-nighters on the weekend," Stewart recalled. "It ran from midnight to 6 a.m. on Fridays and midnight to 7 a.m. on Saturdays. . . . Nobody really wanted the [compère] job. And I took it because I figured that, 'round about four o'clock in the morning when nobody was paying attention, I could sneak myself onstage and get up in front of an audience and practice songs."

The Cousins became a magical place where the talent level of the performers went through the roof. Players included Stewart, Donovan, Bert Jansch, John Renbourn, John Martyn, Ian A. Anderson, Sandy Denny, Wizz Jones, Nick Drake, Davey Graham, Van Morrison, Cat Stevens, and Paul Simon. The club also became a mixing point of sorts between the so-called separate rock and folk worlds. Alexis Korner and Long John Baldry would play there. Even David Bowie turned up one night but was refused entry since he wasn't on the guest list.

After a long night performing and/or crashing on the floor, patrons and performers would stumble outside into the early morning light. Typically, the Tube wouldn't be running right away, so everyone had about an hour to kill before heading home. "There was a woman called Judith Piepe," Anderson recalled, "[and] she used to have a house in the East End where a lot of musicians stayed at different times. Al [Stewart] lived there, Paul Simon lived there, Jackson Frank lived there, and various others. But she also ran a kind of mission place for homeless people in Soho, not far from the Cousins. So she'd quite often get up on the stage roundabout the time the Cousins closed and said, 'If the Tube's not open yet, if anyone wants to come around for a cup of tea.' We'd do that and then we'd get the Tube right out to the west of London and start [heading] back to Bristol."

The Cousins did not set off a firestorm that instantly combined folk music with rock 'n' roll. Rather, it kind of planted a seed, sort of like what the Ramones would do a decade or so later with punk rock, which wouldn't hit the mainstream until Nirvana exploded in the early 1990s. Similarly, folk music seeping into rock 'n' roll had to wait for a year or two before coming to fruition. Within this realm, three major folk/rock groups would begin to emerge from Britain's folk community by the late 1960s: Fairport Convention, the Pentangle, and the Strawbs.

The Strawbs began life as the Strawberry Hill Boys—a creation of Dave Cousins and Tony Hooper. Contemporaries of their R&B relatives, the pair drew from American bluegrass and country instead of black urban blues. Cousins went in that direction despite his enormous affinity for the blues. "I bought Muddy Waters EPs and I bought 'Smokestack Lightnin'' by Howlin' Wolf," said Cousins. "And I sounded absurd singing those songs like that. My voice just didn't suit it. And I didn't have the depth, the maturity or anything like it. So despite [the] fact that I wanted to play that, I gravitated towards white Americana."

Cousins opted for the banjo over guitar, determined to learn Earl Scruggs's distinctive licks. Unfortunately, though, Scruggs played so fast, the individual notes became almost impossible to discern. "Once I heard Flat & Scruggs, I wanted to play like Earl Scruggs," Cousins recalled. "And I found the only way I could work out what he was doing was to slow the record player down to 16 and a half and learn to play [by] listening to the licks he was playing at half speed. And so I learned to play Scruggs-style banjo picking by listening to Earl Scruggs at half speed. And I became the fastest banjo player in Britain.

"I used to go every Friday night to a pub in Isleworth called the London Apprentice on the banks of the River Thames. And a group of people got together every Friday night and sang songs to one another. There was Johnny Joyce who played 12-string guitar and sang Cisco Houston songs. There was Ron Caine who sang the blues. There was a flamenco guitar player. I took my banjo along—Tony Hooper came along with me and we started to play bluegrass instrumentals at 100 miles an hour. And then there was a young guy who turned up one day who was a tinker—of gypsy origin, if you like—that's not disparaging, it's just that was his background. And he sang traditional English folk songs, but he also played mandolin. And so he joined our bluegrass group and he sang the high harmonies. I played the banjo at 100 miles an hour, and Tony was the lead singer. And that was the first incarnation of the Strawberry Hill Boys."

Soon, virtuoso fiddle player Dave Swarbrick, later with Fairport Convention, would join the group. The Boys got their first regular gig at Hylda Sims's Skiffle Cellar. "And they had the City Ramblers," said Cousins. "And they were skiffle origin, but we got booked in there. From there, we gradually got booked in other folk clubs in London, and then gradually it spread out. And in the end, we ended up traveling—I was working during the day—but we'd drive up north to Birmingham. It was 120 miles, and [we'd] drive back overnight. The next morning I'd get up and go to work, again. So, we began to travel. And these folk clubs are springing up all over the place. Folk music was very acceptable to BBC Radio. So they were playing folk music programs because they were easy and cheap to record. And it was very attractive. And all of this was derived from Lonnie Donegan."

The Strawberry Hill Boys would soon meet up with a young nurse who sang traditional ballads in the folk clubs: Sandy Denny. Cousins became enamored with her hauntingly beautiful voice. "There was a guy called Jackson C. Frank, who was an American . . . and his girlfriend was Sandy Denny," Al Stewart recalled. "She was 19 and she was a nurse at the time. So the first time I ever saw her, I think she was in a nurse's uniform. And she showed up, and she was singing the 'Ballad of Hollis Brown' by Bob Dylan—first time I ever saw her. I didn't know that she could sing. I didn't know she could play guitar. Turned out that Jackson didn't like her to sing or play the guitar. He thought that was his job. So Sandy only did it when he wasn't around, but they broke up."

Cousins, who quickly shortened his band's name to the Strawbs so as to symbolize his move beyond bluegrass, saw Denny perform for the first time at the Troubadour. "She was singing a song called 'Fear a' Bhàta' . . . it's a Gaelic song," said Cousins. "And I was just completely mesmerized by this young girl wearing a long, white dress and a straw hat with a Gibson Hummingbird guitar singing absolutely beautifully. And I was completely captivated. And [I] went up to her [and] said, 'Can I introduce myself?' She said, 'Who are you?' I said, 'David Cousins. You want to join the group?' almost flippantly. She said, 'Who are you?' I said, 'The Strawbs.' [She responded,] 'Hmm, yeah, all right.'"

Sandy Denny, who would later gain notoriety with Fairport Convention, had a voice that conjured up images of a sophisticated, world-weary singer. These impressions drew from the sheer beauty and depth of her delivery. Offstage, though, Denny provided a striking contrast. Joe Boyd, who would later manage Fairport Convention, had this to say about the enigmatic singer: "She was very funny, profane, loud, clumsy," Boyd wrote me, "not what you might infer from just listening to her singing. Very confident musically, [but] lacking confidence in her looks and femininity."

Denny's convergence with the Strawbs would lead to one album together, *All Our Own Work*, recorded in 1967 but not released until 1973. "That was Britain's first ever folk/rock record," said Cousins. "So we went over to Denmark, and they said, 'What do you want in the studio?' I said, 'I want a drummer.' And so, that was the first time we'd ever recorded with a drummer. It was the first time we ever recorded in what was supposed to be a proper recording studio. So you get Sandy Denny and the Strawbs singing my songs, but essentially they were pop orientated, if you like. And a totally different feel altogether from what we were doing as a bluegrass group. There's a couple of banjo instrumentals on it, but that was just to prove to people I could still play the banjo. That was a revolutionary record for its time."

England's definition of folk/rock would have a much different feel than the jingly/jangly sounds coming out of the American West Coast. Instead, Britain would begin to draw from its own centuries-old traditions, as it had done in the folk club scene, and then weld it onto the rhythms and drive of rock 'n' roll to create its own distinctive version of folk/rock. Denny again would play a pivotal role in all this when she left the Strawbs for a new group called Fairport Convention . . . but that is a story for chapter 5.

IT WILL GET LOUD

By 1966, British rock's innovators like Pete Townshend and Eric Clapton wanted to take things a step further in terms of sound and volume. For Britain's rock and blues musicians to develop their own identity, they would need more than just their own stylistic or traditional influences. The equipment itself would begin to define how England sounded, as seen with the genesis and meteoric rise of Marshall amplification under its cofounders, Jim and Terry Marshall.

Marshall earned his living playing drums in a dance band; he did so until he opened his first shop in the West End of London in 1960 along with his wife, Violet, and son, Terry. He initially stocked drums and taught lessons to a growing list of pupils, among them Mitch Mitchell (later with the Jimi Hendrix Experience), Micky Waller (later with the Jeff Beck Group), and Mick Underwood, who became a preferred session player—later joining the Herd with Peter Frampton. Underwood recalls responding to a Marshall ad offering drum lessons. "My dad took me over to see him," said Underwood. "And there was this beautiful kit sitting there. And [Marshall] said, 'Well, go on there, Mick. Have a go on it. Sit down there and have a go on it.' I'd never put my foot on a high hat pedal before. And I was a bit nervous, really. I just sat there and played the kit—I went mad on it, to be honest with you. I just went bloody potsy, went bananas. I thought, 'Well, that's it, then, we're out the door now.' And he said to me dad, 'He's an absolute natural player. He hasn't got a clue what he's doing,' which is absolutely correct. 'And I would like to teach him.' And that's how I started with Jim, then, or Mr. Marshall to me. . . . He was a fabulous teacher. . . . He was an absolute delight to be taught by."

Budding R&B musicians soon visited the Marshalls' shop; they asked him to stock guitars as well, which he did. Key players frequenting the Marshalls' store included the Who's Pete Townshend and John Entwistle, Eric Clapton, and Ritchie Blackmore, later with Deep Purple.

During the R&B boom, the Beatles and Stones had helped popularize the British Vox amplifier brand. The problem with the Vox was that it often couldn't produce enough volume for the guitars to be heard over the drums. American-manufactured Fender amps were a possibility, but they were too expensive for most young English musicians to afford. Townshend in particular urged the Marshalls to come up with their own amplifier, one that could generate the necessary volume and fit within a reasonable budget. They then worked closely with the guitar players to come up with a tone they desired but at a more affordable price than Fender.

The process of developing what we now call the "Marshall sound" was quite different from its competitors Vox and Fender. Jim Marshall's son, Terry, a professional saxophone player and part owner of the shop and later the amplification company, possessed an ear for the tonal qualities the musicians desired and, thus, could help translate their requirements to the engineers building the amplifier. "I was trying to give something to the musicians," Terry Marshall said, "rather than make an amplifier [and say], 'there it is.' In the past, if you can think of musicians going to a shop—'This is what's available.' 'OK, I prefer that one to that one.' We wanted something that they could say, 'OK, with that, I can get my sustain. I can get my overdrive.'"

And so the development team coalesced, consisting of Jim Marshall, who had a musical as well as an engineering background; Terry, who would assess the sound; and engineers Ken Bran and Dudley Craven. "Being a saxophone player, I didn't have a leaning towards any existing sounds that were available," said Terry Marshall. "I had the likes of people in the shop, who basically jammed together and played together: Pete Townshend, Ritchie Blackmore, Eric Clapton. I used those three as a reference point. Pete was the most rebellious of the guitarists who were available. He wanted something more. So that was our kickoff. Because I wasn't particularly a guitarist . . . I was looking for a tonal sound that I thought would satisfy the likes of Pete, Ritchie, Eric, [and session guitarist] Big Jim Sullivan."

So the Marshalls and their crew of engineers began working on equipment with the desired tonal qualities. "We basically took an RCA circuit," said Marshall, "which was in common use—it was the same circuit [used in] the Fender Bassman [bass amp]. And what we did was tweaked the amplifier to suit my ears. . . . The pre-amp is the part that you can very easily tweak.

"I was looking at the tonal sounds, rather than what [was] existing. So the Marshall sound, I'm very proud to say, is mine."

Through a largely trial-and-error process, the Marshall team manufactured their first commercially available amp in 1963 called the JTM45; "JTM" stood for "Jim and Terry Marshall." "[The number] 45 was the actual rating, what we call RMS—which is the constant power to suit any guitarist," said Marshall. "Amplifiers used to go a peak power, which is what Pete Townshend was after. He wanted more peak, because most of the amplifiers at the time were rated on their peak power, which meant a 50 watt would only really be a 35 watt. We took our amplifier up to 45 watts as a constant, which meant they could peak—if you had a good Gibson or a good Fender—you would get peak power [i.e., in excess of 50 watts] out of that. But if a guy had a cheaper make of guitar without the sensitive pickups, he would only get 45 watts. We wanted to be honest."

The JTM45 inspired intense loyalty among its customers, as would the Marshall brand for years to come. By early 1965, Marshall listed the Who, Yardbirds, and Moody Blues among its customers.

The new amplification technology combining volume with distortion opened up a new avenue for the earlier R&B groups. Eric Clapton in particular, who played in the Yardbirds and John Mayall's Bluesbreakers, saw an opportunity to take blues to a new level by creating something completely new: the heavy blues power trio. Evidence that something was afoot appeared in early 1966. "I intend to stay with John [Mayall] unless I get the chance to form my own group sometime," Clapton told *Melody Maker*'s Chris Welch in the January 22, 1966, issue. "Some artists I have worked with are not widely known as being great and are to many people obscure. Jack Bruce is definitely one of them. He's the best bass player I know."

Bruce had more than proven his mettle from the early days in the R&B scene, including time with Alexis Korner and Graham Bond, as well as a brief stint with Manfred Mann. His powerful, rhythmic approach to the bass could perfectly suit a band with only one guitar player. Further, his bluesy vocals and songwriting talent would prove to be a much-needed commodity. For a drummer, the band turned to Ginger Baker, who had played with Bruce in Korner's Blues Incorporated and again with Graham Bond.

Cream, initially called "the Cream," were not going to be just three guys bashing it out at high volume, however. Clapton's skill as a blues guitarist is well known, but Bruce and Baker would make Cream into something completely different. The band's rhythm section would benefit from serious jazz experience, technique, and finesse. Great jazz comes from the space between the notes, perhaps even more so than the notes themselves. Thus, Cream would become a loud blues band that would tap into the jazz approach to playing. Terry Cox, who followed Baker into Alexis Korner's band, later cofounding the Pentangle, illustrates the importance of space. "[Space is] exactly what it's all about, yes," said Cox. "Being from a jazz background, this is the secret from my point of view. Lots of space. Miles Davis, listen to him. There's more when he doesn't play than when he does."

"Eric and Jack and Ginger were rehearsing, not far from the [Marshall] shop," said Terry Marshall. And they used to come down—I can always remember, they grabbed a couple of acoustic guitars, sitting around. And I heard every bit of Cream's performance on [that] tour [on] acoustic guitars in the shop. And Eric invited me, for the first time they ever played at the Marquee, in London. We met up at a pub called the Ship, which is quite famous. And then we walked across an alleyway into the Marquee."

Cream's formation, with its prominent members, became the most obvious example of the proto-late 1960s loud, distorted blues boom. The Yardbirds, though, would also begin to travel this path after Jimmy Page joined the band in June 1966. Page, who at only 22 had gained a reputation as an ace session player, made the unusual step from session player to live performer. Page had earlier suggested his friend Jeff Beck join the band when Eric Clapton left. He then became the bass player when Paul Samwell-Smith quit, eventually moving to his natural instrument of guitar when Chris Dreja switched from guitar to bass.

Page's move was unusual because typically guitarists played in bands until that petered out and then, later, made a living doing sessions. Page gained tremendous experience and a reputation in the studio, but the tedious nature of playing exact notes as written by someone else took its toll, and he relished the freedom of playing live.

The inclusion of Page added an unusual dynamic to the band, now fronted by two virtuoso lead guitarists. The two players did not necessarily mesh style-wise, however. "They were completely opposite," recalled Yardbirds drummer Jim McCarty. "Jimmy had been playing recording sessions in London—he was the main session guitar player that played on lots of the top recordings. So he was used to sort of reading a script and doing what he was asked to do and being very faithful to that—trying to please. And I think he was like that when he joined us for quite a time. Of course, Jeff was totally opposite. He played right off the top of his head. He wouldn't care—be totally outrageous. Also, being quite emotional and quite wound up, whereas Jimmy was always quite stable."

On rare occasions, though, when Beck was in the right headspace, the two would click, and the results became magical. In 1966, the Yardbirds did what they called a "package" tour of the United Kingdom, filling the spot between opening act Ike & Tina Turner and headliners the Rolling Stones. The *Melody Maker* gave a rather tepid review of a Yardbirds' performance at the Royal Albert Hall in September:

> "The Yardbirds followed the Turner revue after the interval and proved that they are good enough to fill the unenviable part of the show—just before the Stones. Keith Relf backed by guitarists Jeff Beck, Chris Dreja, and Jimmy Page set up a huge wall of sound and there were plenty of screams. But it was nothing like the screams as Long John Baldry leaped on stage to announce the Stones."—*Melody Maker*, October 1, 1966

McCarty, though, remembered times when his band, armed with two incredibly talented guitarists, upstaged the headliners. "There was a particular night," McCarty remembered, "when [Page and Beck] clicked together and we had this incredible standing ovation. And the crowd wouldn't stop. And the Stones were due to go on. And it was all very embarrassing [laughs]. It was sort of difficult for them. They had to [wait] for half an hour before they went on."

Cream and the Yardbirds, fueled by ever more powerful Marshall amps, would begin to define a new kind of blues that would hit its peak around 1968. This would be uniquely British blues, much more aggressive, distorted, and flat-out loud than what had been done earlier in the decade.

By the time London headed into 1967, it had "matured" musically beyond a simple tweaking of American music. London had led the way toward a British dominance of popular music and now had developed its own identity. This identity took the form of three strands: (1) the heavy blues boom that would hit a peak later with bands like Led Zeppelin, Free, and Fleetwood Mac; (2) English folk/rock, which combined British traditions with rock 'n' roll, exemplified by new young bands like the Strawbs, Fairport Convention, and the Pentangle; and (3) progressive rock that again tapped into European influences and, for the most part, left its blues roots at the door. The year 1967 would become an exciting time indeed.

4

DISCOVERING PROG ROCK

"We were shocking people. . . . And the shock really was—I think—[the audience] had never been exposed to the type of intensity that we were delivering as a band, because we were incorporating the power of European and classical music. And we were integrating it into a form of rock 'n' roll."—Greg Lake, King Crimson

Prior to the 1960s, Britain's musical identity seemed to derive from America. All of the best music, the most authentic music, came from the United States. Even through the R&B boom, when bands like the Stones and Yardbirds popularized British blues, it seemed like an inferior product to the real thing. Then things began to change.

Beginning in 1965 as England began to move beyond R&B, three musical strands began to develop that would bring uniquely British and other European influences to the fore. Traditional British folk music began to slowly weave its way into rock and would steer some London bands in that direction. Others, fueled by the volume, distortion, and the distinctive tone of Marshall amps, began to create the British version of the blues. And then there was a third strand, which would eventually become something called progressive rock.

Progressive rock, or prog rock, became the most European of the genres, openly pulling away from black American influences, sometimes discarding them entirely. The purpose was not only to develop a British identity but also to experiment, to challenge, and to see what could be done that had not been attempted before. Instead of piggybacking off of a Muddy Waters or a Bo Diddley, prog rockers took the rhythmic excitement of rock and blues and melded it onto classical traditions.

Prog has a certain connotation that's not always favorable. The negative stereotype showcases a middle-aged beta male, probably balding with a ponytail, sporting a black Jethro Tull T-shirt he saved from the 1970s. But prog rock deserves so much more than that portrayal. Like psychedelia before it, progressive music freed musicians from the constraints of rock and its rigidly enforced three-minute-or-under song structure of verse–chorus–verse–bad solo–chorus. ("Bad solo" snark credited to Kurt Cobain.)

The creators of prog could do anything. They could have one song take up an entire album side—or even two album sides. Vocals did not have to begin 15 seconds into a song; the singer could wait several minutes before opening his or her mouth. Off-time signatures, weird arrangements, no hooks—all of those notions contributed to the rise of progressive rock. Prog rock fit into the accelerated pace of rule breaking occurring in London. Following the 1967 release of the Beatles' *Sgt. Pepper's Lonely Hearts Club Band*, it seemed anything was up for grabs.

But where did the progression start? The Beatles and *Sgt. Pepper's* certainly played an enormous role—since the Liverpudlians utterly dominated music and culture from 1963 through 1967—but the Who should receive the lion's share of the credit (or perhaps blame?) for creating the ignition that would explode into prog with their nine-minute 1966 composition, "A Quick One While He's Away."

The Beatles, as they had done since 1963, dramatically upped the ante with *Sgt. Pepper's*, released in spring 1967. So much has been written about this record that only a summary bears repeating here—an attempt at a concept album (which never really came to fruition) about a fictional San Francisco band, a cutting-edge George Martin production and the use of orchestral instruments not previously featured on a rock album, lyrics printed on the cover, and so on. The album's finale, "A Day in the Life," essentially represented the Beatles' crescendo, with John Lennon and Paul McCartney connecting parts of the song with an orchestra directed to "go crazy" by maestro engineer Martin.

"*Sgt. Pepper*—that took 700 actual working hours to complete at my end," Martin told *Record Mirror's* Peter Jones in the July 22, 1967, issue. "Working a 24-hour day, it still adds up to a whole month."

Like anything so revolutionary, London music fans' reactions to *Sgt. Pepper's* was mixed at best.

> "It's practically a new art form. Every track is absolutely fantastic, especially 'She's Leaving Home' and 'Lucy in the Sky with Diamonds.' The Beatles going down? Absolute rubbish. This LP shows they are at least five years ahead of everyone else."—Martin Page of Berking, Essex, *Melody Maker* mailbag, May 27, 1967

> "What a load of rubbish and tripe the Beatles have dished out on their LP. Senseless noises, and as for the singing, the cat next door could do better."—Christine Ann Creek of Southgate, *Melody Maker* mailbag, June 10, 1967

> "I find it very hard to believe that the tracks were written by the Beatles. I'm sure they were written by a four-year-old child; perhaps one of you has a devoted sister who thought she'd have a bash at writing music. I'd like you all to know you have my deepest sympathy having to record such rubbish."—Christine J. Brooks of Yorkshire, *Record Mirror* letter from reader, July 15, 1967

Sgt. Pepper's meant many things to people, but for England, it represented the end of the Beatles' reign of dominance. Certainly, nearly every single and album the band released until its 1970 breakup shot straight to number 1, but after *Sgt. Pepper's* the band was viewed more from a distance. It wasn't like, "Hey, what are they doing, let's try to do that." It was more of a detached observation following the band's 1967 seminal release. It was as if the Beatles said in 1967, "Here you go, folks. We've taken you to this point. We're tired of leading. You're on your own now."

The Beatles' record also single-handedly elevated the album format to preeminence. As *Melody Maker* columnist Bob Dawbarn wrote in the October 19, 1968, issue, "Has the pop single had it? Not yet, of course, but the emphasis is swinging more and more towards albums." He went on to credit "progressives" for this trend, since they needed more than four minutes to express themselves.

Tracing progressive rock's early development presents quite the challenge since musicians embarked on different paths. Some brought in their European classical training (think King Crimson and Yes); others started with English folk stylings and expanded their palette from there. Jethro Tull comes to mind; some expanded on psychedelia, like Steve Howe, who ended up in Yes; and then there was the Bonzo Dog Band—who had their own category—but we'll talk about all that later.

If we begin in 1967, the year of *Sgt. Pepper's* release, London, and by extension England, had moved light years beyond its R&B roots. By that point, Britain began to make it a point to tap into anything and everything European. That focus, combined with a number of other factors, created an entirely new awareness, one that will likely never be repeated. Much of this awareness, though, came from those who grew up outside of London's confines, and that is not a coincidence.

London of the early 1960s, as explained in chapter 2, was all about the blues, mostly drawing from Chicago. All of the bands of that era came from that place. That was not so outside of the city. Many of those hailing from the hinterlands did latch onto the blues, but they typically enjoyed much more eclectic, and often more sophisticated, musical tastes. Some of them afforded serious training, for instance, people like Jethro Tull's Ian Anderson, who grew up in Scotland and Blackpool in the north of England.

"My first awareness of music really was the kind of wartime Big Band era," Anderson said. "My father owned a few 78 rpm records of that vintage. So around the age of eight, I heard Big Band swing jazz and then around the age of nine stumbled upon the earliest work of Bill Haley and the Comets and Elvis Presley . . . by the time I was 14 or 15, I was listening to Muddy Waters and Howlin' Wolf and Sonny Boy Williamson and Sonny Terry and Brownie McGhee and all those guys. And shortly afterwards to Charlie Parker and Ornette Coleman and Mose Allison—people [that] came out of that Be Bop era of American jazz. So when I started to play music seriously, when I was about 18, 19 years old, I had a background of everything from church music and Scottish folk music through to early rock 'n' roll, American folk music, and jazz and blues."

"I was knocked sideways by rock 'n' roll, but at the same time, I still kept listening to classical music," said the Zombies' Rod Argent, who grew up in St. Alban's, a town roughly 25 miles north of London, "including what was called modern classical music at the time: people like Stravinsky, Bartok. And also I discovered Miles Davis around 1958 with the wonderful band he had with John Coltrane and Cannonball Adderley and Bill Evans, the piano player . . . and [all of] that had an equivalent impact on me."

Yes's Steve Howe, who grew up in North London, listened to anything from Bill Haley to Tennessee Ernie Ford and everything in between. "I was certainly big on blues, but it came from a different perspective than the blues really that affected rock 'n' roll. . . . Although I got into the early Buddy Guy and Muddy Waters, I [really] liked some of the really way out guys like Blind Boy Fuller—and particularly, the guy I've been listening to today, even, right all the way through my career: I never lost touch with Big Bill Broonzy. So he's my favorite guitar [player, and] I [also] like Chet Atkins [and] Wes Montgomery."

Greg Lake offered a perspective from his formative years in the southern coastal town of Bournemouth, taking in everything from the Shadows to Russian composer Sergei Prokofiev. "Places outside of London—the influences that I first drew on—came to me because of the guitar lessons I had," Lake recalled, "which were really based more on European music. I was doing violin exercises by Paganini and tunes by [French jazz guitarist] Django Reinhardt—a lot of European-based stuff. So I think in a way, young musicians from big cities had a media access to this sort of blues influence, whereas further out in the sticks, there wasn't that media access. And so therefore, the musical influences were more diverse, I think. The interesting thing was [that] during the guitar lessons, I was learning all this sort of—I wouldn't call it classical music—but it was certainly European. And yet, in my sort of spare time, I was playing rock 'n' roll in my little bands. . . . But what I was learning [were] the foundations of European music. The same goes for [King Crimson's Robert] Fripp, the same goes for [the Police's] Andy Summers [who then played in Zoot Money's Big Roll Band]. In fact, Robert Fripp, myself, and Andy Summers were taught by the same guitar teacher—a guy called Don Strike [from] Bournemouth."

As these kids came into London from the hinterlands, another ingredient existed that would fuel progressive rock: competition. Unlike, say, Seattle of the late 1980s grunge era, where bands openly supported one other to further the aspirations of a small music scene, London fed off competition among bands. This competitive atmosphere tended to veer toward the friendly side, but rivalries existed nonetheless. And, for the period from 1963 to 1967, the Beatles set the bar. "The Beatles drove everything," said Yes's Bill Bruford. "Post-Beatles you could do anything. So the whole thing was blown apart by them. If you wanted a sitar, you got a sitar. . . . It was one of those hugely generous times, where you were being encouraged to do that. [And] money in these things is never inert. Either there's no money—which is the usual problem—so musicians try to please the customer. Or there's tons and tons of money—like there was in my day—[and] you don't have to worry about the customer at all. All you have to worry about is the other guys you're playing with. Do *they* want to have a sitar player? It's not whether the guy on the street cares whether you have a sitar player or not, it's 'Do we want to have one?' Or an orchestra, or flutes, or play in 5/4, or a Mellotron. . . . No one [was] watching the studio clock. . . . You just play whatever music you want as long as it didn't sound like the other guys. The trick was to sound different. . . . So if Led Zeppelin were doing *that*, you would probably want to do *this*. Or if ELP or the Nice were doing *that*, then you'd probably want to do *this*."

The tools had become apparent by 1967—the ethos of freedom and experimentation, the money, and a renewed connection to European music. And so did the technology. Musicians began to extract new sounds, not just from guitars but also from the increasing power and diversity of keyboard-based instruments. As early as 1964, the Selmer Company began advertising in the *Melody Maker* for an instrument called the Pianotron, which offered multiple sounds including the piano and marimba. Then came the release of the Beatles' "Strawberry Fields Forever" in February 1967, whose intro featured an unusual sound similar to a flute, but not quite.

> "A Great New Sound using the fabulous new Mellotron. Congratulations Beatles from Mellotronics Ltd., 28/30 Market Place, London, W.1"—ad from *Melody Maker*, March 11, 1967

The Mellotron Mark II, which became the standard-bearer of the instrument, became the first serious prelude to the synthesizer. The new instrument took the form of a keyboard, usually with 35 keys. Depressing a key would activate a taped playback of an instrument, a flute, or any other orchestral instrument. The keys were arranged to allow a player to re-create an orchestral sound in different octaves. Playing the Mellotron required a certain dexterity since the recordings only lasted eight seconds. After that, you had to let up on the key to allow the tape to rewind; it was crude by today's standards, but for the first time, a rock musician could begin to create classical sounds without the expense of hiring an orchestra.

The Moody Blues' Mike Pinder became an early proponent of the new instrument, having worked at the Mellotron factory for a year and a half. "I loved the Mellotron at first sight," Pinder wrote me. "Having worked at the factory I also learned everything about the Mellotron and could take it apart and put it back together, which often proved quite useful. It was a big instrument to move around and because of the tapes inside the Mellotron it was fragile and did not want to be jostled too much. It took time to reassemble the tapes if they were jumbled up. So playing the instrument live onstage was the biggest challenge because of the transport issues. I loved having the Mellotron in the studio because it allowed me the flexibility of the orchestration in our arrangements, as I often had the task of developing the song arrangement for everyone in the band. I could create countermelodies and add my orchestral layers by using strings, violins, violas, flutes, brass, organ, etc. I would often add my signature swoop in a way that only the Mellotron could do."

"We spent all our food money on [the Mellotron]," the Moodies' Graeme Edge told Richard Green in the August 31, 1968, issue of *New Musical Express*. "Mike used to work for the company that makes [them], so he took it all to pieces and did lots of things to it. They're very delicate and you have to be careful how you treat them. Once, the tapes got mixed up inside. It's a two-day job at the factory to sort them out, but Mike did it on stage with a bent coat hanger and a screwdriver in three quarters of an hour!"

Sgt. Pepper's essentially began the journey to prog rock in 1967. One can draw a line from this album to the Who's *Tommy* released in 1969. Following that, the genre we know as progressive rock began to emerge with bands like King Crimson, Yes, and Jethro Tull, among others. But there were stops along that critical 1967–1969 period, and that first waystation was the Moody Blues' *Days of Future Passed*, released six months after *Sgt. Pepper's*.

The Moodies used a combination of the Mellotron and the London Festival Orchestra to create their musical statement. While *Sgt. Pepper's* approached the idea of the concept album, the concept itself never came to fruition. The Moody Blues were one of the first to bring an idea to a conclusion, to tell a story, or at least build an album around an idea of taking a journey—in this case, from early morning through to the evening—that could engage the listener from beginning to end, thus diminishing the importance of the "hit single." Released in November 1967, *Days* became the first symphonic rock album. Encouraged by Decca Records, the London Festival Orchestra backed the band, which also featured the Mellotron throughout. "We wanted to make an LP that went nonstop from beginning to end," the Moodies' John Lodge told *Melody Maker*'s Bob Dawbarn in the February 3, 1968, issue, "with a connecting theme between every number."

"I always had the vision that our music would be something that the listener would want to listen to from beginning to end," Pinder wrote me. "Having the studios at Decca open to us, the Festival Orchestra and the creative freedom to do what we wanted created the perfect storm for *DOFP*. Not only did I now have a Mellotron to add layers of orchestration but we had the Festival Orchestra."

"[The label] had a scheme for producing a fusion of classical-pop to showcase a new recording technique," Edge told Keith Altham in the February 3, 1968, issue of *New Musical Express*, "and wanted us to interpret Dvorak's 'New World Symphony,' so we agreed. Then we went away—locked all the doors in the studio and put our material on tape! Fortunately it turned out very well and the company have given us a blank cheque to produce the next album with the only stipulation that it is out by September."

The year 1967 also featured some significant touchstones by perhaps a surprising source: the Pretty Things. In the first R&B wave, the Prettys became known as a more dangerous form of the Rolling Stones. The band played a raw form of blues, and in some ways their appearance scared their elders, even more than the Stones. Singer Phil May's 1967 shoulder-length hair, worn as early as 1964, symbolized the forward-looking rebellion of this band. By 1967, however, the Pretty Things version 1 had run its course. "If we hadn't have moved on," said May, "we'd have stopped. We had to keep ourselves interested. And that's what drove the changes, I think.

"We'd done the pop thing. We had the hit records. We'd done all that. It saved our life in some ways by being forced out of what you'd call the mainstream. . . . And we became—in some ways—princes of the new Underground. We were back in the Underground, which is a fantastic place to develop stuff."

The Pretty Things inadvertently created another touchstone during this interlude, a rather obscure track called "Defecting Grey." This song never became a major hit, but in retrospect, it resulted in an important if understated turning point in British music. After "Defecting Grey," the journey toward progressive rock would become irreversible.

In 1967, the Pretty Things had finished up their contract with Fontana Records. During this time, the band entered Abbey Road Studios to cut some demos, one of them being "Defecting Grey." "Grey" alternates between dreamy circus-like psychedelia (think of a more twisted version of "Benefit of Mr. Kite") and raw blues, connected at times with backward masked tapes. It's a mess, but a beautifully constructed one . . . a masterful musical moment. Not all critics agreed with that assessment, however.

> "Right in the middle of the sitar, backward guitar, electronics and bits of tape sellotaped together, you can hear a rocking group bashing away. . . . It's a pity groups ever discovered that word 'progress.'"—Chris Welch, *Melody Maker*, November 11, 1967

Pretty Things guitarist Dick Taylor laughed hysterically when I read him that quote in 2014. "It's funny," he said. "We've started playing that again and it goes down an absolute storm . . . so there, Chris Welch. I'm sorry, but we're still doing it."

"Defecting Grey" would not become a hit, but that didn't seem to be a concern of the Pretty Things. "The reason that we were able to do something which was so different," said Taylor, "was the fact that we actually did it just simply for ourselves, really."

The Pretty Things' post-Fontana demos found their way to the ears of producer Norman Smith, who, unlike many of his contemporaries, got what the band was doing with tracks like "Defecting Grey." Because of that, Smith was able to sell the Prettys to EMI (the Beatles' label) and thus provide access to the legendary Abbey Road Studios. That space, along with Smith's support, would lead the band into creating the first rock opera: 1968's *S.F. Sorrow*, released six months before the more celebrated Who work *Tommy*.

The term *rock opera* has been tossed around since *Tommy*, and I've often thought, "Just what the hell does that mean?" If one had to define the term, I would say it tells a story to music, but instead of classical instrumentation driving it, rock musicians provide the base, which of course leads to an edgier and possibly more exciting version of the traditional art form.

Sorrow, whose story originated from singer Phil May, is built on the tale of a stiff-upper-lipped Englishman named Private Sorrow who lives his life in quiet desperation, eventually descending into madness (sound familiar, *Dark Side of the Moon* fans? *DSM*, by the way, came out five years later). "It had its sort of parallels in opera," said May. "We'd got fed up with doing five A sides and five B sides, basically. The story I was writing, anyway, which we used as a sort of kickoff point—there was a theme musically and recurring things and recurring images. It was a whole piece. You could sit and listen to the whole experience.

"It was perfect that we were given Abbey Road. You know, they stiffed us for money, but they gave us the best studio in the world. And I don't know if *S.F. Sorrow* could have been made, A, without Norman Smith, or in another situation without Abbey Road. The two things fell in our lap. And we weren't signing for EMI. In my mind, we were signing for Abbey Road. And they gave us a terrible contract, with absolutely bollocks money. But we didn't care. In Norman Smith, we found the only person we'd ever played our demos to who believed in it. Our manager, when we brought [the] 'Defecting Grey' demo back, he thought we'd lost our marbles. I mean, he completely thought we'd gone. 'Too many drugs, boys,' was his answer. And nobody really seemed to get it. And when we played it to Norman, he got it straight-away. He got up and put it back on."

S.F. Sorrow opens with "S.F. Sorrow Is Born," an Eastern-influenced, ethereal tribute to the story's protagonist, with pretty guitars supplemented by high trumpets, reminiscent of the Beatles' "Penny Lane." At one point, Mr. Sorrow heads off to war. Interestingly enough, while the Pretty Things grew up in the shadow of World War II, and even while Vietnam was raging, this story puts the listener into the French trenches in 1916. This record, and Sorrow's experiences, tell the story of the futility of war . . . and that perfectly matches the unmitigated slaughter of the First World War. "Well, that's kind of what it's meant to be, really," said Taylor. "And . . . the 'Balloon Burning' [song is] meant to be the Hindenburg [after the war]. His girlfriend comes over to America on the Hindenburg, but she dies in the flames."

The Pretty Things' opera provided an important if unintended link between earlier rock and prog. *S.F. Sorrow* took the idea of the concept album, as created by the Beatles' *Sgt. Pepper's* and further refined by the Moody Blues' *Days of Future Passed*, and added a story line to unify the entire effort. This level of sophistication was something completely new in rock 'n' roll, so in essence, *Sorrow* and the Who's subsequent smash *Tommy* helped connect the dots between psychedelia and prog rock, a connection necessary for the new genre to flourish as the 1960s gave way to the 1970s.

The Mod band Small Faces also ventured into the concept album arena in 1968 with the release of *Ogdens' Nut Gone Flake*. Up to that point, the band had enjoyed success as a singles band, having peaked with 1966's "Sha-La-La-La-Lee" and 1967's "Itchycoo Park." "The whole point of recording a commercial [single]," the Small Faces' Steve Marriott told *Melody Maker* in the February 12, 1966, issue, "is to try and get our name really established. If we can score two or three big hits, then we'll start making the kind of records we want to. One day we hope to be doing right weird, far-out stuff."

The band had just returned from a rather unsuccessful Australian tour with the Who and desired to move on and record their own unique conceptual statement. According to keyboardist Ian McLagan's autobiography, *All the Rage*, the Small Faces worked on it for the better part of a year. Drummer Kenney Jones, however, disputes the timing. "*Ogdens' Nut Gone Flake* didn't take anything like a year to record," Jones wrote in his autobiography *Let the Good Times Roll*, "not in terms of hours in the studio. We had the one extended run . . . but other than that, it was a case of finding days here and there when gigs, tours, and TV and radio commitments allowed. If we'd had one straight hit I reckon we'd have been done inside three weeks."

The album centered on the fictional character Happiness Stan, who spotted a half moon and desired to find the other half. "Only seven songs on *Ogdens'* tell Stan's story," Jones wrote in *Good Times*, "side two, plus the title track, the instrumental."

Upon completion, the record still needed a title. Bassist Ronnie Lane liked the idea of a tobacco tin for the cover, so the Small Faces got in touch with a British tobacco company called "Ogden's," who graciously sent over a scrapbook of photos of its original tobacco tins. "We were rummaging through them on the table in [Immediate label owner] Andrew's [Loog Oldham] office," McLagan wrote in his autobiography, "when Steve noticed a rectangular label for 'Ogden's Nut Brown Flake' and fell about laughing. 'There it is!' he screamed. 'Ogden's Nut GONE Flake!'"

Ogdens' would be the Small Faces ultimate and final musical statement as they would begin to splinter and eventually morph into the Faces.

Speaking of the Who, that band had just returned from an exhaustive tour of the United States in 1968 and immediately set [everything] aside to focus on the next album. The previous record, a loose conceptual effort called *The Who Sell Out* released the previous year, was an attempt at a sort of concept album based on made-up commercial jingles. The record seemed a bit rushed, with recording having to take place between gigs. So for the next album, the Who would focus entirely on the studio, with Pete Townshend creating an organized story line stretching over four album sides. The band would record the new record (with the working title *Deaf Dumb and Blind Boy*) in fall 1968. "*Deaf Dumb and Blind Boy* is an opera, and so there have to be a lot of links and connecting numbers. We're all working on it together—the original idea for the story was by Pete Townshend," the Who's bassist John Entwistle told *Record Mirror*'s Derek Boltwood in the October 12, 1968, issue. "It's the story of a deaf dumb and blind boy and all the things that happen to him through his life. Because he's so cut off from the outside world there are two sides to everything that occurs in his life. There's what he thinks is happening to him, and what is actually happening. We talked about the idea a lot in the States, building on the theme, and now we're concentrating on getting it done. It's not a complete life story of the boy—mainly about his growing up.

"Pete made up the whole plot of the story and we're all leaping about the place doing different things to fit into it. I do most of the comedy or sinister numbers in the opera. . . . My songs are all fairy tale things. I don't know why really—it's just that my songs seem to appeal to the seven-year-olds and upwards."

Two creepy Entwistle numbers made it onto the final record (the name of course changed to *Tommy*): "Cousin Kevin" and "Fiddle About" featured childhood torture and abuse, a subject Townshend was unwilling to tackle perhaps because of his own formative experiences.

Tommy made its London debut on May 1, 1969, at Ronnie Scott's, the famed jazz club. "As enormous speaker cabinets were piled high along the walls of the club and hummed ominously at the assembled throng," *Melody Maker*'s Chris Welch commented in the May 10, 1969, issue, "Pete drily explained the story line: 'It's about a boy who is born normal, just like you and me. Then he witnesses a murder and becomes deaf, dumb and blind. He is later raped by his uncle and gets turned on to LSD. The boy then gets turned on to pinball, gets healed, and then becomes the hero of the younger generation.'

"In the confined space of Ronnie's," Welch continued, "a venue used to the refined rhythms of jazz, the overwhelming intensity of the Who's performance left scores of people literally deaf. Some twenty hours after the event, my ears were still singing and I was barely able to sleep without a vision of Keith Moon thrashing like a demon swimming before me. The opera underlined Pete's flair for inventive lyrics and original composition, not forgetting the sense of humor and sense of the dramatic always evident in his work."

"The LP ends with what appears to be a musical philosophical question," wrote *Record Mirror*'s Lon Goddard in the May 10, 1969, issue, "what happens to Tommy after his disturbed childhood? Where went the Pinball Wizard? The Who gave us a good solid hour's worth of quality listening and excellent showmanship, leaving amid chortles of 'more!' 'get off!' and 'to the bar!'"

Others explored more traditional musical themes. The Kinks, for instance, loved to reminisce about an idyllic past that perhaps didn't exist. The band began venturing into more thematic storytelling on the 1966 *Face to Face*, which contains the wistful "Sunny Afternoon."

The Kinks were banned from the United States during the latter 1960s due to an unspecified dispute. Front man and chief songwriter Ray Davies used that time to explore inward-looking British themes. This exploration continued on 1967's *Something Else by the Kinks* and beyond with songs like "Afternoon Tea," "End of the Season," "Waterloo Sunset," and "Autumn Almanac." "Of the many influences on the Davies' song-style, two are perhaps worth special mention," wrote *Record Mirror*'s David Griffiths in the October 28, 1967, issue. "One is his taste for the past: [quotes Davies] 'We do a lot of stompy things. The rhythms are reminiscent of the Twenties. I like the old days. Everybody does—in song.' The other is his birth sign: 'I'm a Cancer and influenced by the seasons—hence *Sunny Afternoon* and now *Autumn Almanac*. I like writing about the Sun, and animals. I'm in a romantic bag! But I don't work to any songwriting rules.'"

Those English-focused themes continued on with 1968's *The Village Green Preservation Society* and 1969's *Arthur (Or the Decline and Fall of the British Empire)*. "It's a shame that the Americans are more interested in our traditional values than we are," Davies told *Record Mirror*'s Boltwood in the May 10, 1969, issue. "Personally, I'm very interested. I'm not particularly patriotic—perhaps I'm just selfish—but I like these traditional British things to be there. I never go to watch cricket any more, but I like to know it's there. And it's bad for people to grow up and not know what a china cup is—or a village green. In other words, I'd rather have the actual things here, not just pictures of things we used to have. It all sounds terribly serious, but it isn't really—I mean, I wouldn't die for this cause, but I think it's frightfully important."

So the concept album became one ingredient for progressive rock. Another took the form of presentation. This notion of presentation, which hadn't meant much up to this point, would begin to rear its head. The Who, with their instrument-smashing mayhem, offered up a step in this direction, but it took others to create an entire production based on

Dave Davies of the Kinks on Carnaby Street with admirers, 1967. *Pictorial Press Ltd. / Alamy stock photo.*

music. And the personification of that idea came to fruition with the Crazy World of Arthur Brown.

Hailing from Whitby, Yorkshire, on the eastern coast about 75 miles south of Newcastle, Brown eventually made his way down to London. After bouncing around the music scene unsuccessfully, Brown found himself embarking to France with his new band, which would feature a 16-year-old drummer named John whose kit was held together with string. "I often used to have to rescue the wandering bass drum," Brown wrote me, "and return it to its place next to his feet."

"We played seven nights a week—three sets," Brown said. "And on Sunday we also played in the afternoon. So it was a proper full-on engagement. And after playing the same stuff for a while, I got bored, and so we started jamming. And I'm bringing bits of theater—you know, come on dressed as the Statue of Liberty or—General de Gaulle had made an edict that anybody crossing the French border with long hair could have it cut off. So we had General de Gaulle cutting the pope's hair.

"And one night, one young boy came in with his mother and we were just sort of chatting, and he suddenly said, 'You should black out your teeth.' . . . And I thought, 'OK, I'll see how well that goes down.' And I did it the next night and people loved it."

> "It all really got together in France about two years ago. I used to come on stage with my suit on back to front, one sleeve to my sweater, no flies to my trousers and wearing nine ties of varying lengths simultaneously."—Arthur Brown in *New Musical Express*, September 7, 1968

Soon Brown stumbled upon something that would become a central feature of his ever-more-outrageous stage act: the notion of the fire god. "A few nights later, in the hotel we were in, I found the remains of a very wild party," he recalled. "Someone had left outside my door a crown with candles in it. So, I lit the candles that night at the club [and wore the crown] with my teeth blacked out. And everybody thought it was fantastic. And that was the beginning of the 'Fire' album. [But] the crown soon broke, and I thought I got to have something more permanent, so I used a vegetable colander with candles. And that stuck to my hair. So [I] hit on the idea of a plate full of petrol [laughs], which used to explode and splatter all over the place and set everything on fire. Wonderful."

By 1968, Brown's band, the Crazy World of Arthur Brown, had returned to London and began to make a dent in the burgeoning Underground scene at the notorious UFO (pronounced YOU-FOH) club along with psychedelic bands like the Pink Floyd and the Move. By this time, Crazy World featured a prodigious drummer named Carl Palmer, who would go on to achieve fame with Atomic Rooster and Emerson, Lake & Palmer.

PSYCHEDELIA AS A PROGENITOR OF PROG

Psychedelia, as originated on the US West Coast and adapted by Britain, would become another ingredient of progressive rock. It would appear both as a predecessor and contemporaneously to it.

Mid-1960s American psychedelic bands like the 13th Floor Elevators, Jefferson Airplane, the Grateful Dead, and Quicksilver Messenger Service would expand what rock 'n' roll could be, both literally and figuratively. Fueled by LSD, or acid, songs became more about a colorful journey than they did about a hook-laden destination.

Whether one wants to admit it or not, drugs were a necessary ingredient in the creative process—at least certain drugs were. Some artists believe there are "good" drugs and "bad" drugs. Good drugs, like pot/hash and acid, open up the mind and possibilities of art. Bad drugs, like coke and heroin, close the user off to the outside and thus often stifle the creative process. "Playing under the influence of hash or grass—you can elevate yourself," said John Alder, aka Twink, who played drums with the psychedelic Tomorrow and the Pretty Things. "If everything is right, all the elements are right, when you're right in tune with each other onstage and with the audience, [it can] develop into a psychedelic experience. Colors just happen."

Acid just added more colors and more possibilities to the life experience and the music. And in Britain, psychedelia, at least for some, seemed like a natural extension of the Mod movement. If Mods were about colors, psychedelic hippiedom was about even more colors.

Begun on the American West Coast, psychedelia challenged the strict hook-laden, verse-chorus-verse song format. Championed by the

Arthur Brown on fire at the Marquee, London, 1968. *Pictorial Press Ltd. / Alamy stock photo.*

burgeoning FM radio format in America, bands like Jefferson Airplane and the Grateful Dead began writing longer and meandering songs that engaged the listener in a whole different way than traditional pop songs did.

In London, the psychedelic movement didn't have the same overt influence, but it was prevalent enough to at least provide some of the groundwork for progressive rock. English psychedelic bands helped create this whole new scene in London called "the Underground." Underground bands would flout the rules, appeal to a younger generation of fans, and continue to break out from the monotony of being tied to a constant release of hit singles.

Late 1960s London Underground has a dramatically different meaning than what it would come to mean in the punk and alternative rock scenes of the next several decades, and just so as to not confuse things, that distinction will be addressed here.

Punk and alt rock Underground scenes sprang up in the United States in rebellion against the mainstream rock culture, which was heavily fueled by MTV in the 1980s. Such scenes were typically tiny, with perhaps only a few hundred participants, including the musicians and fans. The musicians of the US Underground championed a do-it-yourself ethic, starting their own labels, putting out their own records, and publicizing their music through the use of self-published fanzines with a heavy assist from college radio.

In contrast, London's Underground offered a more esoteric approach. Unlike their later US counterparts, English bands roaming this territory were not averse to mainstream success; it was just that the way they went about it was different than their predecessors. They signed with major labels and put out financially successful records, but the ticket to the Underground mainly consisted of a desire to create and break the rules of what constitutes art, even if this art might include drug and perhaps even violent experiences. Such was the danger represented by bands like the Move, the Pink Floyd, and the Crazy World of Arthur Brown.

"Places like Middle Earth, and the Roundhouse, and UFO—you really kind of didn't want to see them in daylight, because they were quite awful," said Fairport Convention's Judy Dyble. "You only ever saw them during the night. They were quite magical places. They were all lit up with the oil/light shows. And it was all quite exciting. . . . They were not the most salubrious of places, but they were fascinating. And it was quite wonderful to come out blinking into the dawn from particularly the Middle Earth, because that was underneath where Covent Garden fruit and vegetable market was. So we'd come out and they'd all be these people selling [fresh] fruit and vegetables.

"[UFO] was a real death trap because you had to go down stairs to get to it and there'd be people sitting everywhere. So it was lucky that nothing ever caught fire.

"The Roundhouse was another very strange place. I have memories of playing there and also I think seeing the Byrds or the Doors or Jefferson Airplane there. But there were so many huge pillars . . . where the trains used to come in. It was kind of a turntable. The train would come in, the turntable would turn round—it would go off in another direction. . . . So you'd be tripping over bits of concrete all over the place if you weren't careful, or catching your feet in the train line. But because it was dark, you didn't really notice. It was a bit claustrophobic, that place."

The Pink Floyd (and it was *the* Pink Floyd in those days) quickly became the torchbearers for London's "psychedelic freak-out" scene.

Floyd began life as a blues outfit during the tail end of London's R& B boom in 1965. Initially calling themselves the Spectrum Five, drummer Nick Mason, bassist Roger Waters, guitarist Syd Barrett, and keyboardist Rick Wright shared a flat with a college lecturer named Mike Leonard. Barrett painted at Camberwell Art School while the others studied architecture at the Regent Street Polytechnic. "I'm always on the look-out for someone who has half a million pounds to spare and wants me to design him a house," Mason told *Record Mirror*'s David Griffiths in the July 8, 1967, issue. "Please tell the readers of the *RM* to get in touch with me if they are affluent enough to need my services."

The band soon began calling themselves the Pink Floyd after American bluesmen Pink Anderson and Floyd Council.

Leonard had been working with lighting effects, and he encouraged the band to integrate their performance to his visual presentations. No one had really done anything like that before in the rock 'n' roll realm, and the blues the band had been doing didn't really mesh with Leonard's lighting work. So Barrett started writing songs that pushed Floyd into the experimental. The light shows and the band's burgeoning psychedelic sound soon found a home at clubs like UFO and the Electric Garden. "We play what we like, and what we play is new," Waters told *Record Mirror*'s Derek Boltwood in the October 21, 1967, issue. "I

suppose you could describe us as the movement's house orchestra because we were one of the first people to play what [we] wanted to hear.
We're really part of the whole present pop movement, although we just
started out playing something we liked."

The band's early UFO shows were not the "psychedelic Floyd" of
lore, at least initially. The experience was kind of a jazzy art school
expression of light and sound. "They were just jamming in the clubs,"
recalled Tomorrow's drummer Alder, who shared a stage with Floyd.
"They weren't playing songs. When I first saw the Floyd down at the
UFO club, they were just jamming."

The jammy, artsy, colorful psychedelic Floyd trips suited the band
much better than the blues, and by 1967, audiences at UFO and other
clubs like the Roundhouse began to get it. "Three years ago, no one
knew what it was all about," Mason told *Record Mirror*'s Boltwood in
the October 21, 1967, issue. "But now the audience accepts us. We
don't feel that we should try to educate the public, we don't want to
push anything onto them. But if they accept what we're offering, and
they seem to be at the moment, then that's great. And we feel good
because our ideas are getting across to a large number of people."

While the Floyd's live experience cemented the band's following,
record sales would require something a bit more structured. That's
where producers Joe Boyd and Norman Smith came in, guiding Barrett's experimental music ideas toward more commercial singles like
"Arnold Layne" (produced by Boyd) and "See Emily Play" (produced
by Smith). The former song, about a character who dresses in ladies
clothes, was cutting edge and controversial for its day. The latter effort
would appear on the band's debut album, *The Piper at the Gates of
Dawn*, released in 1967. That record remains the quintessential British
psychedelic statement. England's version of the music, while drawing
from the journey/LSD aspect of San Francisco, added a childlike British fairy-tale element to the music, making it distinctly European.

While the Floyd got its share of publicity, and the 1970s version with
David Gilmour substituting for Syd Barrett made the band one of the
biggest in the world, another group worked the London psychedelic
circuit that has been vastly overlooked: the Move.

Hailing from Birmingham, the Move transitioned into the London
freak-out scene upon arrival in 1966. The band's outrageous stage antics
quickly won them a following and a regular residency at the Marquee.

"Psychedelic sounds came to London in a new—and explosive—dimension," Nick Jones reported in the October 29, 1966, issue of *Melody Maker*, "as the Move continued their Thursday night residency at the Marquee Club—finishing their act in an ear-splitting and conscious-shattering blaze of celluloid and sound. A projector flicked colours, contrasts, textures and atmosphere onto the group who—as if incensed—jumped, swirled, dived, and thundered in front of the dancing backclock. Then a gigantic explosion. They ripped the film screen off the wall and put a lot of weird smiles on the faces of the audience."

Led by enigmatic guitarist Roy Wood, the band would cement its place in London's scene by the end of 1966 with a New Year's Eve "Psychedelicamania" appearance at the Roundhouse with the Who and the Floyd.

> "The Roundhouse at Chalk Farm was once called 'a derelict barn.' On Saturday it saw in the New Year with little elevation of its stature. The scene was the Giant Freak-Out All Night Rave, where the participants, 'emancipated from our national social slavery' as the ads shrieked, are supposed to 'realise as a group whatever potential they possess for free expression.'"—Nick Jones, *Melody Maker*, January 7, 1967

By that point, the band enjoyed success with its first single, the splendid "Night of Fear." Featuring a riff from Tchaikovsky's *1812 Overture* and sparkling harmonies, the Move enjoyed their entrée into the charts. The band's stage antics quickly overshadowed the music, however. "To the gentle strains of Tchaikovsky's *1812*," *New Musical Express'* Jeremy Pascall wrote in the January 7, 1967, issue, "Birmingham's Move have smashed their way into the charts with their first record, 'Night of Fear.' And I use the word smash advisedly for the Move incorporate little goodies like destroying silver-painted cars (with two chicks stripping in time to the music), axing television sets and exploding thunderflashes into their act. It is NOT psychedelic."

"'Night of Fear,'" Move manager Tony Secunda told Pascall, "is about a guy who takes a stale dose of LSD and has a bad trip—it's a nightmare, and the flip, 'The Disturbance,' is about madness—a guy out of his head who ends up shouting Mother and things. It's 1967 Goodtime music."

The band continued to expand its stage performance and quickly distanced itself from the psychedelic label foisted upon it and the Floyd. "Don't call us psychedelic," singer Carl Wayne told *New Musical Express*' Alan Smith in the January 21, 1967, issue. "The Move have been tagged psychedelic, but we're not and hate it. A lot of groups are calling themselves that, but when that word dies, they'll die. We're not psychedelic, we're showmen.

"It is our life's ambition to start a riot. People love violence. They WANT violence. In our act we wreck cars and stick an axe through TV sets. The kids go wild. Within minutes they're right in there with us . . . WRECKING, SMASHING, breaking things up."

The Move's onstage antics became so extreme that they found themselves banned from London's premier rock club. "[Manager] Tony Secunda had come up with the now legendary idea of the television set smashing," Nick Logan wrote in the March 15, 1969, issue of *New Musical Express*. "While the group was chopping up the set on stage they were letting off smoke bombs and firecrackers that deafened the watching crowd. One went accidentally into the crowd and slightly burnt a girl's coat. Five minutes before the group was due off, there were fire engines and dozens of policemen outside. Inside the club was by now just a mass of dense smoke. The Marquee had never emptied so quickly before. In minutes the crowd was out on the street and the Move and Tony Secunda were being asked to go the same way. It was chaos. It was a year before they played the Marquee again.

"Roy Wood was dispatched with orders to write the most commercial single he could and he came up with 'Blackberry Way,' the single that made No. 1 and saved the Move."

"Blackberry Way," as a sort of chuckling reference to the Beatles' "Penny Lane," would become the Move's only number 1 single. The band would not make much of a dent in the American market, but later Wood would gain some notoriety when he formed the Electric Light Orchestra with Jeff Lynne.

Unfortunately for the Move, the band's emphasis on outrageous stage craft overshadowed their accomplishments on record, which showcased Wood's developing songwriting. Wood even did things like playing his guitar with a violin bow in 1966, years before Led Zeppelin's Jimmy Page made that technique famous.

A band called Tomorrow also wove its way into London's psychedelic scene. Originally called the In Crowd, Tomorrow's vision emanated from singer Keith West and guitarist Steve Howe. Tomorrow became part of the Roundhouse/UFO community occupied by the Pink Floyd and the Move by 1967. Initially a cover band, by 1967, Tomorrow forged ahead in a new direction. "Keith said at this rehearsal, 'I got a couple of songs'—this was at the end of '66," said Howe, "because to get ready for '67, you could feel [change] coming. And so he said, 'Maybe it's time to change. Why don't we do our own songs?' So we all said, 'Yeah.' We got down to it, started rehearsing out new material that was improvised, much more—long improvised solos by me. This became a sort of trademark of the band. And we went out and did this stuff and sometimes people would come up afterwards and tell us they were completely blown away, and I'd say, 'Well, why?' [laughs]. [We] realized that we were becoming a force. We were risking it all with our own material. And Keith was the primary writer. I got the idea of writing songs from Keith, really."

The band also joined with artistic efforts by the Who and Pretty Things with an attempt at a mini-rock opera called *Excerpt from a Teenage Opera*. While West's ambitious project of acts and characters never came to a *Tommy*-like fruition, it did lead to the band's sole self-titled album, released in 1968. The record featured "My White Bicycle," which showcased an early use of backward phasing with the guitar. It also led Howe into a more progressive direction following the band's breakup that same year. Howe would move on to a band called Bodast, which crossed the lines between progressive rock and psychedelia, and into Yes by 1970.

THE ZOMBIES' *ODESSEY AND ORACLE*

The Zombies, a band who had some success earlier in the decade with such hit singles as "She's Not There" and "Tell Her No," would use Abbey Road to make one of the 1960s most enduring musical statements: *Odessey and Oracle*. The record offered up some of rock 'n' roll's most beautiful songs, culminating in an eventual hit, "Time of the Season." *Odessey and Oracle* featured Mellotron heavily throughout. The band ventured into the studio in June 1967, intending to make a final musical statement and go on their merry way. "My memory of it was that we walked into Abbey Road, virtually as the Beatles were walking out after recording *Sgt. Pepper*," recalled Zombies keyboard player Rod Argent. "And John Lennon's Mellotron was left in the studio. And I just used it. I didn't ask anybody. I just used it. It was just 'cause it was there. And I thought, 'We can't afford to pay for real strings. So this is great. This is a way of using a string orchestra,' not thinking of it as an instrument in its own right. Although we hadn't heard any *Sgt. Pepper* [yet], but we had heard 'Strawberry Fields' and been knocked out with the vibe on that. So I just jumped on it. And we used it quite extensively. I mean, that's my memory. And I'm pretty sure it was John's Mellotron, because I've subsequently seen pictures of it. And that's the instrument that I remember playing in the studio. So it was only 'cause the Beatles left some things lying around that we took advantage of it. [Laughs.]"

Compared to modern computer sampling, the Mellotron seems quite primitive, especially since the player could only hold down a key for a maximum of eight seconds at a time. After that, you had to wait until the tape rewound before hitting the same key. "You're limited by the boundaries of the instrument," said Argent. "And, in a way . . . those limiting factors can actually be a creative force in themselves, I think. And maybe that was so in the case of the Mellotron."

PROTO PROG BANDS

Three strands basically led into prog rock: those coming from a folk direction that ventured off into further European influences, à la Jethro Tull and the Strawbs; those that ventured from a psychedelic direction, notably the Pink Floyd, Tomorrow, and Yes; and those who directly wanted to connect with their European roots, such as King Crimson and Deep Purple. And there was the Nice, which mixed it all in a blender with no idea where it would head.

Initially performing as a backing band for American singer P. P. Arnold (referred to as "Pat"), the Nice quickly began to develop their own eclectic identity. Beginning as a four-piece, the Nice consisted of David O'List on guitar, Brian "Blinky" Davison on drums, Lee Jackson on bass, and Keith Emerson on keyboards. Arnold allowed the band to play what it wanted, so the Nice mixed in soul covers and then began to combine jazz and classical influences.

The band's first recorded effort, *The Thoughts of Emerlist Davjack*, reflected those influences. Released in 1967, the album title is a combination of the band members' last names, as shortened by O'List. Quickly, the standout track became the eight-minute opus "Rondo," adapted from jazz musician Dave Brubeck (originally called "Blue Rondo à la Turk"). O'List had been a Brubeck fan as a child since his mother brought home his records. "I decided to make one of his tunes into a rock song, as anything seemed possible after these jazz records hit the charts," O'List wrote me. "I remember feverishly changing the tempo in 'Rondo' to 4/4, writing a different bass line, which was a simple one to hook the listener, changing the jazz feel to a rock fusion of classical, psychedelia, rock, blues, funk, and sound effects as might happen in film music. I introduced this song to the Nice . . . and directed them how it should be played and constructed."

The Nice quickly gained a name for themselves in Britain, becoming regulars at the Marquee. By 1968, the band became major players in London. "[The Nice are] only the best group in the country," Chris Welch wrote in the March 2, 1968, issue of *Melody Maker*. "This may stun fans of Hendrix, Mayall and the Cream. . . . The main effect is created by the driving creative forces of organist Keith Emerson and drummer Blinky Davison. Keith is a classically trained musician who plays jazz piano. Combining these influences in a progressive pop mould results in singularly exciting and novel music."

Emerson initially shunned the spotlight. "I was very reserved at the time," the keyboardist mentioned in the September 28, 1968, issue of *Record Mirror*. "During the day I worked in a bank. At night I played the pubs along with a drummer and bass player. We were on our own scene. We had no contact with the music scene except through records. It didn't interest me much—I didn't want to know."

The keyboardist quickly became the group's focal point, however, as he evolved into the first true British keyboard showman. His classical and jazz talent notwithstanding, Emerson would create otherworldly sounds on his Hammond organ at times by sticking knives into the keyboard (some of which reportedly belonged to future Hawkwind and Motorhead front man Lemmy Kilmister), tipping the instrument down onto himself while continuing to play, and sometimes creating strange sounds by opening up the back of the organ and striking various strings to create percussion. Emerson's act quickly drew the attention of Jimi Hendrix, who had become a huge celebrity in England in 1967. In December of that year, Hendrix told *Melody Maker* the Nice were his favorite group in the country. "Keith Emerson, their organist, has been hailed as the Jimi Hendrix of the Hammond organ," Chris Welch wrote in the July 13, 1968, *Melody Maker*. "Young, good looking, and visually exciting as he works himself into a frenzy, girl fans are already mobbing and pulling him off stage as he reaches a climax on their arrangements of 'Rondo' and 'America.' In wild, unashamed showmanship, Keith dances on the keyboard, throws knives into his amplifiers, cracks a whip over the heads of the crowds, plays with his feet, and even gets inside the Hammond to produce 'space' noises from the intricate electronic equipment. The crowds go wild."

> "[Emerson's] interest was centred in classical and Church music— Vivaldi, Bach, Sibelius. Two things brought him into Pop. One was a boring, watershed afternoon in the Bank when he suddenly put down his pen and thought: 'What the hell am I doing here, when I could be playing?' The second was in the bank's manager agreeing with him. 'You're looking tired,' said the boss. 'You'd better choose between banking and music.'"—*Record Mirror*, September 28, 1968

"We supported Jimi Hendrix at the Marquee and we got an encore," O'List wrote me. "Hendrix had been watching when we came off the stage. It was sublime to see Hendrix standing there saying he would like us to support him on his UK tour. Hooray, we had made it."

"The Nice were my favourite group on the tour—their sound is ridiculously good, original, free, more funky than West Coast," Hendrix told *Melody Maker*'s B. P. Fallon in the December 23, 1967, issue.

The Nice's popularity increased to the point of reportedly breaking the all-time box office record at the Marquee set by Hendrix.

To expand what was possible in rock music, the Nice, anchored by the classically trained Emerson, played an expanded piece backed by classical musicians in 1969. An event like that would never had been attempted, even a year prior, as the thought of "serious" musicians making music with "lay" pop pretenders seemed pretentious and outrageous. But now with the level of musicianship reaching ever higher, such a project came to fruition.

"In a courageous blow against the huge barriers between pop music and the classics, the Nice played three pieces in conjunction with 41 string and horn players, including members of the London Symphony Orchestra. It was a nerve racking experience for the musicians and their fans. Many silent prayers were offered that (a) the music would work and (b) the bulk of the crowd would react favorably. At the end of the experiment the cheers drowned sighs of relief. 'It worked!' was the cry backstage later as Nice manager Tony Stratton-Smith bought drinks for Keith."—Chris Welch, *Melody Maker*, August 16, 1969

For most American music fans, the Nice are a footnote to Emerson's arena rock staple of the 1970s: Emerson, Lake & Palmer. But in the late 1960s, the Nice were enormous in England. One of the issues that perhaps created a disconnect for the band in the United States was an adaptation of a Leonard Bernstein song from his musical *West Side Story* that it called "America." Emerson's furious attack lent an aggressive edge to the song, and it became the Nice's finale. "I had lent some scores to Keith to study," O'List wrote me, "one of them was *West Side Story* [and] he came up with the idea of doing 'America.' We got the arrangement together at a rehearsal at the Marquee Club. I came up with the idea of using 'Yo Ho Heave Ho' for the beginning, which was an old pirate song from my childhood. Obviously, we changed it around until it sounded right. I still had my treble choirboy voice and recorded the choir on different tracks on top of that at the studio singing harmonies."

"I went away and thought about an arrangement and decided to use Debussy's New World Symphony to depict the pure side of America and the 'West Side Story' theme to depict the brutality," Emerson told Richard Green in the July 6, 1968, issue of *New Musical Express*.

"Even the presence of The Nice as guest stars at the Second Prague Beat Festival was a part of it; only a week or two before Moscow had been berating 'decadent Western music.' But the show went on, brilliantly and riotously in the great Luzerna Hall, gilded remnant of a long-ago empire. In it were packed three and a half thousand young Czechs . . . and they roared approval as a whole series of Czech groups performed, and sometimes openly cocked a snook at their 'masters'—such as having a scrawled 'Ivan Go Home' on their amplifiers! . . . As the last note [of the Nice's set] was played there was a brief, pregnant silence . . . and then the whole Hall erupted in a roar the like of which, admitted Keith, he had never heard before."—*Record Mirror*, January 11, 1969

For the finale, the band would set fire to an American flag, which of course created an enormous controversy, getting the Nice banned from the Royal Albert Hall. "It was an anti-[Vietnam] war protest about the senseless killing," O'List wrote me. "We were trying to influence people in politics to change their stance and become peaceful. The worse the war became the better we played it. At one performance, several American guys in the audience who had run away from the draft invited us to burn their draft cards with the US flag, which we did for them on the stage." The band also turned off promoters in the United States with a controversy over a poster.

"The Nice has asked its record company to withdraw [a] controversial poster advertising its single 'America'—because, the group claims, its bookings and record sales are suffering as a result of the poster's adverse effect on the public. The Nice has requested a written undertaking from Immediate [Records] that in future no more of the posters will be distributed. The poster shows the group members with small boys on their knees—and superimposed on the children are the heads of the late President Kennedy, Senator Robert Kennedy and Dr. Martin Luther King. A spokesman for the Nice commented: 'Several record stores have refused to stock our current disc, and some promoters will not book the group because of this poster. The Nice feels that if the posters are issued in America they will do considerable harm. The group has been offered a U.S. college and TV tour in September and it has no wish to create ill-will from the outset.'"—*New Musical Express*, July 27, 1968

Atomic Rooster were sort of cousins to the Nice. A three-piece formed in 1969, the Rooster consisted of Vincent Crane on organ, Nick Graham on bass, and Carl Palmer on drums. Palmer's debut came as a 18-year-old prodigy in the Crazy World of Arthur Brown. During a US tour, that band imploded due to personality conflicts and equipment malfunctions, and Palmer moved on. While Crane would take the role of songwriter and visionary, Palmer's intricate propulsion would drive Atomic Rooster to new heights.

The young drummer quickly made a name for himself as an up-and-coming percussion virtuoso, capable of off-time signatures most rock drummers could not touch. By this time, Palmer had befriended legendary jazz drummer Buddy Rich, an elder who had little time for musical incompetence.

"I met him when I was 16. He was playing in London at Ronnie Scott's [jazz] club," Palmer said. "He was staying at the Dorchester. I went down and walked up to his secretary and I said, 'I'd like to speak to Mr. Rich, please.' And [he] said, 'Does he know you?' I said, 'Yes, he does.' [laughs] . . . When I said that to the guy behind the desk, he went to make the call. As he made the call, I turned 'round and the elevator doors are opening and out walked Buddy Rich. And I walked up to him and said, 'Hi. My name's Carl Palmer. I'm a drummer. I'm a big fan. Would you sign my album? And could I come and see you later?' He said, 'Yes, kid. You can come and see me later and I'll sign this for you now.' And I said, 'When would you like me to come back, Mr. Rich?' He said, 'Come back tomorrow evening. About five o'clock.' I went back and I went up to his room and there were all these other great English drummers. When I say English drummers, I don't mean rock 'n' roll drummers. I'm talking about people like Kenny Clare, Ronnie Verrell, Jack Parnell. These are all the great big band drummers. . . . [I said to him] 'What do you think I should [play]?' I don't know if you know much about Buddy Rich, but he [couldn't] really teach you or tell you anything. He just [said], 'Just watch, look, and listen.' . . . [It] started from there. I bought his daughter a box of chocolates to say hi—she was about three years younger than me—to say thank you. I remained friends with the family for years. When I played at Madison Square Garden with ELP, I sent a car to pick him up. He came out and it just went on from there. But the real deal with him was, you had to be polite. And you had to be well-mannered.

"When I did play with his orchestra for the second time, he asked me what I wanted to play. And I said, 'Whatever you'd like me to play.' . . . So he said, 'Let's play *Shawnee*.' And when he said that, I was trying to think, 'What album's that? I don't know *Shawnee*.' He looked up, he said, 'This is a new one. You don't know it.' . . . We counted it off and off we went and it got recorded and it ended up on the album [Carl Palmer's *Anthology*, released in 2001], so it couldn't have been that bad. That's what life with Buddy Rich was like."

While the band's sound, exemplified by their 1970 debut LP *Atomic Roooster* (misspelling intentional), does not really constitute progressive rock, the record introduced complex time signatures and jazz stylings. Palmer's dexterity come to the fore on "Decline and Fall" and "Play the Game." The record did not set the world on fire (reference to Arthur Brown is intentional) but had some commercial success, reaching number 49 on the charts in the United Kingdom.

As the band began to become more prominent in the London scene, Atomic Rooster found itself frequently crossing paths with Keith Emerson's Nice, and the bands began overlapping musically.

> "Atomic Rooster were a sensation at London's Marquee Club recently, stunning the crowd with the most exciting new group sound since the Nice. Essentially an organ band, in the tradition of the Nice et al., they have a unique approach—how else with the phantom Vincent Crane at the organ and Carl Palmer on drums?"—Alan Lewis, *Melody Maker*, September 27, 1969

"The Nice were sort of a bit more poppy than what Atomic Rooster was—slightly more commercial sounding," said Palmer, "but more in the way that I wanted to play because Keith was already using classical adaptations, which is definitely something I wanted to do. I wanted to introduce [classical] music into rock."

Emerson and King Crimson's Greg Lake crossed paths during a 1969 Nice / King Crimson American tour and hit it off immediately. Requiring a drummer, the pair was introduced to Palmer by Cream manager Robert Stigwood. The three-piece would conquer the 1970s as the prog rock supergroup Emerson, Lake & Palmer.

And then there was the Bonzo Dog Band. This group unintentionally provided a link between the early proto-prog bands, the theater of Arthur Brown, and progressive rock . . . and had a great time doing it.

Visionary and songwriter Neil Innes joined the band while attending Goldsmith's Art College in London. Upon Innes's 1966 graduation, the Bonzos would turn professional. Innes, along with singer Vivian Stanshall, would steer the band toward a sort of comedy rock entertainment project rooted in post–World War I Dada culture. In fact, the band originally called themselves the Bonzo Dog Dada Band but changed the name to the Bonzo Dog Doo-Dah Band since the players got tired of explaining what Dada is. The Bonzos, unlike many of their early

1960s peers, embraced trad jazz as well as the theater of vaudeville. "We had old gangsters pinstriped suits and two-tone shoes and awful ties," said Innes. "We used to hold up cut-out comic speech balloons with 'Wow! I'm expressing myself!' and things like that. And Vivian Stanshall used to wear sort of [a] gold lame suit and be sort of right over the top."

The Bonzos' outward rejection of their peers' embracing blues over trad jazz made them kind of punk rock in a way. "We were kind of punk trad jazzers [laughs]. That's a good way of describing it," said Innes. "Rodney [Slater] took more pleasure in making his clarinet sound like a chicken."

> "The only serious facet of the Bonzos is their skill and hard work in producing one of the funniest sights and sounds on the scene. They hope to become professional on leaving art school in July, and are already packing out huge London pubs five nights a week. The material is culled from old 78s and song sheets dating from 1900 to 1930."—Chris Welch, *Melody Maker*, April 16, 1966

Around that time, the Bonzos' trumpeter, Bob Kerr, came in contact with a producer named Geoff Stevens. Stevens had just put out a record called *Winchester Cathedral* by the New Vaudeville Band, a group that didn't actually exist. Session musicians played on the record, and Stevens asked Kerr if he and his band wanted to become a real "New Vaudeville Band" and promote the album. "And Bob came to us [and said], 'We can be the New Vaudeville Band,'" Innes recalled. "'We can be on *Top of the Pops*!' And the rest of us looked at him and said, 'Why?' And he said, 'Well, I'm gonna do it.' We said, 'Well good luck to you then.'"

Shortly thereafter, Kerr's New Vaudeville Band showed up on television looking and sounding like the Bonzos. "And then we sort of realized that they'd stolen the whole look of everything . . . to promote this rather ordinary record, really, I think," said Innes. "And then everywhere we went, people said, 'You're like the New Vaudeville Band.' So we had to do something. [And we said,] 'We'll do any kind of music now.' It did us a favor in a way, because we hadn't dreamt of writing any stuff ourselves. So we started writing stuff that was more satirical, more from where we were, and having great fun doing it. So that's how we changed. And pretty much from Year 1, when we went professional, playing sort of cabarets and things like that, we turned into more of sort of like [a] bizarre rock band."

The band's onstage performances became ever more outrageous with costumes and comedy bits interspersed with the music. And some of the more prominent musicians on the London scene took notice. "[Jimi Hendrix] came to see us," Innes remembered. "And he was in the [men's room], and I thought, 'Bloody hell. Jimi Hendrix.' We were both having a pee, and he said, 'You know, we're doing the same thing.' And I said, 'What do you mean? Having a pee?' He said, 'No, on stage.' Because he saw himself—at the time he was lighting guitars [on fire]— he was just doing over the top things as well.

"Eric Clapton played with us [and he] said, 'I wish I could muck about like you guys. I've always wanted to come onstage with a stuffed parrot on my shoulder.' I said, 'Well, Eric, you've gotta [make] a choice. You can't have posters made with you in a permed hairdo under the saying, "Clapton is God." It's the stuffed parrot or God.'"

By the late 1960s, the increasingly eclectic London music scene began to feature bands of all kinds on a single night. For example, if you went out one weekend in January 1968, say to the Middle Earth Club in Covent Garden, you'd catch the Bonzos headlining on Saturday, supported by bluesman Alexis Korner, along with colorful DJ Jeff Dexter. If you ventured out on that Friday, you would have seen English folk/rock pioneers Fairport Convention, along with Robert Plant's Band of Joy, his last group prior to forming Led Zeppelin.

Putting out three albums from 1967 to 1969, the Bonzos created such classic song titles as "Death Cab for Cutie" (a name taken by a Bellingham, Washington, band in the late 1990s) and "Can Blue Men Sing the Whites?" By 1969, in the spirit of the times, the band decided a concept album was in order, and thus *Keynsham* was born. "I was sitting in a dressing room. It was one of those quiet moments," said Innes. "We were all there. And the idea popped into my head. I said to everyone, 'Suppose this isn't really happening, and we're in a loony bin. And we're all on some sort of sedatives. And we *think* this is happening.' I was just sort of opening my mind, and words coming out, but everyone got what I was dribbling on about. And we quickly got bits of paper and we started formulating the idea of *Keynsham*. . . . So we were sharing the loony bin with everybody."

"The title came from the town near Bristol where [advertiser] Horace Batchelor is always telling us to send our pools coupons," Stanshall said in the December 13, 1969, issue of *Record Mirror*. "It strikes my mind as a sort of money-laden fairyland where the streets are paved with gold. I hear that it is actually a very boring suburb of Bristol, but I don't want to go there or think of it as that. Keynsham is the starting point of the LP, a sort of middle-class fantasy.

"There are two lines of thought running parallel, one being that paradise vision, infested with veiled, luring trickery and utopian goblins, while the other is the story of the five of us neurotic students who suffer mental breakdowns and then form the group to go out and do all the good things we dreamed.

"Idealistic, young and hopeful, we then run into the management problems, business hassles, clubs and all the drudgery that goes with the profession. Eventually, it turns us into the very things we set out to destroy. We become sacred cows and get all the decency kicked out of us. Toward the second half, we try to regain what was lost. The track 'I Want to Be with You' is representative of that . . . when you get too covered in sequins, you want to rush out and do very ordinary things."

While *Keynsham* might have signified a venturing into progressive rock, the Bonzo Dog Band, being the Bonzo Dog Band, were not going to become another King Crimson or Yes. Instead, the group's penchant for mixing musical and comedic creativity would lead them toward a now iconic British comedy troupe: Monty Python.

In 1968, Innes and company began appearing on a British television show called *Do Not Adjust Your Set* along with future Pythoners Eric Idle, Michael Palin, and Terry Jones. Eventually, a fourth and key figure, American Terry Gilliam, would join the crew. The following year, as the Bonzo experience became exhausting for its members, Idle phoned Innes and asked for his help in the formation of *Monty Python's Flying Circus*. "Terry Gilliam made Python different, really, if you want a single thing," said Innes. "Because most sketch shows and things had to have a punch line. With Terry Gilliam, you didn't need a punch line. You could go—to their catch phrase, 'and now for something completely different.' It's a bit like the beat arriving. On television, all of [a] sudden, a stream of consciousness, and rebellious humor, and intelligent stuff as well. . . . It's a bit like a surfer catching a wave."

The Bonzos also crossed paths with the Beatles, having shared Abbey Road Studios to record *Gorilla*, the 1967 predecessor to *Keynsham*. That meeting led to cameos in the Beatles' 1967 film *Magical Mystery Tour* and, eventually, to the late 1970s Beatles parody titled *The Rutles*. "[George Harrison] said, 'What should have happened was the Beatles and the Bonzos and the Rutles and the Pythons should have all got together and [had] a good time,'" said Innes.

By 1969, the experimentation with the concept album, with storytelling, and with more advanced musicianship and instrumentation began to manifest itself in what then fell under the banner of "progressive" music. We now call it progressive rock, or "prog." That year, a new experimental band began to lead the way into this new phenomenon: King Crimson.

King Crimson represented a new breed of experimental bands typically hailing from outside of London and consisting of middle-class kids with serious musical training combined with a desire to meld that into the world of rock. Crimson was guitarist Robert Fripp's vision of launching rock music into a new realm, free of rules that govern pop, jazz, or anything else. After a few iterations, King Crimson came into existence in late 1968; joining Fripp were Michael Giles on drums, Ian McDonald on guitar and keyboards, and Greg Lake on bass and vocals. The band debuted the following year with *In the Court of the Crimson King*, still one of the most highly regarded records in progressive rock.

Featuring complex arrangements, Fripp's eclectic guitar work, Lake's distinctive vocals, and McDonald's Mellotron throughout, ultimately the record just told a tale in the tradition of the medieval storyteller. "This was the sort of minstrel element. . . . Slightly medieval, green sleeves, that kind of medieval lute playing essence—the wandering minstrel thing," said Lake. "That is quite natural. You think about it—guitar player, stringed instrument, song, ballad . . . boom. There it is. And you weave that in. And that's how that arrives. When you listen to a song like 'Court of the Crimson King'—that is a very minstrel-ish song. The whole structure of that particular song was very minstrel-ish: the chords that were used, the storytelling, the sort of plaintive—a couple of sad chord movements under a storytelling ballad. That is what minstrels did."

For those in King Crimson, the music and experience was a natural one . . . and the timing was perfect. "We never talked about progressive music," Lake continued. "There was no such thing. It was just the music we were making. And also, I have to say, there was a sense of effortlessness about it. It wasn't like we were trying to be something. We were just on this voyage of discovery. It was an adventure."

King Crimson, within a few months of formation, found themselves playing in front of 500,000 people at a free concert at Hyde Park, opening for the Rolling Stones. "In the early days of King Crimson," said Lake, "one week we would go and play to 200 people. The next week, it would be 2,000. And a month after that, it would be 500,000. You know something, King Crimson never had one penny spent on paid publicity. Nothing. It was just word of mouth. Even though ELP, in terms of volume, was a far bigger band—you know, in terms of record sales and mass audiences and so forth. But I have never seen anything in my life like that response—that word of mouth, wildfire response—[that audiences had] to King Crimson."

By summer 1968, another band emerged in London that would become synonymous with progressive rock: Yes (initially advertised as "Yes!" in the *Melody Maker*). Consisting of singer Jon Anderson, bassist Chris Squire, drummer Bill Bruford, guitarist Peter Banks, and keyboardist Tony Kaye, Yes would soon define everything that was progressive rock: virtuoso musicians playing long, winding compositions based on classical themes and odd time signatures, all pulled together by beautiful song-lets that kept the listener's interest. Early on, though, Yes sounded nothing like that. "We were [initially] a covers band," said Bruford. "That's never underlined enough—the stuff I've read, never underlines fact that we were a covers band. I like covers bands, *except*, these days a covers band means you play it exactly like the record. In my day, 'covers band' meant you applied your style, your technique, your vision to the thing—to make a different kind of sound."

An example of Yes's approach to covers appears on the band's first eponymous record, released in fall 1969, where Yes does their take on the Beatles' "Every Little Thing." Unlike the original, which features a sweet acoustic guitar accompanied by Lennon and McCartney's trademark harmonies, the Yes version offers forth their vision of not only the song but also of progressive rock. First, the idea of a then little-known London band covering a Beatles song on record was incredibly ambitious and risky. Second, instead of playing a brief, pretty intro followed by the vocals, the prog rock pioneers offer up a rough-sounding minor-based guitar jam anchored by Bruford's rolling drum line. Not until 1:45 does the listener begin to recognize the chords of the Beatles classic . . . but wait, not too fast. First, the players segue into an organ-laced part and then the opening riff from "Day Tripper." Finally, at 2:06, Jon Anderson's high tenor vocals appear: "When I'm walking beside her . . ."

"I just loved the idea [of] changing music around, experimenting like crazy," Anderson wrote me. "Vanilla Fudge had done it so well at that time—the thought of transforming a classic Beatle song was just fun to do, and people enjoyed it onstage. That was what Yes was all about: to entertain the people and be a bit adventurous."

The band's dynamic changed dramatically with the third record, 1970's *The Yes Album*. Banks left, replaced by eclectic virtuoso guitarist Steve Howe. Then, for 1971's *Fragile*, keyboard phenom Rick Wakeman took Kaye's place. Wakeman not only brought an instrumental expertise but also contributed a folk sensibility after having played with the Strawbs. Meanwhile, Howe possessed a guitar style differing from most of his contemporaries. He loved the blues, like the Claptons of the world, but he preferred the more open stylings of jazz. Even his blues playing came from more country-oriented influences like Big Bill Broonzy. All of that combined to make Yes sound different and European. "It was almost like we wanted to sound British," said Howe. "And we picked things like the major key emphasis that a lot of Yes music had—was a turn away from the minor keys of blues. So we were very major-ish. We were very symphonic at times. We were bringing classical and bits of jazz. Yes most probably got me to do—in the course of 10 years—several retakes on guitar breaks because they were too jazzy. So, I understood that. Because we were never going to be a jazz band, as much as King Crimson kind of developed into something that was more jazzy, you know with Bruford [who joined King Crimson later] and [guitarist Tony] Levin doing their pieces with [Robert] Fripp. But basically, Yes had another mission. It was about entertainment, in a way. It was about arrangements that featured everybody in the band, but you had the three-part harmonies and you had these words that were like no other words."

In some ways, the crystallization of what would become known as progressive rock occurred in September 1969. Deep Purple, then still finding their identity, decided to do something then unheard of in the world of popular music. The band scheduled a full concert with the Royal Philharmonic Orchestra at the Royal Albert Hall based on a piece composed and arranged by keyboard player Jon Lord. While such musical combinations have become more frequent, if not commonplace in recent years, this melding of two seemingly opposite musical approaches was an anomaly in 1969. The World War II generation, by the late 1960s, had just begun to acknowledge, if somewhat begrudgingly, that some of the pop musicians had serious musical chops. Nevertheless, to "legitimize" rock 'n' roll music by placing it within the sacred realm of a symphony orchestra was a whole other thing.

> "[Deep Purple organist] Jon Lord believes that the musicianship in pop is getting so good that this kind of cooperation in music can happen more and more often."—BBC newscaster discussing the concert, as posted on YouTube

The classically trained Lord, along with composer Malcolm Arnold, put together a 53-minute piece divided into three movements. "What's it feel like playing with us squares?" Arnold asked Lord. "Wrong word. Wrong word. It's great, actually," he responded.

Several months prior, Purple had added two members from a psychedelic band called Episode Six: vocalist Ian Gillan and bassist Roger Glover. "The first thing [Lord] told us was, 'In September, we're gonna be doing a gig with an orchestra at the Albert Hall,'" Glover recalled. "I went, 'Wow. What kind of band am I joining?' . . . It was just an idea [Lord] had based on a Dave Brubeck album. Dave Brubeck was a jazz guy [and] did a [record] with an orchestra. And [Lord] had this kind of vague dream of doing it with a [rock] band. At the time, the importance of it was lost on me a little bit; although Jon did explain that it was a kind of battle between two opposing forces: rock music and orchestral music. Which at that time were—I wouldn't say bitter enemies, but certainly on different sides of the coin."

According to Glover, the orchestral players' self-importance was on full display. "The attitude [of] some of the classical musicians to us was not very nice," he said. "A few people in the orchestra walked out. One of them said—apparently, 'I didn't spend all those years learning my instrument to play backing to some third-rate Beatles.'"

Nonetheless, Lord's concerto was a legitimate stab at integrating the two diverse musical styles. "It's in three movements," said Glover. "The first movement demonstrates the differences between the two genres or the two styles or whatever [you] want to call it. And the middle movement is a sort of calming down period where we kind of experiment by being together. And the third movement is a kind of joyous bringing together of the orchestra and the band." Local media reaction to Lord's ambitious project varied.

"Organist Jon Lord's Concert for Group and Orchestra was a bold and inventive piece, probably the most advanced piece of writing produced by a pop musician. The structure was in three movements, the first depicting the group and orchestra in conflict and the other two as allies."—Chris Welch, *Melody Maker*, October 4, 1969

"The various recent attempts to wed rock and classical music are one of the strangest and, to my mind, more disturbing aspects of recent months . . . by attempting to graft classical forms on to their music, the rock musicians are more likely to destroy exactly what is valid in their own thing."—Bob Dawbarn, *Melody Maker*, November 1, 1969

["The gulf remains wide and unabridged." "Pop and classics just don't mix . . . so the pop group had its fire steadily dampened."] "The above are just two quotes from reviews in our national Press which appeared the morning after the Deep Purple's appearance with the Royal Philharmonic Orchestra at London's Royal Albert Hall last Wednesday evening. Now I don't suppose there is much doubt that the two critics concerned have a far wider experience and understanding of classical than myself, but I do feel that they have somewhat missed the whole point of the exercise. Music isn't meant to work; it is to be listened to and enjoyed, to arouse emotion and to borrow a phrase from Shakespeare, soothe the savage beast. Perhaps it is my own musical naivety, but [Jon] Lord's 'Concerto for Group and Orchestra' was a resounding success, not only in my book, but also for the large crowds of youngsters and older folk present."—Gordon Coxhill, *New Musical Express*, October 4, 1969

Despite the misgivings of joining together two forms of music coming from differing points of origin, Deep Purple's experiment ultimately provided a jumping-off point for decades of musical experimentation. In some ways, this concert represents the legitimization of what would become known as progressive rock. "Looking back on it now," said

Glover, "it was an incredibly brave thing to do. And I think [it] helped in many ways to bring together two opposing forces. I mean, you wouldn't think twice now about heavy bands, or rock bands, or even heavy metal bands working with an orchestra. It's almost commonplace. But then it was unheard of."

The increasing level of talent and sophistication began to create another dynamic in the music world: the "elder generation" began to actually respect the rock 'n' rollers. Beginning with *Sgt. Pepper's*, older jazz and classical musicians started to believe some of the kids could actually play more than four chords. By the time progressive rock began to flower, however, these "serious musicians" began to actually respect their younger counterparts . . . even from the legendary Buddy Rich. *Melody Maker* used to run a feature called "Blind Date," where a musician would listen to several songs and comment on them, without being told who the artist was. Rich heard Yes's cover of a Leonard Bernstein / Stephen Sondheim composition called "Something's Coming."

"Is that Blind Faith? No? Then it isn't [Ginger] Baker. Hey, that's a good drummer [Bill Bruford] . . . good hands. I enjoyed that. They've

Deep Purple, rehearsing with the Royal Philharmonic Orchestra, Royal Albert Hall, London, 1969. *Keyston Press / Alamy stock photo.*

taken a difficult piece of music by Bernstein, they went at it differently and pulled it off. If we were giving records a star rating, I'd give this five stars—for choice of material, conception, arrangement and professionalism in the performances."—Buddy Rich, "Blind Date" review of Yes's cover of "Something's Coming," *Melody Maker*, November 15, 1969

Arising out of Scotland via Blackpool via London came another progressive rock titan . . . well, at least a band that would become a progressive rock titan: Jethro Tull. Formed in Luton, North London, in winter 1968, Jethro Tull initially presented themselves as a blues-oriented band . . . thus aligning with the popularity of the blues boom of 1968–1969 and other bands working that territory including Fleetwood Mac, Chicken Shack, and the Savoy Brown Blues Band. Only the minstrel-like vocal delivery and flute playing of front man Ian Anderson distinguished Tull from their blues contemporaries. Jethro Tull's ability to entertain their audience with Anderson's flute playing while kicking up a leg quickly earned them an audience at London's biggest clubs, including the Marquee.

"I think the underground has now become an established musical form. One of the groups who've helped to do this is Jethro Tull. They present their music with a great deal of excitement which is what is needed these days."—Jimmy Page, as told to *Record Mirror*'s Ian Middleton, September 20, 1969

The band's blues-oriented approach appears on its first record, *This Was*, released in fall 1968, and sounds nothing like their later records that evoked images of traditional British folk, storytelling, and classical stylings. *This Was* the blues, especially with the hit single off the record, "A Song for Jeffrey." "It really was a bit of a—not entirely cynical exercise," said Anderson, "but it was one that was pragmatic at the very least. It was an entrée into being a professional musician since the subculture of music in the UK at that time was quite strongly based on what we called back then—we still call 'rhythm & blues.' . . . And it was our—certainly *my*—pragmatic career option to try to exploit that growing niche in music—at least to get started. But I always felt too indebted to blues and, to a degree, jazz, to ever want to persevere with music that was really more properly celebrated within a different continent, let alone race or culture. So, as soon as it was possible to do so—which was in 1969—I started to try and bring more of my own European influences to bear: classical music and church music and folk music—even to some degree, some Asian music slipped into the mix, too, as early as 1969. So I felt more emboldened to be a little broader in my influences to take on some of the more European flavors which were not necessarily popular in the USA, although it turned out that that quickly became the case."

Tull would venture into a sort of proggy rock meets folk band, anchored by Anderson's minstrel-like baritone vocal delivery, his flute playing, and the heavy guitar work of Martin Barre (who joined the band following *This Was*). In the early 1970s, Tull, like some of their contemporaries Yes and Nektar, would write one or two songs that would span an entire album, taking progressive rock to its zenith. For Tull, that approach would result in 1972's masterpiece, *Thick as a Brick*. Was the Tull effort influenced by the likes of Yes and Nektar? "Not only were we not talking to other bands," Anderson said, "I wasn't even talking to the rest of *my* band. It was something really that was just engineered by me. And to give the guys in the band the credit due to them. I mean they trusted me to have this vision of something bigger. They couldn't possibly have known what was coming next because they only got the next three minutes of music when I arrived for rehearsal at lunchtime and we would work through the afternoon into the evening rehearsing a piece of music that they had never heard before until that day, largely because I'd only written it during that morning before I went to rehearsal. So it was done in a very spontaneous and quite an organic way, [because] we just built the album up day by day. And then we went straight on to record it a couple of weeks later. I don't think the band would have heard even then most of the vocals until they actually heard the finished record because they wouldn't have been in the studio when I was doing vocal overdubs or mixing. I didn't like having people around me when I was doing the slightly more personal and intimate part of the recording. They were very trusting and it paid off on that occasion. They did their job admirably without really knowing necessarily how it all fitted together."

By the end of the 1960s, rock music had arrived. Progressives had pushed the boundaries of the genre perhaps to the limit and, in doing so, gained the respect of the elder generation of musicians. Much has been written about the arrival of punk rock in the United States, with the Ramones' first album in 1976, or the Sex Pistols in the United Kingdom with their debut showing up the following year. But the seeds of discontent, or at least the questioning of where rock had arrived at, and perhaps if it had lost its soul, arrived before 1970 in England.

> "We're not interested in dexterity, in this big technical thing represented by people like King Crimson. That's so sterile. The function of rock and roll is to get out and have a good time, not to stand in groups marveling at the guitarist's technique. The scene at the moment reminds me of the British jazz scene of the Fifties, when everyone stood around seeing who could play the fastest."—Mick Farren of the Deviants, as told to Richard Williams, *Melody Maker*, September 20, 1969

"Suddenly, some musicians decided, 'Let's impress other musicians,'" said Herman's Hermits' Peter Noone. "That changed the whole game. And we sat down with [our producer] Mickie Most and said, 'Let's make sure we never ever try to impress other musicians. We're impressed by them, so we'll let them play on our records so *they* can impress other musicians. We're just gonna be a pop band who sings songs that young girls and young boys want to buy.'"

YOU CAN ALL JOIN IN
(PROGRESSIVE FOLK)

"We're gonna create this new repertoire of things that have never been done before to folk songs. We're gonna take traditional songs and make them sound as if they were written yesterday. And we're gonna have new songs and make them sound as if they're a couple of hundred years old."—Simon Nicol, Fairport Convention

Then there was Sandy Denny. Before reading further, go to YouTube and listen to "Fotheringay" or "Who Knows Where the Time Goes." If her voice doesn't make the hair on your arms stand up, you're not human. "Probably the greatest singer I've ever worked with," said Richard Thompson, who played with Denny in Fairport Convention.

Denny represents in many ways a symbolic connection between Britain's folk club scene and rock music. She was such an immense talent, but her untimely death in 1978 has obscured her accomplishments. She was, to put it simply, a force.

Denny made a name for herself in the folk clubs and was noticed by musicians such as the Strawbs' Dave Cousins and folk artist Al Stewart. She was a study in contrasts: she was beautiful but insecure about her looks; she possessed a pure, lovely voice yet could curse like a sailor.

Dave Cousins of the Strawbs took notice of Denny performing at London's Troubadour Club in November 1966 and asked her to join the band. She agreed.

Cousins invited Denny to his house to do some rough demos. "We recorded our first demos on my Grundig tape recorder," Cousins wrote in *Exorcising Ghosts.* "We hung blankets over the windows and dangled the plastic mike from the ceiling light. I asked Sandy if she had any songs we could try. She sang 'Who Knows Where the Time Goes,' and our jaws dropped."

The Strawbs, then known as the Strawberry Hill Boys, consisted of Cousins and Tony Hooper, who occasionally brought in other musicians. They were a folk act. That would change with Denny's addition to the group. Cousins desired to venture beyond the folk clubs, and Denny's powerful, soulful voice seemed like the perfect vehicle to inject some rock 'n' roll into traditional music. So he shortened the band's name to the Strawbs to disconnect it from its bluegrass roots and headed over to Denmark to record an album.

Sandy Denny and the Strawbs' 1967 record, *All Our Own Work* (not released until 1973), mixed the tradition with contemporary music. "That was Britain's first ever folk/rock record," Cousins asserted.

The Strawbs opened the gates in a sense, but it was another band Denny touched that really created and defined British folk/rock: Fairport Convention.

Fairport Convention began life at rhythm guitarist Simon Nicol's home in North London. Joined by bassist Ashley Hutchings and lead guitarist Richard Thompson, the three began playing out in local folk clubs, discovering the sometimes rigid enforcement of the Ewan MacColl–led tradition, while finding themselves exposed to the varied sorts of music being played all over London. As a result, they enjoyed more eclectic influences, and especially in the case of Thompson, more European influences than their Rolling Stones and Yardbirds counterparts.

By 1967, the three-piece had added drummer Martin Lamble and singer Judy Dyble to the mix, and they found themselves wanting to strike out in a more serious fashion. In their early days, the players just teenagers, the band's songwriting tended to draw from the US West Coast, à la the Byrds, as well as singer/songwriters such as Joni Mitchell and Bob Dylan. After going through a series of names, the band decided to come up with one that reflected their West Coast outlook. "[Fairport Convention] was suggested by a friend of mine, a neighbor, who I still see to this day," said Nicol, "because Fairport was my old family home and it was the venue for our get-togethers and practices. He just came up with that idea. And there was something right about the polysyllabic nature of the name, which really fitted the tenor of the times, with the band names that were coming out of the alternative story of music on the West Coast, I think. There were a lot of really quite odd names and there was always a sort of a noun and an adjective. . . . There was something very West Coast about 'Fairport Convention.'"

The first eponymous record, released that year, and again with the players as teenagers, reflected the open and naive nature of the musicians. The album featured Dylan and Mitchell covers, and even a Dylan parody song called "It's Alright Ma, It's Only Witchcraft," so named after Dylan's "It's Alright Ma, I'm Only Bleeding." The presence of a second vocalist, Iain Matthews (then known as Ian MacDonald), brought in at the suggestion of manager Joe Boyd[1], created yet a more West Coast dynamic to the band, which can especially be noticed on the opening track, a cover of California songwriter Emitt Rhodes called "Time Will Show the Wiser." As a result, on tour, especially in the United States, some weren't sure if Fairport Convention was American or English, resulting in the band being referred to as "the British Jefferson Airplane." Dyble took issue with the comparison. "That was a really stupid thing for that DJ to say," she said. "It was a Radio One DJ, and he was trying to think of something that we were like and he [came up with] that. And it stuck. We weren't. The only real reason there was any similarity was we both had female singers. And that was about it."

Something was afoot on that first record, however. An odd song called "The Lobster" appeared, cowritten by Hutchings, Thompson, and author George Painter. Beginning with an unusual autoharp introduction, the guitar comes in amid a recorder, and the song seems to blend the West Coast with the medieval. Thompson's intricate guitar work prevails, but nary a vocal appears until almost two and a half minutes have elapsed. In a way, the track is like the "Tomorrow Never Knows" of the record, signifying that something different, and perhaps unprecedented, is about to come. "I remember that song was a bit of a mystery to me," Nicol recalled. "Just as [Thompson's] own interest in melodic music, if you will, extended beyond my parameters. . . . He was even less shackled than the rest of us by current expectations of what made a song or what made music. So he was able to come up with things like 'The Lobster.'"

"I think the first Fairport record pulls in so many different directions," said Thompson. "I mean, it shows how eclectic our taste was. We hadn't quite found ourselves as a band, so every track sounds different. And you get strange tracks like 'The Lobster.'"

Fairport played a number of the psychedelic clubs like UFO and Middle Earth (although they weren't really psychedelic themselves), as well as the Speakeasy. It was there that Fairport crossed paths with Jimi Hendrix. "If he liked the band that was playing that night," Dyble recalled, "he would want to go play with them, because he was that kind of musician. He just loved to play. . . . He would just very politely say, 'Can I jam? Can I sit in?' And Richard would give him his guitar, Richard would take Simon's guitar. Simon would pick up something and I'd be offstage [knitting], because they were just jamming, so there was nothing for me to sing to."

Dyble, who had been dating Thompson, left the band after the first album. So for Fairport's second record, the band enlisted the services of Sandy Denny. For four polite, nondescript, middle-class boys from North London, Denny's addition to the band was a bit of culture shock. "At that point in Fairport, we were kind of shy, retiring North London lads," Thompson recalled. "And Sandy was definitely not shy and retiring. I think she helped to bring us out of our shells a bit. She could swear and drink—keep up with the lads quite easily. And I think at that time it was quite tough to be a woman in the music scene. In a sense, there weren't that many women, and Sandy was one of the pioneers. And she had to be tough. She had to be outwardly tough to withstand all the shit that was thrown at her in basically a man's world at that time.

"She was a larger-than-life personality. . . . She was sometimes very vulnerable, very insecure. Immense talent . . . a great writer, a very intelligent musician. Sometimes Sandy could go from confident to insecure in like two seconds. And she could go [from] happy to angry in two seconds. She had a very volatile personality. She could be a pain at times, but when I think of her, I think of her just laughing. She had a great, infectious laugh. And was usually a lot of fun to be around. And it was a pleasure and privilege to know her and to work with her."

"No group has worked harder for a hit than Fairport. The diminutive sandy-haired Sandy [Denny] was a solo folk singer before she joined Fairport just over a year ago. The possessor of a beautifully clear voice and of a reputation for consuming Scotch in large quantities, she also has a nice line in facial expressions, one of which is a melting smile."—Nick Logan, *New Musical Express*, August 16, 1969

Fairport receives a lot of credit—and properly so—for "inventing" British folk/rock. But that mixing, which of course would completely blow up the traditionalists like Ewan MacColl, was not a conscious musical shift. As manager Boyd was booking the band on a 1969 tour, Fairport had little time to record and rehearse for their upcoming albums *What We Did on Our Holidays* and *Unhalfbricking*. "To a certain extent, that embracing of the folk culture was a bit of a—not compromise—but it was a happy accident," said Nicol, "because we didn't have a lot of time once Sandy was taken on board. We didn't have a lot of time before our first sort of rash of gigs. And rather than getting her to do all the learning, we thought we'd meet in the middle. So we would learn songs she knew inside-out from the tradition and vice versa. [So] by finding that middle ground, we were actually standing on fresh ground."

Denny brought some beautiful compositions to both records, notably the traditional sounding "Fotheringay" and the haunting ballad "Who Knows Where the Time Goes." But Fairport would reach its apex in combining the traditional and contemporary on their fourth record. And that would happen only because of a horrible accident.

In spring 1969, while on the M1 motorway, the band's tour van crashed, killing 19-year-old drummer Lamble and Jeannie Franklyn, Thompson's girlfriend. Thompson and Hutchings survived but were seriously injured. Only Nicol emerged relatively unscathed. Denny was not in the van at the time. The impact on the band was understandably traumatic, as Fairport seriously considered calling it a day. Fortunately, despite the devastation, the band decided to continue on, bringing in new drummer Dave Mattacks as well as fiddle virtuoso Dave Swarbrick, a veteran of the Ian Campbell Folk Group. "[Mattacks and Lamble] were such different musicians, such different players," said Nicol. "And then you had this existing leadership relationship between Sandy and Richard; [it] had become . . . a triangle, with Swarbrick at the other point. It was like musical chairs, really. Everybody had to sort of stand up, run around the room, and find a new place to sit down."

For Thompson, the accident forced the band to focus on advancing its vision to combine old folk songs with contemporary musical stylings. It was something the players had been thinking about, but they now confidently took off the gloves and ventured wholeheartedly in that direction. "After the accident," Thompson remembered, "we thought, 'Well, we don't really want to go back to the repertoire that we did with

Martin. It seems like that's water under the bridge now. We've kind of done that. So why don't we take the traditional/rock concept and pursue that. It'll give us something to focus on. It'll keep us together as a band. It'll keep our minds focused on the present rather than the past.'"

The result, *Liege & Lief*, arguably the penultimate document of British folk/rock, was released in December 1969. The record contains updated versions of traditional folk songs like "Tam Lin" and "Matty Groves," as well as new songs like the rocking "Come All Ye" and the lovely "Crazy Man Michael." Fairport Convention fully realized its exploration by this record. It had successfully blurred the lines between the traditional and the modern.

> "I don't know who it is, but it's bloody good. Just to help me, is it English or American? She's got a lovely purity to her voice. Is it Fairport Convention? Didn't they do 'Chelsea Morning'? Oh, Dave Swarbrick's in this group. He's a damn fine violinist, and the girl must be Sandy Denny. If the rest of the album is as good as this, it should be a big seller for them. It would make someone a very nice Christmas present."—Jimmy Page, "Blind Date" review of "Come All Ye" from *Liege & Lief, Melody Maker*, December 27, 1969

As mentioned previously, the Strawbs did their first record with Sandy Denny before she moved on to Fairport Convention. While Denny had a significant impact on Fairport, her influence on the Strawbs is debatable, as that band had already been heading away from the folk club circuit prior to bringing her on board.

Unlike Fairport Convention, which more consciously combined folk music with rock 'n' roll, the Strawbs' evolution was much less deliberate; it did not end up in a particular spot and certainly not within the neat confines of folk/rock. By the time the band was ready to make its second record, simply titled *Strawbs* (which incidentally featured Led Zeppelin's John Paul Jones on bass), things had changed dramatically. It was 1969, Denny had moved on to Fairport, and the band was beginning to carve out an identity. "The reason why the songs became so different," Cousins recalled, "was I started to put banjo tunings—I realized that people like Clarence Ashley in the Appalachian Mountains was playing his banjo in a modal tuning. So I put my banjo in a modal tuning and I wondered what that would sound like on the guitar. So I started to put my guitar in all these banjo tunings and suddenly a whole

Sandy Denny with, from left, John Bonham, Robert Plant, and Jimmy Page of Led Zeppelin, 1970. *PA Images / Alamy stock photo.*

different repertoire opened before my eyes . . . and I started to write different style songs. And so [as a result] the current repertoire that we were doing . . . was so totally removed from the stuff we were doing in the folk clubs."

Strawbs began to display Cousins's songwriting talents, most notably on the controversially titled "The Man Who Called Himself Jesus." Here the guitarist shows not only his instrumental innovations but also Dylanesque lyrical poetry:

> He asked me if I knew a place where he could start to preach. And I said, "Well, try a church or maybe Brighton Beach." And I was trying

to be serious, but he didn't seem impressed. He said, "You think I'm crazy. You're just like all the rest."

Strawbs concludes with a six-minute-plus epic track called "The Battle," which featured the organ work of future Yes superstar Rick Wakeman. Wakeman was introduced to the band during a performance on Radio One on John Peel's *Top Gear* program. "I asked Tony Visconti to come along as our musical director," Cousins wrote in *Exorcising Ghosts*. "Tony turned up with cellist Clare Deniz, and a lanky organ player with long blond hair who he introduced as Rick Wakeman. We played our epic, 'The Battle,' the six-minute-long closing track on *Strawbs*, and I knew we had recorded something special. After the session, we adjourned to the nearest pub for a celebratory drink. Rick was wide-eyed, enthusiastic, enjoyed several pints, and was one of the lads, as we say. I made a note to stay in touch with him."

Wakeman's presence would make a more pronounced impact on the next record, 1970's *Dragonfly*. Wakeman, like Denny before him, would quickly draw the most attention, notably for his showmanship in addition to his virtuosity. Wakeman brought trained musicianship into the fold—something that rock music was not inherently about but would change with the progressive movement of the late 1960s and early 1970s. "The theory side of [music] was very important to me," Wakeman wrote me, "as I wanted to compose and orchestrate. And that meant a thorough knowledge of the theoretical side of things, so I studied that very hard."

Wakeman took that musical theory knowledge, still somewhat foreign to most folk and rock musicians, and brought that into the Strawbs. So unlike Denny, who peripherally touched the Strawbs, Wakeman completely changed the band's musical dynamic and evolution. "It was Rick coming into the band," said Cousins, "that gave me the idea of [marrying] his classical music stylings to my strange modal chords [and it] gave us a unique sound . . . we didn't sound like anybody else."

The first rehearsal with Wakeman would portend a life-changing moment for the Strawbs. "I started to play a new song, 'Song of a Sad Little Girl,' written about my daughter Joelle," Cousins wrote in *Exorcising Ghosts*, "in one of my D modal tunings. Rick looked puzzled and asked me to play the individual notes of my opening chord. He played them on the piano and declared: 'I can't play that, it's a discord.' Once Rick appreciated that my modal guitar chords provided a texture, he started to ripple single notes over them—it was the beginning of the Strawbs' 'sound.'"

The Cousins-Wakeman partnership can perhaps best be symbolized by "The Hangman and the Papist" from the album *From the Witchwood*, released in 1971. Beginning with an almost baroque organ introduction and weaving keyboard and acoustic guitar throughout, "Hangman" tells the story of the "troubles" of Irish Protestants and Catholics. "That's a story about Northern Ireland, if you like," said Cousins, "with the IRA bombing mainland Britain at the time. . . . It was a religious war equally as much as anything else: Protestant vs. Catholic. Now that happened in my own family. I'd been baptized as a Catholic. Mum [remarried] and my brother and sister were brought up as Protestants because my dad insisted on it. So we had a mixed religious situation in my own family. So I then imagined—there you are in a family with two brothers fighting on opposite sides of the religious fence, one a Protestant, one a Catholic, which is alluding to my own family background. And so, the story of 'The Hangman and the Papist' is two brothers: one who is the papist, so a Catholic supporter, and his brother's fighting on the other side and he's elected by drawing lots to become the hangman and he walks out on the scaffold to find out that he's got to hang his brother. And he's forced to do it in the name of God."

Wakeman's live performances also brought him tremendous attention and, eventually, would lead him to joining Yes. "Rick's stage show became wilder each night," Cousins wrote in *Exorcising Ghosts*. "He had the economy version, Hammond L100 organ at the time, which he smashed around to make the reverb explode. When he clambered on top of it, still playing, it looked in danger of toppling over at any moment. Rick mostly wore bright pink trousers with yellow or purple T-shirts, and, with his considerable height, slim waistline, and long blond hair, he stood out a mile."

While Wakeman's addition helped push the Strawbs toward progressive rock, a third British folk/rock act would help fill the vacuum: a supergroup of sorts called the Pentangle.

Fairport Convention were able to successfully blur the lines between the folk tradition and contemporary rock. The Strawbs took the folk storytelling and incorporated the sophisticated sounds of Dave Cousins's modal tunings and Rick Wakeman's classical training. The Pentangle brought something else. In addition to off-the-chart musicianship, the Pentangle's five players—singer Jacqui McShee, guitarists Bert Jansch and John Renbourn, bassist Danny Thompson, and drummer Terry Cox—took folk storytelling and combined it with blues and jazz influences.

Much has been made of the supergroup concept in the 1960s. Most point to Cream, formed in 1966, which featured virtuoso ex-Yardbird/Bluesbreaker guitarist Eric Clapton, stellar ex-Bluesbreaker bassist Jack Bruce (who was also briefly in Manfred Mann), and Ginger Baker, who previously drummed with Graham Bond. The first supergroup, arguably, was a band called the Steam Packet, which predated Cream by about a year; the band featured another set of all-stars: singer-guitarist Long John Baldry, singers Rod Stewart and Julie Driscoll, and keyboardist Brian Auger. The Pentangle, formed in 1966 or 1967 (accounts vary),[2] also brings that supergroup aesthetic.

The issue with supergroups, of course, is that they're fielding an all-star team. Great players for sure, but can they play together? Without any role players, "super" bands face a similar issue. How can they manage to coexist and perform without stepping on one another's toes? How do you avoid disaster, à la Blind Faith, the Clapton-led all-star band that imploded after one record? How do you create enough space to allow the musicians to use their creative talents? That's it. Space. Thompson and Cox, coming from a jazz background, know all about space. That was our philosophy if you'd like—certainly Danny and me, which rubbed off on the other [players] in the same way as what they played rubbed off on us."

The success of the Pentangle, despite the obvious talents of the lead instrumentalists, heavily depended upon the jazz and blues backgrounds of its rhythm section. Cox and Thompson cut their teeth with Alexis Korner's band. Thompson joined up with Korner, and he recruited Cox to be his drummer. Like with previous Korner band members such as Cream's Ginger Baker and the Rolling Stones' Charlie Watts, Thompson and Cox learned a great deal as musicians while playing with him. "He always had a good band," said Cox. "Always. We used to play . . . completely across the range of blues: urban blues, country blues, whatever.

"It was very good training, I have to say. The most [important] thing, for me, was to play very slowly, which is the hardest thing to do. People can play fast, but when you can play really slowly—very hard."

Cox also brought something else to the mixture, which also would become critical to the Pentangle's success. He always played drums with brushes, not sticks. "The reason I played brushes all the time," Cox said, "is because [jazz drummer] Chico Hamilton played brushes all the time. And also, being with a folk/blues group, it doesn't want to be loud from the drummer's point of view because it takes over everything. And also if you're recording and the drums are in a certain position, they leak on everybody's mic. So all you get is drums.

"The other reason for it was that we lived in a semi-detached house [aka a duplex in the American lexicon] . . . so, if I'm playing drums, everybody's going crazy and shouting and all that. So I thought, 'OK, so I'm going to play exclusively with brushes and just be quiet.' So that's why—that's the thing I do. And I got a lot of work because nobody else did it."

With Cox and Thompson providing a bluesy/jazzy backbeat laden with subtlety and space, the other 60 percent of the Pentangle brought more of a sensibility that emanated from Britain's folk clubs, not the least of which was from singer Jacqui McShee.

Like in America, British folk music of the 1950s and 1960s often associated with causes. In the case of McShee and many of her cohorts, that cause was joining the CND—the Campaign for Nuclear Disarmament—which arose after nuclear and thermonuclear weapons were invented and detonated by the United States and the Soviet Union. "Because of all the students [I met] on the CND marches, I ended up going to folk clubs with some of them," McShee recalled.

"I used to go and see Peggy Seeger and Ewan MacColl at [their club]," McShee continued. "It was very accessible—in every town in England and Scotland, and Ireland, for that matter, you'd get three or four pubs in a town that would [have] music pubs. There was just a wealth of places to go and people to see."

Due to McShee's vocal talents, which she honed during the CND marches, she soon found herself singing with some of the student musicians. These frequent gigs led her to cross paths with a 12-string acoustic guitar player named Chris Ayliffe, and they struck up a friendship. Ayliff worked in a music shop and sold guitar strings to Jansch and

Renbourn. "And unbeknownst to me, he was pushing me towards them," she said.

One summer, Ayliffe ventured to busk in the South of France, which left McShee back home gigging and helping to run a folk club. "And John Renbourn had come to the club to play. I'd met Bert before that anyway. I'd met [both of] them sort of socially. And John said, 'I'm making a second album. Do you fancy doing some harmonies on it with me?' So I said, 'Yes, OK.' 'Do you think Chris would mind?' 'Well he's not here. He's buggered off for about six months.' So I did that and then we started working together. And Chris [had] said, 'Well I intended that to happen anyway.'"

Renbourn, like a number of his contemporaries he rubbed elbows with—Wizz Jones, Davey Graham, and many others—put in his time hitchhiking around Europe, busking, and playing small gigs. By the early 1960s, he settled in London and began to become a prominent member of the British folk club scene. Through the efforts of Ayliffe, he collaborated with McShee on his second solo album, 1967's *Another Monday*.

Perhaps the superstar of the band, if there is such a thing, was guitarist Bert Jansch. Jansch also worked the traveling European minstrel circuit before gigging at the London folk clubs during the 1960s. Jansch had an unusual finger-picking style and became one of the early folk singers, like Bob Dylan in America, who wrote original material. Crossing paths with Renbourn, Jansch cut an album with him called *Bert and John* in 1966. The pair, although fully emerged in the British folk club community, fell on the modern, non–Ewan MacColl side of the spectrum, and they desired to expand their horizons, enlisting the services of singer McShee and the rhythm section of Thompson and Cox. "The traditionalists didn't like us at all," said McShee. "Because [they would say,] 'You can't have drums and electric guitars in a folk group.' [So we'd respond,] 'We're not really a folk group.'"

"The way [Jansch] played," said McShee, "it was a very percussive way of playing. And it really drove the songs. And John just—what John would actually say is [that] he'd noodle around Bert's playing. And that was just the way he said it. But it was actually far more intense than that. It wasn't just noodling around. It was just complementary. . . . I'd started researching different songs—traditional songs and working with John singing blues things. So he and I brought the duo side that we were working on. We brought that to Pentangle. And also, John had worked with Danny and Terry before. He worked with Danny before, on a TV show. Everybody except Bert had played with Alexis Korner. So there were sort of lots of different ties for everybody coming together. Danny and Terry did lots of sessions—jazz sessions. And Terry did quite a lot of pop sessions."

By the time the Pentangle got rolling in a major way in 1968, the climate of musical openness had fully blossomed. The Jansch-Renbourn guitar virtuoso team was open to the jazz and blues musical stylings and influences of the other players. Thus, the Pentangle became the rarest of musical acts, a group of superstar-level musicians, a supergroup, if you will, playing together as one while venturing off into multiple genres.

> "Ever since the underground thing started a couple of years ago, people's tastes have been broadening. You can have a group like the Pentangle, who are into a light, folky thing on one hand, and us [Led Zeppelin] on the other. The scene is broad enough to take us all in, and I don't see why that situation can't continue."—Jimmy Page, as told to Richard Williams, *Melody Maker*, September 13, 1969

Arguably the pinnacle of the Pentangle's catalog, 1968's *Sweet Child*, is a double album, half done in the recording studio and half recorded live at the Royal Festival Hall in London. The record explores the vast range of the band's musical vocabulary. "Bruton Town," for example, is a traditional folk song about a servant falling in love with an aristocratic woman. Not approving of the romance, her brothers arrange to take the servant on a hunting trip, where they proceed to murder him in the woods. "No Exit" is a short, Celtic-influenced instrumental piece penned by Jansch and Renbourn. The band explores European classical stylings on "Three Dances" and offers a bluesy rendition with "No More My Lord," which even features an electric guitar. The band plays quietly during the live performance. The audience sits and listens and claps enthusiastically but politely after each song.

The band's understated performances sometimes drew odd pairings, especially when coming to America. "[American concert promoter] Bill Graham . . . he brought us over," Cox recalled. "But [we were paired with bands like] Grateful Dead and all that, which is very loud. So in between the sets, when we came on the stage, Bill Graham came up and he said, 'I've brought these guys over from London, and it's very quiet. So if you don't want to listen, go away. And if you do, shut up.'

"Imagine playing brushes opposite the Grateful Dead. They must've thought we were mad."

Despite the band's quiet and understated performance, as exemplified by the live portion of *Sweet Child*, it could potentially be boring, but it's anything but. "After [us], there's never been a band anything like [the Pentangle]," said Cox, "because they don't have the same philosophy. Truthfully, I don't know any other band that plays like that."

If you chat with English folk or rock musicians (or folk/rockers, for that matter), most of them will insist the folk club community and the rock scene were two mutually exclusive entities. There wasn't a whole lot of crossover. That statement is true on a superficial level, but there was some crossover, if not overt then at least in an understated way. And that crossover wasn't just limited to the Fairport Conventions, Strawbs, and Pentangles of the world. A band like Traffic, for example, doesn't conjure up images of acoustic guitars played in smoky folk clubs. Yet they tapped into the folk aesthetic almost without even realizing it.

Traffic came about at the expense of the Spencer Davis Group, who had two huge hits in 1966: "I'm a Man" and "Gimme Some Lovin'"; both songs were credited to keyboardist/vocalist phenom Steve Winwood but actually cowritten by Davis. The elder member of his band, Davis had a calming influence upon the musicians, but Winwood, who joined at just 15, remained the outstanding talent. "Steve Winwood was some talent," Davis offered. "Still is. You stick an instrument in front of him and he'll play anything. He was a child prodigy. There's no doubt about that. This is my comment: When he learns to join the human race, he'll have a better understanding of life."

Then at the height of the Spencer Davis Group's popularity, the band received an offer to tour America, and Winwood left to form Traffic. For Davis, Winwood's departure stung. "We played the Marquee, and Micky Dolenz—the Monkees—were in town," Davis recalled. "Micky Dolenz came down to the Marquee to see us. And the picture hit *Seventeen* magazine over here. And then the offers to play the States came in. And that's when Steve Winwood left the band. As soon as we'd really hit it . . . Steve Winwood decided—timing was what I always call 'immaculate.' Stupid. We could have done the shows and then he could have gone on his way. He wasn't manacled to the Spencer Davis Group."

Winwood felt he had outgrown not only the Spencer Davis Group and the blues but also the need to make hit singles. His desire to experiment led him to form Traffic in 1967. "I think different people listen to [record albums]," Winwood told *Melody Maker*'s Nick Jones in the July 15, 1967, issue. "Most people when you mention a group immediately think of their single. But if you're interested in the group as people then you'll probably listen to their albums. I think [albums] are getting more and more important in England."

Traffic's inherently unstable nature drew from the twin songwriting talents of singer/organist Winwood and singer/guitarist Dave Mason. The band also featured flautist Chris Wood and drummer Jim Capaldi. Unlike many of its contemporaries, Traffic had little musical commonality among its members. "We all had eclectic tastes," said Mason. "I mean, mine was a pop sensibility. Steve tended to be more R&B. Chris Wood was an art student. Jim was basically a Bob Dylan devotee. [Jim and I] were both very pop orientated."

Traffic gigged heavily in London throughout 1967 and 1968. The band was tapped by Chris Blackwell's Island Records (Blackwell also managed the Spencer Davis Group).

Traffic's first album, *Mr. Fantasy*, featured the iconic title track as well as a hit penned by Mason called "Hole in My Shoe." The pop nature of Mason's songwriting conflicted with Winwood's sensibilities and resulted in Mason leaving the band after the first record. Mason rejoined for the band's third album, *Traffic*, and wrote songs that subconsciously connected the band to the folk scene: "You Can All Join In" and "Feelin' Alright?" "Feelin' Alright?" became famous with Joe Cocker's 1969 cover.

For Jethro Tull, a folk sensibility came more from Ian Anderson's eclectic tastes rather than a specific connection to the folk clubs. Anderson originally hailed from Scotland, moving to Blackpool, England, at age 12 before heading to Luton, North London, in 1968.

Tull made their first record, the bluesy *This Was*, in 1968 during the London blues boom, but moved on from there as discussed in chapter 4.

Anderson's vision began to illuminate with Tull's second record, 1969's *Stand Up*. By that point, original guitarist Mick Abrahams had been replaced by Martin Barre, who would become a longtime staple in the band. Barre, originally from Birmingham, kind of came in on the ground floor with Anderson, in the sense that he was hungry to move beyond the blues. "I was never really a pure blues guitar player," said Barre. "There was a lot of them in England at that time—in '68— and . . . I was playing with these different styles, kind of a melting pot and I think that suited Ian more than having a pure blues guy in the band. And he realized, in '68, that the way to go was to move on from the blues and write your own music. Find your own direction. He was very very clever to get away from the blues when he did. And the first two or three months [of the European tour], people were coming to shows and expecting a blues band, and they weren't getting it. They weren't sure if they liked the music. And, of course, the main perpetrator—the difference—was me. They had a blues guitar player and there I was, not playing the blues. It was pretty hard the first few months. And then gradually people got to like what we were doing and it turned around."

Barre does have a distinctive sound, at least on electric guitar, where his heavily distorted, yet precise playing becomes instantly recognizable, almost in the way Hendrix's sound does. How did he craft that unique sound? "I've got no idea," said Barre. "I never hear myself in that way. I don't want to be restricted by [a musician saying] 'Come and play on my record. I want that *sound* you got.' I'm like, 'Really?' I just pick up a guitar, and I plug it into an amp."

Stand Up showcases Barre's versatility as well as Tull's evolution, although the first track, "A New Day Yesterday," is heavily indebted to the blues. "Jeffrey Goes to Leicester Square" follows. This track begins to show the band's experimentation with folk music and medieval influences. Anderson recalled picking up an unusual Russian stringed instrument called a balalaika at a pawn shop. He attached a pickup to it and used it on the track. It gave the song both an English and world music feel at the same time.

Next is an interpretation of Johann Sebastian Bach's "Bourrée," which showcases the band's entrée into classical music stylings, and thus, prog rock. The folk influence—in particular the carrying on of the English folk tradition—heavily displays itself with the beautifully haunting and acoustic-oriented "Look into the Sun" and "Reasons for Waiting," which showcases Anderson's minstrel-ish vocals.

"Back to the Family" begins to perhaps best show where Tull was headed musically, where the rockiness picks up, the folksiness maintains, and the music gets more and more complex, with sudden tempo changes and shifting dynamics. Unlike some of the prog musicians—like Keith Emerson, for example—who had classical training, Tull did not possess that, at least initially. "We were all learning on the same scale," Barre recalled. "In the early '70s, there was a lot of groups that were sort of a bit pompous, and more into the glamor side of rock 'n' roll—you know, partying. They saw music as a vehicle to have a big party. Whereas we took the music really seriously. We worked really really hard on what we were doing. But we were all maturing at the same rate . . . and we went in different directions, different influences. We were very insulated in the early years. We didn't sort of mix with the other bands. We didn't live that rock star life. We were very disciplined as a band—self-disciplined. Maybe that's why the band went on for so long."

Which brings us to Led Zeppelin. Zeppelin? Folk/rock? Seriously? Yeah, seriously.

Listen to that first record, *Led Zeppelin*, released in early 1969. In between the blitzkrieg of "Dazed and Confused," "Communication Breakdown," and "How Many More Times" sit acoustic folk gems like the traditional "Babe I'm Gonna Leave You" and the Indian-themed "Black Mountainside" that was influenced by Pentangle guitar wiz Bert Jansch. The folk/English tradition influence would follow with the Tolkien-themed "Ramble On" on *Led Zeppelin II* and even more pronounced on the band's third record, released in 1970.

Led Zeppelin III was composed in the Welsh countryside, in a cottage known as Bron-Yr-Ar.[3] Perhaps inspired by their surroundings, the second side of *III* opens with a traditional ballad, "Gallows Pole," and finishes with the bluesy distorted tribute song, "Hats off to (Roy) Harper," which extols the virtues of the enigmatic British folk guitarist.

All of these traditional folk and rock fusions—be they by Traffic, Jethro Tull, Led Zeppelin, or anyone else—were not a conscious mixing between Britain's folk club culture and London rock clubs. But the aesthetic of the English tradition permeated everyone. You couldn't help but feel a part of the weight of history, even if you weren't overtly tapping into it. Take a trip to Oxford and walk around the town. You can't help but feel the roots of an institution that first began assigning homework in the 12th century. It is similar with Britain's folk tradition, which has developed and has been passed along for centuries.

6

BLUES REVISITED

"The man for whom the words 'Wild One' were invented has hit us! Jimi Hendrix, 22, from Seattle, Washington, U.S.A., courtesy of ex-Animal Chas Chandler—debuts in the NME chart at No. 24 with his self-arranged 'Hey Joe' (Polydor). Hendrix is a one-man guitar explosion with a stage act which leaves those who think pop has gone pretty with their mouths hanging open. What this man does to a guitar could get him arrested for assault."—Keith Altham, *New Musical Express*, January 14, 1967

As London progressed and rediscovered its identity with traditional folk music and integrated psychedelia and classical stylings, one constant remained: the blues. In 1963 and 1964, the Brits called it the "R&B Boom," but by 1968, a new round of blues bands including the Jimi Hendrix Experience, Free, Cream, Savoy Brown, Fleetwood Mac, Chicken Shack, the Groundhogs, Led Zeppelin, and (eventually) Deep Purple had reinvigorated and, in some cases, reinvented the genre.

But why did blues "re-happen"? Why in the late 1960s? How was it different from the R&B version earlier in the decade? We historians love to find one magical link to provide us a neat line that takes us from one era to the next. Unfortunately, life doesn't always work that way. A number of occurrences contributed to London becoming reacquainted with the blues in the late 1960s, including the arrival of Jimi Hendrix from America, John Mayall's dedication to keeping the blues alive, reactions to the overindulgent hippy-dippiness of psychedelia, improvement of amplification technology as led by the Marshall Company, and just a new crop of British kids discovering the blues for the first time and bringing their own personalities to the mix.

Hendrix's arrival in London in 1966 had an immediate impact. He had been bouncing around the United States, pretty much unknown and unappreciated, a black musician facing prejudice in 1960s America. Fortunately for Hendrix and the world, Linda Keith, then dating the Rolling Stones' Keith Richards, discovered the guitar wizard in Greenwich Village, New York. She convinced ex-Animal Chas Chandler to check him out. Chandler had decided to move into band management by 1966. Sufficiently enthralled with Hendrix's talent, guitar histrionics, and overall showmanship, Chandler brought him to England and formed a band around the maestro, a power trio called the Jimi Hendrix Experience. Rounding out the three-piece would be bassist Noel Redding and Mitch Mitchell on drums, the latter a protégé of Jim Marshall.

> "Mick Eve, sax player for Georgie Fame's Blues Flames, was mooching around the musical instrument shops in London's Denmark Street as one did in 1966. His friend Chas Chandler, whom Mick had known as a bassist for the Animals but who had recently returned from a talent-fishing trip to America, ran out of a guitar store and said excitedly in broad Geordie: 'Mick! Mick! You got to come and hear this bloke play; I found him in New York!' 'I don't need to go into the shop, Chas,' replied Mick in droll Cockney, 'I can hear 'im from 'ere.'"—Ed Vulliamy, *Guardian*, October 25, 2014

> "Bill Harry and I dropped in at the Bag O'Nails club in Kingly Street to hear the trio working out for the benefit of Press and bookers. An astonished Harry muttered: 'Is that full, big, blasting, swinging sound really being created by only three people?' It was, with the aid of a mountain of amplification equipment."—Peter Jones, *Record Mirror*, December 10, 1966

Unlike in America, in Britain Hendrix was revered, even by rock royalty like Eric Clapton, the Beatles, and Pete Townshend. Nobody had ever seen anything like it. The guy played guitar with his teeth for crying out loud. "About that thing of playing the guitar with his teeth: he says it doesn't worry him," writer Peter Jones commented in the December 10, 1966, issue of *Record Mirror*. "He doesn't feel anything. 'But I do have to brush my teeth three times a day!' [he said]."

"I was in a band called the Shame [in 1967] and we were supporting
Jimi," King Crimson's Greg Lake remembered. "And no one knew
who he was. It was at Brighton University and I remember—we all
thought he was one of those [Motown-Stax] bands with the trumpet,
six/seven-piece soul band. That's what we thought he was. We
thought Jimi Hendrix was a kind of soul band, saxes, all of this. And
when he eventually got up on the stage, there was only three of
them. That looked really weird. I don't think I'd ever seen a three-
piece band before that. And there were these huge stacks of Marshall amplifiers. And that looked very impressive. And then the three
of them with these Afro haircuts. I mean it looked almost comical . . .
until they opened up. . . . I was standing above the audience on a
balcony at the back. . . . And as Jimi started playing . . . you know
when you shake a blanket and sometimes a ripple will run right down
the blanket—well that's what happened to the audience. A shock-
wave—literally, I watched it—run right from the front to the back of
the audience, where they physically were knocked back by him. . . .
And everybody was left just stunned. When we went back home in
the van, not a word was spoken. There was silence. . . . The whole
platform of rock 'n' roll just changed right there and then. . . . It was
as if somebody just swept the game off the table, put a new board on
and said, 'There you go. Start from there.'"

Hendrix continued to leave British audiences in a state of shock. No
one had seen anyone take a stage act to that degree before. "More and
more often during his act, I was reminded of the early days of the Who
when Pete Townshend was at his most violent," Richard Green wrote in
the January 14, 1967, issue of *Record Mirror*. "Except that Jimi takes it
several stages further. He kisses the guitar, sits on it and treads on it.
Quite apart from belting it with his elbow and caressing the amplifier
with it."

Hendrix the man contrasted sharply with Hendrix the performer.
Onstage, he was a shamanic wild man. Offstage, he was the opposite.
"He was such a polite young man," remembered Fairport Convention's
Judy Dyble, who used to hang with him at London's Speakeasy club.
"He was very sweet."

Hendrix did have a dramatic impact upon London, and arguably, he
ignited the blues boom of the late 1960s. But John Mayall would dispute that assessment. He would state it never went away. His Bluesbreakers carried the torch for the blues as the R&B boom waned and

The Jimi Hendrix Experience at the Marquee, 1967. *Pictorial Press Ltd. / Alamy stock photo.*

London ventured into folk/rock, psychedelia, and progressive rock. During all of that musical evolution, Mayall refused to budge from the blues. "There's nothing else I can play," Mayall told *Record Mirror*'s Wesley Laine in the October 28, 1967, issue. "It's all I can do, and of course all I want to do."

"I'd like a hit record," Mayall told *Melody Maker*'s Alan Walsh in the October 7, 1967, issue, "but I'm not prepared to sell-out just to get one. I'd be glad to make the chart—but only with a blues number."

Mayall's band would feature a rotating cast of musicians, many of whom would achieve fame and success post-Bluesbreakers, including Eric Clapton, Peter Green, John McVie, Jack Bruce, Andy Fraser, Mick Taylor, and Aynsley Dunbar. The musician turnover never seemed to bother him, however. "I can usually tell when someone—the lead guitarist especially—is unhappy with the group and wants to leave," Mayall told *Record Mirror*'s Laine. "You see guitarists reach a peak within the

group, and then they start to slacken off, become discontent and generally want to do their own individual things. I've never been unhappy
with anyone leaving though—but it is a task to find new members."

Mayall was always around, keeping the flame alive, and Hendrix
helped spread the fire in a dramatic way. And then there was Cream,
who came to life in 1966. Regardless of the intense level of talent in the
three-piece, Cream would be much more than the sum of its parts.

Eric Clapton had grown bored in Mayall's Bluesbreakers, having
always felt he was the best musician in every band he was in. So he
challenged himself when joining up with bassist Jack Bruce and drummer Ginger Baker, both stellar players. Bruce had spent time in the
Bluesbreakers as well as a brief stint in Manfred Mann. Baker had
provided percussion for the Graham Bond Organisation. "I had met my
match with both of them," Clapton said in a TLC special called *Standing at the Crossroads*. "Up until then I'd really been able to kind of
manipulate and dominate situations musically speaking. Around these
guys I felt like a younger brother. And I was very aware of the dynamic
being out of my control. And that interested me. No doubt about it.

"It was un-describable. It wasn't jazz. It wasn't blues. It wasn't rock
'n' roll. And it definitely wasn't pop music."

"I didn't see the point in recreating [a] kind of Chicago blues band,"
Bruce stated in the TLC special. "And I remember discussions with
[Clapton], saying, 'Well I wanna take it somewhere else,' which is really
presumptuous, very daring and kind of arrogant and everything, but you
know, I was young."

"I'm a blues guitarist and Jack is a jazz man and Ginger is rooted in
rock 'n' roll," Clapton told *New Musical Express*' Keith Altham in the
October 28, 1966, issue. "I say that of him because he is at the bar and
cannot hear it!"

Baker would clearly disagree, given his jazz training. "I started with
trad [jazz] bands in 1955—Bob Wallis, Terry Lightfoot and others,"
Baker told *Record Mirror*'s David Griffiths in the July 29, 1967, issue.
"Toured around Germany and Scandinavia for a while, mostly with
mainstream [trad] bands."

Also, Clapton wouldn't want Baker overhearing him for another reason. He was just someone you didn't mess with. I had attempted to get
an interview with Baker for years without success. In 2015, as I was
traveling to London, I suggested to his manager that I meet him for

coffee. His response: "Ginger is mercurial at best. Even if he said yes, he would likely not show up. If he did you could likely have a different set of problems."

Peter Noone of Herman's Hermits can attest to Baker's mantle of frightfulness. As a teenager in London, Noone found himself at a casino, gambling, quite drunk. He was hanging out with Bruce, who had become a good friend. Out of nowhere, Baker got up in Noone's face and growled, "Aaaaahhhh!" Noone took exception. "I basically said, 'I'm gonna kick your ass! I'm gonna beat the shit out of you!'" he remembered. "So, [Baker] leaves to get ready and Jack Bruce comes up to me and he says, 'Peter, Peter, he'll fuckin' kill you.' So I said, 'I don't care. He just insulted me. He went, "Ahhhh" to me.' He said, 'No, Peter, Peter. He'll fuckin' kill you.' Years later, when I saw Jack Bruce, I said, 'What was that all about?' He said, 'Oh he would've killed you. I mean, *killed* you. He wouldn't have just beat you up. He would've fuckin' killed you, so I stopped you.'"

Jack Bruce's mellower persona sharply contrasted with Baker's aggression. He also could play a variety of musical styles. "I used to sing a lot as a kid," Bruce told *Record Mirror*'s Griffiths, "got interested in music seriously and wanted to learn double bass. But I wasn't big enough, so I learned the cello. Left home at 16, played with anything I could, learned electric bass, got interested in jazz and joined Alexis Korner."

Clapton's enormous presence combined with Bruce's multitalented instrumental background and Baker's jazz training and volcanic personality made Cream an explosive combination in a literal sense. "I don't believe I've ever played so well in my life," Clapton told *Melody Maker*'s Nick Jones in the October 15, 1966, issue. "More is expected of me in the Cream—I have to play rhythm guitar as well as lead. People have been saying I'm like Pete Townshend, but he doesn't play much lead."

Arguably, Cream's penultimate recorded statement came with their second album: 1967's *Disraeli Gears*, which featured bluesy numbers like "Strange Brew," "Sunshine of Your Love," "Swlabr," and the ominous storytelling of "Tales of Brave Ulysses," along with a traditional music hall tune, "Mother's Lament."

Clapton told *Record Mirror*'s Bill Harry about the songwriting process in the November 18, 1967, issue. "Tales of Brave Ulysses": "My flat-mate Martin [Sharp] wrote the words to this. We went into the studio with just the lyrics and I wrote the music and made a rough arrangement in about an hour in the studio. He is very fond of the Mediterranean islands and he wrote the song last winter in his cold rooms, wishing he were out in the sun." "Swlabr": "The full title of this is 'She Was Like a Bearded Rainbow' and it has a typical Pete Brown lyric—Jack wrote the music. This was originally going to be released as a single." "Sunshine of Your Love": "This was written by Jack and me and Pete Brown. It's a pop stage number that we do. Peter is a poet who wrote our first record 'Wrapping Paper'—and he writes most of the lyrics for our songs."

Even given Hendrix, Mayall, and Cream, there is another argument for the resurgence of blues in late 1960s London. "My own theory about the current ascendancy of the Blues," Bob Dawbarn postulated in the October 5, 1968, issue of *Melody Maker*, "is that it is a reaction against the psychedelic, hippy, drop-out scene. Blues has always dealt with reality—its whole subject matter has been the problems of living."

That notion, the rejection of the ethereal psychedelia and embracing the reality of the blues is probably best exemplified by the Rolling Stones. In May 1967, in the wake of the Beatles' groundbreaking *Sgt. Pepper's Lonely Hearts Club Band*, the Stones tried their hand at whirling a psychedelic masterpiece by releasing *Their Satanic Majesties Request* that December. The Stones' latest effort drew tepid reactions. A panel of critics at the *Melody Maker* made comments such as "tragically trivial" and "nothing is particularly exciting," finishing off with "pop groups enter the big league of music at their own peril" in the December 2, 1967, issue.

Even Keith Richards acknowledged as much in his autobiography, *Life*. "None of us wanted to make [the record]," Richards wrote, "but it was time for another Stones album, and *Sgt. Pepper's* was coming out, so we thought basically we were doing a put on . . . [it] was all a bit of flimflam for me."

The Stones' faux experimentation with psychedelia would end when they would return to their blues/rock roots with the follow-up record, 1968's *Beggars Banquet*. To signal this directional change, the band released the single "Jumpin' Jack Flash" in May. "Mick Jagger denies it was a deliberate move backwards," Bob Dawbarn wrote in the May 25, 1968, issue of *Melody Maker*, "but it certainly stirs memories of the group a year or two back—wild, exciting, bluesy with that massive furry sound."

Both "Flash" (a single not released on an album) and its sister tune, "Street Fighting Man" off *Beggars Banquet*, featured a fascinating, accidental recording innovation. Richards explained in *Life*: "I'd discovered a new sound I could get out of an acoustic guitar. That grinding, dirty sound came out of these crummy little motels where the only thing you had to record with was this new invention called the cassette recorder. And it didn't disturb anybody. . . . Playing an acoustic, you'd overload the Philips cassette player to the point of distortion so that when it played back it was effectively an electric guitar."

But the Stones' moving on from *Majesties* to *Beggars Banquet* was not an overt reaction to psychedelia like punk rock would be to arena rock in the 1970s. Rather, it was more of an understated response to the excesses of psych and its bastard offspring, progressive rock.

It was a new crop of bands that would most effectively tap into the blues revival. Leading this new generation would be Fleetwood Mac, yes *that* Fleetwood Mac. For those who became familiar with Mac and their massive success in the mid-1970s with their self-titled LP and *Rumours*, the previous decade's version of the band was completely different and totally rooted in the blues.

Mac is a fascinating band, and unfortunately most know them only from their most commercially successful lineup with Stevie Nicks and Lindsey Buckingham. But nearly a decade before *Rumours* erupted, the band was centered on a gifted guitarist named Peter Green, who had himself graduated from John Mayall's Bluesbreakers' finishing school. Green, who some say had outshone Eric Clapton in the Bluesbreakers, would be the star. In fact, in *Fleetwood*, Mick Fleetwood's autobiography, the drummer would quote B. B. King: "Peter Green, he's the only [white guitar player] that ever gave me cold sweats. He had the sweetest tone I ever heard."

Green joined ex-Bluesbreakers bassist John McVie and drummer Mick Fleetwood (*Fleetwood Mac*Vie, hence the name) to form a heavy blues-based combo. "The first thing [Green] did was name the band Fleetwood Mac," Fleetwood told Anthony DeCurtis in an August 2017 interview. "And the first album, it says, 'Peter Green's Fleetwood Mac.' And he was so angry about that.

"I learnt this ages and ages after the fact. [Green] said [in an interview], 'I always thought that at some point I probably won't be in the band. I will have moved on,' which of course he sadly did. 'And I want John and Mick still to have a band.'"

Green made quite an impact on Mick Fleetwood right away. "Peter Green came in . . . looking like a character from that film, *The Gangs of New York* or something, like hardcore, plugged in and he had a Les Paul. In our world, we're going like, 'Wow! He's got a Les Paul!' . . . Myself and [friend, later A&R man] Dave Ambrose said, 'I don't think he's got enough ability. He only plays like a few notes.' It was like the world's worst mistake, when I look back on it. And [friend and keyboardist] Peter Bardens turned around and said, 'You're both wrong. This guy is so special.' It was the first time I heard the expression, 'less is more.' . . . It was a terrible mistake, and one I actually remember and always like mentioning because I am such a huge advocate of what I learnt from Peter."

"I like to play slowly, and feel every note," Green told *Record Mirror*'s Norman Jopling in the August 19, 1967, issue. "It comes from every part of my body and my heart and into my fingers, I have to really feel it. I make the guitar sing the blues—if you don't have a vocalist then the guitar must sing."

Paul Rodgers of Free caught an early Fleetwood Mac show at the Marquee and was taken with Green's methodical approach to manipulating the sound within a song. "You'd watch Peter Green," said Rodgers, "and he would [sing] and [then] he [would look] down at his Les Paul. He [then] hit a switch . . . and he [made] a different sound. Each bit that he played, he changed the sound."

Desiring another guitarist to complement him, Green asked an Elmore James–obsessed slide player named Jeremy Spencer to join. Green was impressed with Spencer's playing mostly because he wasn't a speed demon. Prior to Mac, Spencer had been playing blues and had been repeatedly told, around 1965, that the genre was out of fashion. "When I was first playing [the blues]," Spencer said, "people were shouting, 'Beach Boys! Rolling Stones!' from the audience, but then John Mayall came out with Eric Clapton [and] the Bluesbreakers and all of a sudden what we were doing was hip."

Peter Green's Fleetwood Mac, advertised as such, would take London by storm in 1967, playing a heavy blues combination with Green's brilliant lines and Spencer's distinctive slide work. Mac would make its debut at the National Jazz Pop Ballads & Blues Festival in August 1967. The three-day event would also feature Cream, the Small Faces, the Pink Floyd, Donovan, Zoot Money's Big Roll Band, the Crazy World of Arthur Brown, the Move, Jeff Beck, John Mayall, and Chicken Shack. (The last band possessed a young keyboardist singer/songwriter named Christine Perfect. Perfect would later marry Mac's bass player, change her name to Christine McVie, and join Fleetwood Mac.)

> "Chicken Shack's blond haired pianist Christine Perfect had married Fleetwood Mac's bass guitarist John McVie—and to celebrate the event John and Pete Green, just back from their triumphant tour of the States, sat in with the Shack for a completely impromptu performance."—Pete Barra-Clough, *Melody Maker*, August 10, 1968

Mac's debut went so well that the band soon found a regular residency at the Marquee, London's preeminent music club. According to Fleetwood, Spencer's quiet personality soon blossomed into outrageous behavior onstage. "He'd fill condoms with milk or beer," Fleetwood wrote in his autobiography, "and hang them from the pegs of his guitar and swing them out over the appalled audience of blues purists."

Spencer has a different recollection. "There was maybe two or three times we did that in places where . . . it was like more informal," recalled Spencer. "And of course the press just loved that."

"He [Jeremy Spencer] was and is one of the greatest slide players ever," Fleetwood told DeCurtis, "and worshipped Elmore James . . . and basically was Elmore incarnate.

"Being, in a way, a copyist [of James], but he wasn't. He was so into Elmore James that he became Elmore James. . . . He's a tiny tiny tiny chap. And he always insisted on having these giant guitars."

Regardless of the band's debated escapades onstage, Fleetwood Mac represented a new generation of London blues bands. This wasn't a reconstituted Yardbirds or Rolling Stones. Fleetwood Mac didn't attempt to re-create Muddy Waters's "Got My Mojo Working." Instead, the band played a slower, more intense version of the blues, with Green taking the lead role as singer and guitarist. "It wasn't so easy to put a band together and have a [lead] singer/guitarist," Spencer said. "That wasn't so common."

The band would soon add another guitar player, a young talent named Danny Kirwan. "Danny Kirwan [was a] young lad that used to come and sit in the front row and watch Peter," said Fleetwood.

By 1968, with the London blues boom in full force, Fleetwood Mac would lead the way. At this point, the band was huge in the United Kingdom but had yet to make a major dent in the American market. Kirwan's addition to the band would help bring Mac much-needed commercial success. In 1969, Fleetwood Mac released their third album, *English Rose*, which contained a surprising number 1 hit in the slow instrumental dirge penned by Green titled "Albatross." "Obviously lyrics are important," Green told *Record Mirror*'s Ian Middleton in the January 4, 1969, issue. "But I think that with an instrumental, you can make your own story—I called it 'Albatross' because that's what it meant to me. It can mean something entirely different to each individual."

The record would also contain another Green classic, "Black Magic Woman," made famous by Santana when they covered it the following year.

> "Me, I like to sing the blues to people who don't know anything about it. Don't know the band, have never seen the band. Because they will get the message much better than people who are waiting to see how fast I am going to play."—Peter Green to Nick Logan, *New Musical Express*, August 3, 1968

In 1969, with the three-guitar attack of Green, Spencer, and Kirwan, Fleetwood Mac would make their classic album of this blues era, *Then Play On*, featuring the Green-penned "Oh Well," a raucous blues number. "Half of that album is Danny," Fleetwood told DeCurtis, illustrating the point of how gracious Green could be despite being the band's star. "[It] was very unusual in a band [to have three guitar players]. You often had maybe a couple of rhythm guitar players and you have the *lead* player. They all worked in duality. We became three bands in one, really."

"We don't all play lead at once," Kirwan told *Record Mirror*'s Middleton in the August 31, 1968, issue. "If Peter is featured, Jeremy and I accompany him. If Jeremy or I am featured then the others back. When the others are soloing I might get a riff going and this all adds to the performance. Peter Green writes and I compose too."

The ascendancy of Fleetwood Mac as a blues powerhouse not only lit up the genre in London again but also gave notice to the record companies that this new generation of slower blues could sell.

> "In the large cities and towns, new blues groups seem to be continually starting up. The larger record companies are now tending to take blues seriously and are beginning to realise it is a saleable product."—Chris Welch, *Melody Maker*, March 2, 1968

During this blues boom era, yet another supergroup appeared that has been somewhat buried in the mist of history: Humble Pie. Everyone thinks "Cream" when they hear the word *supergroup*; however, rarely does the Pie come up, and that is a shame.

Pie would emerge at the intersection of two phenomenal talents: singer/guitarist Steve Marriott from the Small Faces and singer/guitarist Peter Frampton, who had been in a pop-oriented band called the Herd. Frampton, already a gifted player at only 16, started jamming informally with the Herd in 1966. "At the end of the summer vacation, things were starting to happen for the Herd," Frampton said. "They came to me and said, 'Would you think about joining the band?' And I said, 'I would love to. But my dad's a school teacher. I don't think he's going to allow me to drop out of school at 16.' My dad did a financial deal with me that if I went and got a 'regular' job [like at] the post office, I'd get £15 a week. So they had to sign something that they would pay me £15 a week, which they did. Until we started earning more money, that they could afford to pay me more, but they didn't. They paid themselves more and kept me at £15 a week. So I fired my dad as my manager. [Laughs.]"

The Herd initially played more bluesy rock with a touch of jazz, led by a young, talented, and photogenic Frampton, who quickly became the star. That's when the band's management decided to capitalize on his looks to move the Herd into pop single territory. By late 1967, with the Herd enjoying a residency at the Marquee, the group was promoted with Frampton's name in a larger font than the band name.

> "It's not surprising, then, that Peter Frampton, seventeen-year-old singer and guitarist with the chart high Herd, is being hailed by experts as a potential pop giant."—uncredited, *Melody Maker*, October 28, 1967

By 1968, Frampton had grown bored of the Herd and wanted to move on. By that point, he had become enamored with the Small Faces, in particular the band's 1968 psychedelic masterpiece, *Ogdens' Nut Gone Flake*. So Frampton wanted to join the Small Faces and found himself in an informal jam session with singer/guitarist Steve Marriott and bassist Ronnie Lane. He then received a phone call from producer Glyn Johns, who was recording the Small Faces in Paris. Peter Frampton said, "So Glyn calls me up and says, 'Steve asked me to ask [if] you'll come over as another guitar player.' I think he said, 'Eric Clapton or Jimmy Page were a little busy. Could you come?' I didn't know whether that was a compliment or a backhander [laughs]. So I'm living my dream. I'm now in a Paris studio recording with Small Faces and loving every minute—I joined the Small Faces for a week.

"Came back [to London]. I was at Glyn Johns's place. He said, 'I gotta play you this band—we just did this whole album in 12 days.' I said, 'Oh, wow, that's quick.' And he said, 'You've heard of Jimmy Page, right?' I said, 'Yeah, I have. Great session player, right, and with the Yardbirds and everything else.' 'Listen to this album—two sides of this album—it's called Led Zeppelin, the band.' So I'm halfway through listening to *Led Zeppelin I* and my jaw is on the floor, not even from the guitar playing. Just from the bass drum of Bonham, marveling at the drumming, and just the whole production, obviously. And the phone rings as we get halfway through and it's Steve. He says, 'Can I speak to Pete, please?' Glyn says, 'It's Steve!' [Marriott said,] 'I just played my last gig with Small Faces. I walked offstage and I wanna know if I can join your band?' Because he was helping me form a band. And I think now I realize what he was doing was, he was trying to persuade the Small Faces—the other three—that I should join the band. Because we had so much fun at the session and whatever, [but] they didn't want another person because it's a five-way split now. So he said, 'Well if he can't join the band, then I'm leaving.'"

Adding the rhythm section of Greg Ridley (Spooky Tooth) on bass and Jerry Shirley on drums, the new band would quickly try to shed the dreaded "supergroup" tag. Marriott would suggest the name "Humble Pie," and it stuck. A headline in the July 26, 1969, issue of *New Musical Express* screamed, "Don't Think of Humble Pie as a Supergroup, plead Steve Marriott and Peter Frampton."

"Will these people PLEASE stop writing in and saying Humble Pie is not a supergroup because we KNOW we are not," Marriott told *New Musical Express*' Nick Logan in the September 27, 1969, issue.

Humble Pie's beginnings, notwithstanding the supergroup tag, were a bit awkward for Frampton. Shortly after getting together with Marriott, Ridley, and Shirley, Ronnie Lane called Frampton up to ask if he could stop by his London flat. So the three remaining Small Faces—Lane, Ian McLagan, and Kenney Jones—came over. "So I said, 'Hey guys, what's up?'" Frampton recalled. "And I'm sort of dreading what they're going to say because I had a funny feeling what's coming. And they said, 'Steve's left the band. Would you join in his place?' I said, 'Awfully large pair of shoes to fill [and] you're a little late. The thing is, I was hoping we could all be in the same band together. But Steve left and we're forming a [new] band together.'"

As far as the Herd went, Marriott had little time for that band. "I don't want to be rude to Pete or to the Herd," Marriott told Nick Logan in the July 26, 1969, issue of *New Musical Express*, "but he was in a Mickey Mouse band before. No one had a chance to hear him play guitar."

"There you go," Frampton said. "I totally agree with [that statement]. But we became a Mickey Mouse band from being a very well respected—the Herd were very well respected [initially]. Once we were taken under the wings of [new management]—they wrote these pop songs for us. We didn't even do our own material. It was different. And in a way he's correct."

Besides his guitar prowess and soaring voice, Marriott brought a theatrical element to his stagecraft. Between Frampton and Marriott, Humble Pie would either be an unstoppable creative force or a train wreck. In truth, they were a little of both. The band's first record, 1969's *As Safe as Yesterday Is*, featured tracks as diverse as the acoustic/ folky/storytelling title song and an offbeat tune called "I'll Go Alone." Beginning with a little over two minutes of psychedelic-inspired Eastern sounds featuring a sitar, flute, and bursts of electric rhythm guitar, the record suddenly explodes into a three-chord riff that resembles Led Zeppelin's "Communication Breakdown" until Frampton's distinctive vocals make an appearance.

The band's exploration of acoustic folk styling, psychedelia, and blues/rock would evolve into a heavy blues motif on the band's 1971 release, *Rock On*, featuring a giant metallic riff and Marriott's brilliant vocals on "Stone Cold Fever."

Another band that gets lumped in with the blues boom but went way beyond that is Tony McPhee's Groundhogs.

The Groundhogs first made a name for themselves backing blues legend John Lee Hooker in 1964. Originally John Mayall's Bluesbreakers were supposed to play with Hooker, but his popularity led to an extended United Kingdom tour that Mayall couldn't fulfill. So the Groundhogs filled the spot. "I saw John backed by John Mayall at [London's] Flamingo Club," McPhee wrote me, "and I thought he looked so serious. I didn't know how he'd like being backed by us. We had no rehearsal. He just asked me if we knew 'I'll Go Crazy' by James Brown in E. He just played the riff's three notes and then John vamped the song all in one key—no changes at all! At the end of the gig, I felt disappointed that we hadn't backed him well. But he said to me, 'You guys know my shit.' I said, 'We're fans!'"

Hooker's distinctive finger-picking style influenced McPhee. "I was using picks which were teeth from plastic combs," McPhee wrote me, "but I saw John playing fingerstyle as did Hubert Sumlin playing with Howlin' Wolf, so it seemed the way to go."

In 1966, the Groundhogs would morph into the psychedelic Herbal Mixture in 1966, but that fizzled out after a couple of years; they eventually re-formed the Groundhogs as a power trio by 1969. By that time, the blues boom was in full force. What distinguished this generation of blues from the earlier R&B boom? One word: "Heavier," McPhee exclaimed.

The evolving equipment, including the Marshall Super 100 head featuring 100-watt power, had something to do with it as well. "With the invention of the fuzz box used on the Stones' 'Satisfaction,' [plus the Taste's] Rory Gallagher had used a treble boost for ages, so changing or modifying the guitar sound was necessary even in the '60s," McPhee wrote me. "Heavier sounds was the next step, so amps and speakers had to get louder and bigger. I made or modified my own amps and made my own speaker cabinets. I made [bassist] Pete Cruickshank's cabinets also."

The Groundhogs would break out of the blues mold in a major way with the release of 1970's *Thank Christ for the Bomb*. The band's stab at a concept album would turn out to be a masterpiece. Written during the worst years of the American war in Vietnam, *Bomb* takes place during the First World War and touches on the Cold War–era nuclear standoff between the United States and Soviet Union.

> The thermo nuclear threat they say
> Presents a cleaner way to die
> For were not our fathers skinned alive
> When in other days the serpents thrived
> —from the inside cover of *Thank Christ for the Bomb*

"I hate the glorification of war," McPhee stated in Martyn Hanson's book, *Hoggin' the Page: Groundhogs, the Classic Years.* "I hate how people were duped into fighting. Not much changed between World War I and World War II for the soldier."

As the 1960s crawled to a close with the London blues boom in full force, three of those bands would foreshadow the sounds of the coming decade: Free, Deep Purple, and Led Zeppelin.

Free would soon find itself out front of the blues boom, with a powerful musical lineup of drummer Simon Kirke, guitar wizard Paul Kossoff, soulful singer Paul Rodgers, and prodigy Andy Fraser on bass.

Kirke and Kossoff, heavily into the blues, were in a band called the Black Cat Bones. Kossoff checked out a London blues band called Brown Sugar, finding himself drawn to lead singer Rodgers. "[Kossoff] was a Jewish kid with a famous father, actor David Kossoff," said Rodgers. "And he had a Les Paul and we hit it off immediately. We had a jam session at the Fickle Pickle Blues Club. And we found we had a lot in common. He loved Cream, Hendrix, and all of the blues: B. B. King, Howlin' Wolf . . . Hubert Sumlin, Willie Dixon, all those guys. And so we decided we'd form a band."

Kirke's straightforward drumming approach would fit well with this new blues band. "My influences [included] Ringo [Starr], Levon Helm," Kirke wrote me, "but my number one influence was Al Jackson Jr. from Booker T and the MGs—the Stax house band—I loved his muscular approach, but also his simple style.

"Drumming in a blues band, you had to be simple," Kirke continued. "I'm not a great technician. [I] couldn't play like [Rush's] Neil Peart or [session virtuoso] Vinnie Colaiuta."

Looking for a bass player, Kirke, Rodgers, and Kossoff talked to Alexis Korner, who knew a young teenage talent named Andy Fraser. Fraser was dating Korner's daughter, Sappho, and had gotten quite close with her dad. Fraser felt closer to him than his own father. He would hang out at the Korner household and play whatever instrument he could get his hands on. "Alexis was one in a million," Fraser said. "Very intelligent guy. Could speak 14 languages. And invited me into the family like I was one of them."

In 1967, John Mayall found himself looking for a bassist and asked Korner if he knew one. Fraser wasn't an expert on the instrument, but Korner recommended him anyway, given his innate talent and sheer determination. "One day John Mayall called up and says, 'I need a bass player. Like yesterday,'" Fraser said. "[Korner] said, 'Oh I got this kid hangs around the house. He's pretty good.' That was Saturday. I went over Sunday. And Monday I quit college, bought a new guitar and amp, went to 'court,' swore up and down to the 'magistrate'—[the notoriously straight-edged] John Mayall—that I'd be in bed by eight o'clock. Tuesday we were in Amsterdam trying Amsterdam's finest. That was me and Mick Taylor. If John Mayall knew out about that, he probably would have fired us."

"I just had so much to learn from people who were way older than me," Fraser wrote on his website. "The only person close to my age was Micky Taylor, who was 18 at the time, and an incredible guitarist even then, and the only one I could sneak off with behind the building for a quick toke—everyone else being 'tea-totalers.' John Mayall would have been horrified, although Alexis thought I rolled a pretty good joint. Of course Mick Taylor went on to do great things with the Stones, and I'm sure I was just not in the same league as Keith Richards, when it comes to showing Mick Taylor how to get 'whacked.'"

The experience with John Mayall, as it was for many of his talented protégés, became a finishing school for Fraser. "I could just like soak it up," Fraser said. "Learn from everybody. See how things were done. See how John Mayall organized things."

Fraser's Bluesbreakers gig only lasted for a few months before he was tapped to play bass with Rodgers, Kirke, and Kossoff. That was 1968. The four-piece began rehearsing, and the chemistry emerged rather quickly. "We were actually playing ['Moonshine,' the first song Rodgers cowrote with Kossoff] in the Nags Head," Rodgers said, "which is a pub—the room above the pub—when Alexis Korner walked in and I hit high notes [sings] *I sit here alone and cry* and I'd never hit such a high note with a band before, so it was really great for me. And then he walked in right at that point. And we all took a break at that moment.

"[Korner] said, 'Well, you've got a band now. All you need is a name. I used to have a band with Cyril Davies and we called it Free at Last. I don't know if that helps you.' And we all sat around. And we all were thunderstruck with this idea. [We said,] 'It's gotta be Free then, [doesn't] it?' And that fit right in with the scene at the time because it wasn't *the* Cream. It was Cream. So we weren't *the* Free. We were just Free. And it was perfect."

Dropping *the* from the band's name became an early harbinger of the 1970s. All of the 1960s bands had *the* in front of their names. It was *the* Beatles, *the* Kinks, even *the* Pink Floyd. But this band would start out as just "Free" (although to be fair, some of the *Melody Maker* gig advertisements did refer to the band as "the Free" in the early days).

The band soon secured a regular residency at the Marquee in addition to playing other key London clubs like the Roundhouse and Middle Earth. Free then began working on their first LP, *Tons of Sobs*, which would be recorded in fall 1968. It featured a slow, heavy blues, as exemplified by the track "Worry," which displayed Rodgers's powerful vocals.

In addition to Rodgers, a couple of other traits distinguished Free from their contemporaries: their groove and, quite frankly, their good looks. "My father was from Guyana," Fraser recalled. "So he was a product of the Fraser clan going over and fucking the slaves. . . . That's why I've got a bit of calypso or reggae in me. The songs gotta have a groove for me. And I always try to put one in there. And it was a good combination with rock, blues, soul, R&B. I think that sort of sums up Free."

"We were good looking, so to a degree I believe [there was a certain] amount of sex appeal," Kirke wrote.

Free obtained some degree of popularity within the London scene, but it was their third album, 1970's *Fire and Water*, that took the band to a new level. That record, and this is difficult to explain in words, just *feels* like the 1970s. It's clear that the 1960s were over when this album came out. In some ways, *Fire and Water* paved the way for the arena hard-rock sounds of 1970s bands like Foghat (which featured Savoy Brown's Roger Earl on drums) and Bad Company (with Rodgers and Kirke). "On *Tons of Sobs*, though, I was still finding my drumming niche and my playing was a little busy," Kirke wrote me. "It wasn't until *Fire and Water* in 1970 that it all came together for me."

The album featured the standout 1970s classic "All Right Now." And, like a lot of classic songs of the era, this one came almost as an afterthought.

Kirke wrote, "We were playing in Durham University and our repertoire was pretty much medium-paced blues material. And [we had] a bad gig. In fact, we walked off stage to the sound of our own footsteps. And when we got back to the dressing room, there was some talk—primarily from Andy—that we needed an up-tempo song . . . and here he started ad-libbing, bopping around the dressing room singing 'all right now.' Paul and Andy were the main songwriters and over the next few weeks they wrote what would become 'All Right Now.'"

Rodgers said, "The one song that we could not drop from the set, it was called 'The Hunter.' It was by Albert King. It was really an anthem. It was almost bigger than anything we could write. And I said, 'We have to write a song that is stronger than "The Hunter"—something really simple like [sings] *all right now, baby*.' And I said, 'That's it!' So I grabbed a guitar. We worked the chords out from there. Then Andy took that away and came back with the verse chords. And now I had to say, 'Well, what's *all right now*?' So I [wrote,] *There she stood in the street*.

"It's interesting because the words just flowed out of me. I was actually—in my mind—standing in the street, looking at the girl. *There she stood in the street*. Well, what happened next? What was she doing? She was *smiling*. How big was it? *From her head to her feet*. I thought, 'Oh yeah. I'll write that.' *I said hey, what's this, maybe she's in need of a kiss*. And I still like the line, *Let's move before they raise the parking rate*, because that still happens today. If you stand still long enough, you'll get a parking ticket."

Deep Purple would experience something similar with "Smoke on the Water." But before we get into that, we have to delve into how that band evolved from a sort of prog band into a bluesy rock outfit.

Formed in 1968, Deep Purple struggled a bit with their identity early on. With core members Ritchie Blackmore (guitar), Ian Paice (drums), and Jon Lord (keyboards), the band was quickly labeled as "progressive" by the *Melody Maker*–driven media, particularly in light of the band's landmark 1969 orchestral concert with the Royal Philharmonic Orchestra at the Royal Albert Hall. But that direction didn't suit new members Ian Gillan (vocals) and Roger Glover (bass). "We were a rock band just dabbling in this orchestral world. We just wanted to support Jon," Glover recalled. "Seemed like a good idea at the time. But we were then seen as some kind of progressive band, which didn't go down well with everyone in the band, especially Ritchie and Ian Gillan. They felt that the direction the band was going in was being thwarted by this misconception."

The reaction against this progressive rock label drove Deep Purple to become Deep Purple, which is heavily reflected in the band's 1970 landmark effort, *Deep Purple in Rock*. "By the time we did the concerto," Glover continued, "we were already writing songs that would later appear on *In Rock*. 'Child in Time' was already written at that point. 'Speed King' was in its embryonic form."

By 1969, the band's live shows became more ferocious as the band found its heavy blues/rock voice. But that vital power was not reflected in the studio, so the approach to recording began to change for *In Rock* to reflect the live feeling. "With virtuosos like Ritchie Blackmore and Jon Lord and Ian Paice—all on fire—the live shows were getting louder and heavier and more exciting," said Glover. "And yet a studio is a difficult place to re-create that. Studios being sort of stagnant, clean, unexciting places to record. They were kind of dead. And we found that by abusing studios, by doing things it wasn't designed to do, that we actually achieved more results. But certainly by the time we recorded 'Hard Lovin' Man' [and] 'Flight of the Rat,' the live shows were coming into the studio, the excitement. I remember Jon Lord in particular was slightly frustrated by the fact that he couldn't bend a note like Ritchie could on the guitar. But he found a way of doing it by switching the organ on and off [onstage]. And if you listen to his solo in 'Hard Lovin' Man' you hear exactly that. You hear what he was doing onstage." (Check it out around 3:26 to hear what he's talking about.)

Besides the sheer talent of standouts like Blackmore and Lord, it's the band's percussion that often sets it apart from its heavier cousins. Paice, like earlier English drummers Charlie Watts and Ginger Baker, came from a jazz background. But perhaps more than any other drummer of his ilk, Paice could *swing*. "Buddy Rich is Ian Paice's absolute hero," said Glover. "Ian Paice is at heart a big band drummer . . . to this day [he] plays with a swing that most drummers don't have or are incapable of. And he doesn't hit the drums hard. You see a lot of drummers now just bashing the hell out of the kits. As Paicey says, 'You can only hit a drum so loud. It's not gonna get any louder.' But when you're playing it loud, you're not very fluid. But by hitting the drum correctly, you get the ring out of the drum, the real smack out of the drum. But you're also playing it light enough to be able to move quicker."

Paice's feel can be felt throughout Purple's heavier work, notably on the band's signature tune, 1972's "Smoke on the Water," arguably the most recognizable riff in all of rock, if not all of music.

(As an aside, the day after I interviewed Glover, I met up with a couple of friends who aren't familiar with rock music. Their tastes tend toward smooth jazz and Motown. When I mentioned I interviewed someone from Deep Purple, they said, "Never heard of them." I tried again. "How about 'Smoke on the Water'?" Blank stares. Then I did the riff. "Bah bah bah! . . ." I hadn't even made it through half the notes when they said, "Oh yeah, we've heard of that!")

Blackmore came up with the classic riff. "I thought [I'd] play [Beethoven's fifth symphony] backwards, put something to it," Blackmore stated in a 2007 interview. "That's how I came up with it. It's an interpretation of inversion. You turn it back, and play it back and forth, it's actually Beethoven's fifth. So I owe him a lot of money."

That may have been a joke given Blackmore's sense of humor, but one thing isn't. He wrote the riff in something called "fourths," which is a medieval style of writing. He had played around with that type of writing for a few years before stumbling upon what would become the iconic riff of "Smoke on the Water."

The story about the song's creation somewhat mirrors that of "All Right Now" and other classics written as toss-offs and in a hurry.

Deep Purple were in the midst of recording their seminal 1972 album, *Machine Head*, at a casino in Montreux, Switzerland, when some moron set off a flare gun and burned the building to the ground. This was during a performance by Frank Zappa and the Mothers of Invention. So Deep Purple had nowhere to record. "The guy who was in charge of the casino and kind of looking after us, came to us," Glover recalled, "and he put all his problems aside and was worried about us. Our equipment was there. We were there. We had no place to record. So he arranged to have us move into a small theater nearby the old casino—the ex-casino, I should say."

The band set up on the stage and ran cables out to the Rolling Stones' mobile studio. Recording began in the afternoon. The musicians took a break for dinner and returned to the studio around 9 or 10 p.m. "We started jamming a bit," said Glover. "And Ritchie just started this riff. I don't know if he had the riff beforehand or whether he made it up on the spot, but it was a kind of mid-tempo, ploddy kind of riff. It came together fairly quickly. 'Well this is a verse, we need a chorus. How about this? How about that? Let's do a solo.' And by the time we started recording it, it was [about] midnight. We were doing the first take of this song—well, it wasn't a song yet. It was just a jam with a kind of rough arrangement to it. And what we didn't know is that the police were trying to get in and stop us because we were keeping the whole town awake. Montreux was then a very sleepy town populated mostly by old ladies who had tea in the afternoon."

So now the band had to find yet another place to record in this small, idyllic, quiet town. There weren't many options, and it took a few days to find a suitable space. "So we came across the Grand Hotel," Glover recalled, "which was then closed for the winter. A cold sort of place, I mean it was freezing cold, after all [it was] November, December time. We arranged to have a carpenter put a couple of walls up. We threw some mattresses against the windows, brought a couple of industrial heaters to heat the place before we arrived there during the day. And [we] basically recorded there. We did 'Highway Star' and 'Lazy' and 'Pictures of Home' and all those. And we finished all those and we were still short of a song. 'Well what about that one jam we did at that other place?' 'Yeah, OK. Well, what are we going to do with it?' 'Let's write a song about the adventure of actually coming to try and record, and the place burning down and ending up doing it in a hotel corridor. Let's write an autobiographical song.' And Ian [Gillan] and I sat down and we listened to the song. We said, 'Right, well let's write some lyrics.' And we wrote them quite as conversationally as I'm talking to you.

"I came up with the title a day or two after the fire," Glover recalled. "I said it half asleep as I was waking up; I realized I just said something out loud in the hotel room—to no one. There was no one there, just me. And I thought, 'Did I just say something out loud? What was it?' 'Smoke on the water.'"

"We never thought for a minute it was going to have the kind of future it was gonna have," said Glover. "We didn't think that much of it.

We thought, 'Mid-tempo, slightly boring.' We put all our efforts into another song on the album called 'Never Before.' We thought that was going to be the single. But it wasn't us that chose 'Smoke on the Water.' It was first of all some DJs, and then the public at large turned it into the song it's become. Now, listening to it, it's obvious. The riff is so simple and yet so different to anything else. And I know, Ritchie himself has said it's like Beethoven in a way— Beethoven's fifth. What Beethoven does with just very few notes, that riff does it with very few notes, too. But it's got a hint of Eastern mysticism in it, just by the semitone lift. Instantly recognizable and yet nothing like anything else."

In retrospect, "Smoke on the Water" is pretty hilarious. It's like writing a song about any mundane daily activity: "I went to the grocery store / To buy some cheeeese." But in this case it turned into an all-time classic.

In all the 1968 London blues boom hype, no band loomed larger than Led Zeppelin, a group that formed by accident from the ashes of the Yardbirds.

By 1968, the Yardbirds had been touring and recording for more than half a decade and were on their fourth lead guitarist: Jimmy Page. After going through a psychedelic period under Jeff Beck, the band ventured back into the blues under Page.

Most music fans associate Page with the creative histrionics of Zeppelin, but they don't realize that this persona took years to evolve. Page, a guitar prodigy who came through the skiffle channel like many of his contemporaries, quickly became an in-demand London sessions player in the early 1960s. He had built his career as a self-taught maestro from a young age. "When I was at school, I had my guitar confiscated every day," Page told Chris Welch in the February 20, 1970, issue of *Melody Maker*. "They handed it back to me at 4 p.m. I didn't have any guitar lessons because there was nobody to teach me, and I couldn't get up to London.

"Originally I used to jam with a group at the old Marquee when Cyril Davies was still alive," Page continued. "One day someone asked me if I wanted to play on a rock session—and that's how it started. At that time only Big Jim Sullivan was around and if there were three sessions, he could do only one, and others would end up with—well, no names mentioned. Without Jim they were desperate. From then on, work for me escalated. I couldn't read [music] at all when I started session work. I had to teach myself on a crash course. There was no individuality involved at all. The arranger said, 'This is what you play,' and that's what I played."

Singer P. J. Proby recalled Page as a rhythm guitarist when he did session work on an early Proby record. "He learned," Proby said. "Lead guitar didn't come easy to Jimmy. He taught himself."

Having tired of the rote work of sessions, Page eagerly joined the Yardbirds as a bass player in 1966, then quickly switched to lead guitar after Chris Dreja moved over to bass. "I got fed up [with session work]," Page told Welch. "It began to be a pain in the neck. When the Yardbirds came up—that was it. I was a good friend of Jeff Beck who had replaced Eric Clapton. I was there when Paul Samwell-Smith had a great row and left the group, so I had to take over on bass. I had never played one before. Then Chris Dreja swapped from rhythm guitar to bass and the idea was for me and Jeff to get a stereo guitar sound."

For a brief window, the Yardbirds had two otherworldly talented lead guitar players. As discussed in chapter 3, this lineup had mixed results as the two guitarists' styles often did not mesh; Beck's freewheeling approach typically did not click with Page's more methodical style. In late 1966, the combustible Beck left the band, leaving Page in charge.

Yardbirds Jimmy Page in 1966 was not the Led Zeppelin Jimmy Page of 1969, at least according to drummer Jim McCarty. "With Jimmy, it was almost polite" [laughs], McCarty recalled, "which is a crazy thing to say considering what happened afterwards. We just didn't have the range of ideas. We were quite busy, so we didn't have much time to sort of sit around and make up songs. I think the songs that we did write, they weren't so classic as the earlier ones."

By July 1968, McCarty, bassist Dreja, and singer Keith Relf had had it. The band, having toured and recorded for six years straight, hit the proverbial wall and quit mid-tour. "I don't think we could have sustained it, what we were doing," McCarty said. "It was just too much for us. We were all completely shattered when we broke up."

With gigs to fulfill, Page went scrambling to find players to finish the tour. He knew bassist John Paul Jones from his sessions days, so he was tapped. Next to find a singer. A couple of names popped up. Steve Marriott of the Small Faces was one, but he was committed to Humble Pie with Peter Frampton. Terry Reid was another, but he also was under contractual commitment. Word got out about a fabulous 19-year-old blues wailer named Robert Plant, who had been playing London with a group called Band of Joy in 1968. Page went to check him out and was duly impressed, wondering why the kid hadn't made it yet. (That's funny, a 19-year-old kid hadn't "made it" yet. The Brits started out young in those days.) The guitarist and Yardbirds manager Peter Grant visited Plant in Birmingham. "I played kazoo and washboard in the sort of bands which, if they had been based in London instead of Birmingham, would probably have become the Rolling Stones," Plant told Richard Williams in the September 27, 1969, issue of *Melody Maker*. "We used to do the whole country blues thing: Memphis Minnie, Bukka White, and Skip James numbers which at that time, about six years ago, were really deep blues—and they are now, too. This sort of music turned my mind to the ideal that I could really express myself through the medium of the blues. I had a certain freedom, and while other singers were copying all the pop records I could get up on stage and sing blues with any group."

Plant and Page quickly developed a bond when the singer visited the guitarist's home on the Thames. "I rummaged through his record collection," Plant told Williams, "and every album I pulled out was something I really dug. I knew then that we'd click."

Plant recommended old Birmingham pal John Bonham on drums, and the four-piece rehearsed in a London basement in August 1968. "We first played together in a small room on Gerrard Street, a basement room, which is now Chinatown," Jones stated in a 1990 interview cited at LedZeppelin.com. "There was just wall-to-wall amplifiers, and a space for the door—and that was it. Literally, it was everyone looking at each other—'what shall we play?' Me doing more sessions, didn't know anything at all. There was an old Yardbirds' number called 'Train Kept a Rollin'.'. . . The whole room just exploded."

Calling themselves the New Yardbirds, the band would record what would become their first record together in London that October. In August 1968, two months before recording *Led Zeppelin*, however, the boys would make a little-known LP with a singer from Texas who relocated to London in the early 1960s: P. J. Proby. Proby was ready to record another album and got in touch with an American friend of his named Steve Rowland. Rowland came over to England to produce the new Proby record. Instead of the orchestral arrangements Proby used in the past, he asked Rowland to find him a backing band in tune with the zeitgeist of 1968. Little did Proby know, Rowland had booked Jimmy Page, Robert Plant, John Paul Jones, and John Bonham. "The day came, and we all showed up at the studio," Proby recalled. "And in walked guys I had worked with on my first record: Jimmy Page, he was my first rhythm guitar player. The rest of them I didn't know that well. But after the session was over, it went so well that I said, 'Guys, that was a really really good session. I'm looking for a band. Would y'all be interested in backing me? I've got work.' They said, 'Sure, we'd love to. But we've got two gigs we've gotta do in America now [in] San Francisco.' And I said, 'Really? Where are you playing in San Francisco?' They said, 'The Fillmore.' I said, 'I've just come back from there with my old band, Canned Heat. You're gonna go down great.' In fact, I said, 'You're gonna go down so well that I'm gonna say good-bye right now. Y'all won't be backing me anymore. Y'all probably won't be coming back from America for a long time. That's how successful you're gonna be.' So they went over there and I never saw them again for 20 years."

While the exact dates of Proby's recollection might be off (Zeppelin wouldn't tour San Francisco until 1969), his point was well taken. Even at the early stage, it was clear and apparent to most that this band was going to be big. But something had to be done about the name. Everyone knew "the New Yardbirds" was awful. There are a number of stories about how "Led Zeppelin" came to be, but the one that seems to stick is a conversation that Page had with Who drummer Keith Moon. (That version is also referenced in an April 5, 1969, feature in *New Musical Express*.) When Page told Moon about his makeshift Yardbirds lineup, the Who's drummer dismissed it, saying the band would go over like a lead zeppelin. According to an old Robert Plant interview, the *a* was removed from *lead* so stupid Americans wouldn't mispronounce the group's moniker as "Leed Zeppelin."

> "Lead guitarist Jimmy Page has re-formed the Yardbirds with Robert Plant (vcls), John Paul Jones (bass gtr) and John Bonham (drs). In future Jimmy plans to produce the Yardbirds' discs himself and negotiations are currently going on for their release. The new Yardbirds' first British date will be at London's Marquee club on October 18. The group starts a six-week American tour on November 14."
> —*Melody Maker*, September 21, 1968

The band's impression on its home country would be mixed, however.

> "So Led Zeppelin are the next Cream. But in what sense? Best British blues-based group? Not while we have Keef Hartley, Jethro Tull and Taste."—David Walker to the *Melody Maker* mailbag, March 29, 1969

> "When Jimmy Page formed Led Zeppelin, he [said he] chose as his co-musicians the most talented available at the time. Would he please note that now there are better musicians available for regular work? Jack Bruce is a vocalist and harpist of far higher standard than Robert Plant and he's an infinitely superior bassist to John Paul Jones. Mitch Mitchell or Jim Capaldi could replace John Bonham on drums. Backed by Bruce, Mitchell or Capaldi, Page could realize his full potential."—Rick Ainsworth to the *Melody Maker* mailbag, September 6, 1969

> "Led Zeppelin don't do anything that is so revolutionary or new. They just do what the public want very well. They play heavy rock the best, and no arguing!"—Chris Welch, *Melody Maker*, October 18, 1969

By 1969, the band found the audiences in America were much more receptive than those at home, and that's where Led Zeppelin broke. "In America the audiences get into their music more," Jimmy Page told Nick Logan in the April 5, 1969, issue of *New Musical Express*. "They are more appreciative. They will listen to the sort of patterns you are playing. In Britain all they are interested in is the way to the bar."

Armed with powerful albums like *Led Zeppelin*, *Led Zeppelin II*, *Deep Purple in Rock*, and *Fire and Water*, Led Zeppelin, Deep Purple, and Free would lead London and the world into the 1970s. Those bands later were considered 1970s bands, even though they began life in the 1960s, but they just feel and *sound* like the 1970s. The 1960s were dead. These new bands were ready to take the mantle and lead London into the new decade and beyond.

EPILOGUE

"When the '60s came in, it was like a tiny little flower, like a spring crocus if you like, just poking its head through the soil."—Stan Webb, Chicken Shack

By the time the 1960s ended, London had brought so much to the musical table . . . it was staggering. If you closed your eyes at the dawn of 1963 and opened them again as 1969 waned, you wouldn't be able to process the absolute explosion of the creative muse. When has humanity had such an intense concentration of artistic expression? Perhaps never again will the forces of the universe converge on one town and give us an eternity of timeless art.

From the ignition of Liverpool's Beatles to London's Rolling Stones and the R&B boom through the various incarnations and explorations and mixing of American and European influences, the world has been gifted something precious for generations to come. And London was at the center of it all.

Everything just converged at this one point and place in time. Arguably, other cities were more important to the birth and development of rock 'n' roll—Memphis, New York, San Francisco, and Los Angeles, for example—but none of those towns contributed the embarrassment of riches London gave us.

Despite the Nazis' best efforts, London remained standing after the devastation of World War II. And because of that war, because of the generation that would grow up in its shadow, a new and a fantastic era would come to fruition. It took an unprecedented tragedy of the world's

bloodiest war to create the beauty that followed. When you place ugli-
ness against beauty, the ugly becomes more brutal and the pretty becomes more enchanting. Such was London's postwar musical contribution to the world. Its beauty so contrasted with the cruelty and evil of
the Nazi regime that it made London not only more beautiful but also
highlighted the joy of the era.

That unbridled joy—the ecstasy of living, of just living—is what
made postwar London so special. Those children—whose parents
served in the British military during the war, or died fighting the Germans, or perished in pubs from Nazi bombs or V-1 or V-2 rockets—
knew. They knew they had a special opportunity their parents never
had. And, boy, did they ever take advantage of it.

Whether they experienced American blues and started a band, à la
the Rolling Stones, or ventured down to London—as an underaged
Peter Noone did—and had drinks with John Lennon. Whether they
hung out with the Who's Keith Moon and watched him pour brandy
into the mouth of a ventriloquist dummy dressed as Hermann Göring
("Well, he likes a drink. You know what they're like, these Germans,"
Moon told perplexed observer Stan Webb from Chicken Shack) or
temporarily stole a bus with Webb and the Kinks' Mick Avory and Dave
Davies.

Or maybe they just made music. Like maybe they sliced an amplifier
speaker as the Kinks' Dave Davies did to get that muddy sound on "You
Really Got Me." Or maybe they showed up at Abbey Road Studios and
played John Lennon's Mellotron on their record, as the Zombies did
with *Odessey and Oracle*. Or perhaps they made a modest living at
England's folk clubs, then headed down to Les Cousins later to hang
out with Al Stewart or Paul Simon, staying all night and then having a
friendly neighbor make them breakfast before taking the Tube home.
Maybe they got swindled into playing a harpsichord on a single, like the
Yardbirds talked Brian Auger into doing. Perhaps they went big and
composed a piece for orchestral accompaniment, then played with the
Royal Philharmonic, like Jon Lord and Deep Purple did in 1969.

Speaking of Purple, maybe those kids made up a song on the spot
out of a loose jam with "Smoke on the Water" and Free did with "All
Right Now"; both tunes became classics.

The possibilities seemed limitless. Once the shackles were broken,
by say 1964, anything was possible. Anything.

And audiences were open to it all. That's what made it work. Unlike in today's world, where no one would think of promoting a warm-up act in a different genre than the headliner, in 1960s London audiences possessed no such hang-ups. They'd go out on a routine night in 1968 to catch a Saturday show at the Middle Earth featuring the newly formed Led Zeppelin, John Lee Hooker, and the Deviants. Then the next Saturday they'd catch the Who, Arthur Brown, the Small Faces, and Joe Cocker. Maybe the vaudevillian Bonzo Dog Band might show up on a bill with psychedelic Pink Floyd. Or Zeppelin might have a show with the acoustic folk/blues Pentangle. It didn't matter. It was all good.

It was like a ride, literally, London of the 1960s. It ebbed and flowed between blues (OK, R&B, whatever, Brits . . . it's just blues as Sonny Boy Williamson said), folk, folk/rock, psychedelia, conceptual album–based rock, progressive rock, theatrical rock, and back to the blues again. You rode London back then like you rode the Tube, experiencing something completely different at each stop.

And the people. Oh, the people. There was Pete Townshend smashing his guitars during performances and then throwing sandwiches at reporters' heads afterward. There was Keith Moon. Freaking Keith Moon. One interviewee described him as "certifiable." Keith could be sweet but reckless as hell. And a force. He could outplay you on drums and outdrink you in the pubs. Jimi Hendrix showed up in 1966 and quickly won over the town with his musical gifts and his soft-spoken demeanor. Unlike your typical super-dominant male lead guitar player, Hendrix was an absolute sweetheart. Shy, even.

Eric Clapton somehow formed a band with the two outsized personalities of Jack Bruce and Ginger Baker. And Baker would proceed to make Cream swing while intimidating the hell out of everyone else.

Incredibly gifted musicians popped up like Clapton, Yes's Steve Howe, and Led Zeppelin's Jimmy Page. A young Peter Frampton made a dent in the world, years before *Frampton Comes Alive*, with his eclectic Humble Pie, along with ex–Small Faces bandmember Steve Marriott. Massive guitar talents like Bert Jansch and John Renbourn combined their gifts in the acoustically masterful Pentangle. The classically trained, outrageous showman Keith Emerson demonstrated how it's done with the Nice. And a then scraggly haired, maniacal singer named Ian Anderson added a flute to the repertoire in Jethro Tull.

And then there were the bands.

Led Zeppelin formed by accident. Think about that for a moment. One of the biggest bands the world has ever seen came about by happenstance. If not for all of the Yardbirds, save Jimmy Page, quitting mid-tour, Zeppelin never would have happened.

And what about the Who? The Beatles dominated the world for sure, but the Who led London for most of the decade (and the world along with it). Pete Townshend, Roger Daltrey, and company elevated raunchy blues-based rock music into a conceptual form and did so in perhaps the most violent way possible.

Sublimely gifted guitarist Peter Green gave us Fleetwood Mac and a whole new way to interpret the blues. Little did he know his band would be taken in many different directions on the way to the pop-oriented mega-version of Mac in the mid-1970s.

The Davies brothers essentially gave us punk rock with the Kinks and "You Really Got Me." Then Ray Davies got in touch with his British roots to tell us stories about Arthur and village greens gone long ago.

Arthur Brown created what we now know as shock rock by blackening his teeth and literally wearing a ring of fire.

The Bonzo Dog Band showed us that we could maintain a sense of humor through it all, eventually gifting us the beloved *Monty Python's Flying Circus*.

The Pink Floyd added their own theatrical element, with then elaborate light shows fueled by acid and the exploration of the beyond.

Then there were the supporting players who made it all happen. Jazz trombonist Chris Barber brought Muddy Waters and Sister Rosetta Tharpe to the United Kingdom, recorded the first skiffle single with Lonnie Donegan, and opened the Marquee club where everyone played. *Melody Maker* photographer Barrie Wentzell covered it all, providing classic shots of everyone from Jethro Tull to a visiting Diana Ross. Reporters like *Melody Maker*'s Chris Welch and Royston Eldridge and *New Musical Express*'s Keith Altham told us all about what was going on.

The pirate radio stations, at least until the BBC closed them down in 1967, exposed millions of British kids to rock, blues, jazz, and everything in between. Radio Caroline DJs like Keith Skues and Tony Blackburn made sure the kids got the proper exposure to the music ignored by the BBC.

The Marshall Amplification Company, which started out of a small drum shop in the West End, changed the sound and, literally, the face of rock 'n' roll. Father and son Jim and Terry Marshall, along with a small team of engineers, created the British sound of blues and rock.

Perhaps more than any British player, an American musician can provide us with a proper perspective. Geno Washington, an African American born in Indiana, found himself stationed in the US Air Force in England from 1961 to 1965. Assigned to a base near London, the young Washington frequented the town. Even though he had no background as a musician, he tried his hand at singing in various clubs, particularly the Marquee and Flamingo. "I'd hang around in both [clubs] because I knew the guys: Clapton, and Ginger Baker and Jack Bruce from Cream. I knew all those guys before they became famous," Washington said.

Washington was present in 1963–1964 when the London scene flipped from trad jazz to R&B. "When they moved to the R&B thing," Washington said, "well my family owned a juke joint. I already heard those records, but you got groups going around doing that shit, so I said, 'Hey, why not me? I'm black and I'm a real American. Why not me try this shit?' I never sung in my life, but I could always talk shit and I was a great dancer."

To pursue this new direction, Washington headed down to London clubs where sometimes American GIs would get up onstage to sing. To get onstage, Washington would spin a tale when asked if he could carry a tune. "I said, 'Sing?! My auntie is Dinah Washington and my sister is in Martha and the Vandellas,'" Washington recalled. "They said, 'All right. We know you're a bad motherfucker' [laughs]. So they would let me sing. And I'd use that lie. I'm lyin' out of my ass. So I go down to this club, the Flamingo. That's where I'd meet Eric Clapton, Jack Bruce, and Georgie Fame. I'd meet them all down there. They would let me get up and sing two numbers with them.

"I started out singing with Rod Stewart, Long John Baldry, Georgie Fame, the Animals."

Like Jimi Hendrix, Washington soon found out he was treated significantly better in England than the United States as a black American. As a result, he stayed in London after his 1965 air force discharge and soon formed a soul group called the Ram Jam Band. "We had to find a name for the band. On a main road in England back in the day called the A1, there was a garage and a restaurant. And the garage was called the Ram Jam Garage and the restaurant was called the Ram Jam Inn. We thought it was a silly name. We was laughing because we was thinking, 'What if the guy who works in the Ram Jam Garage is serving you steaks when you eat in the Ram Jam [Inn]?'" [laughs].

Washington met his future wife at London's Bag O'Nails club, the same place where Paul McCartney first encountered Linda Eastman. Washington's wife just happened to have a sister who was married to Peter Noone of Herman's Hermits, so Washington and Noone became brothers-in-law as well as lifelong friends.

Geno Washington and the Ram Jam Band would become an integral part of London's music scene through the Mod years, the psychedelic era, and beyond. Washington's group would share the stage with some of London's biggest bands, most notably at the Barbeque '67 festival along with Cream, Jimi Hendrix, Zoot Money, the Pink Floyd, and the Move.

Perhaps Washington's penultimate experience reflects London's vibrancy in the 1960s, not to mention his own popularity. During a music festival attended by about 5,000 people, the Ram Jam Band pulled up nondescriptly in a van. The Small Faces were onstage, entrancing the crowd. That all changed once Washington exited the vehicle. Instantly the crowd stopped paying attention to the band and began chanting, "Geno! Geno! Geno!" "We had no control, you know what I mean?" said Washington. "The place is packed. People are so glad to see us. They're going crazy. [They] picked me up, put me on their neck and shit, split my pants, took me up to the stage, put me on the stage while the Small Faces are doing their show. They're actually doing their show, trying to get into a groove. You got a big crowd [of people carrying me], at least about 25, rolling me to the stage, 'Get out of the way! Get out of the way!' and put me on the stage. Steve Marriott was so pissed off. He said, 'If you want [him], you can have him!'" [laughs].

And that was London in the 1960s. Anything could happen, and it did. And we're all the better for it.

NOTES

1. OUT OF THE GRAY AND INTO THE BLUES

1. The proper pronunciation of Davies, a common Welsh surname, is "Davis." Welsh musicians like Cyril Davies and Spencer Davies (no relation) were persuaded to change the spelling of their last names to the English "Davis" to avoid mispronunciation. Others, like the Kinks' Ray and Dave Davies, kept the original spelling.

2. Note to Americans: the pronunciation is "Twickenim," not "Twicken-HAM."

2. R&B BOOM!

1. Pronounced "lester."

2. Despite that image, the reality of the Beatles and Stones was quite the opposite. The Beatles, hailing from a rough port town of Liverpool and cutting their musical teeth in the rough port town of Hamburg, Germany, were the true bad boys. "The hard men of rock 'n' roll were the Beatles," Noone observed. "They were the ones who you didn't want to fuck with. The Stones were easy."

3. Beck would replace Eric Clapton as lead guitarist in 1965 (as recounted near the end of this chapter).

3. IT WAS JUST BLOODY WEDNESDAY

1. According to Kenney Jones's autobiography, *Let the Good Times Roll*, the name came from a friend of Marriott's called Annabelle. Annabelle commented that, since the players were physically small and had little faces, they should be called the "Small Faces." Regardless, the name fit the band members' stature and status perfectly.

5. YOU CAN ALL JOIN IN
(PROGRESSIVE FOLK)

1. According to Iain Matthews, "I didn't really have an audition, per se. We set up a meeting at a recording studio, a place called Sound Techniques in Chelsea. I walked into the meeting with my suitcase in one hand and about a dozen LPs under the other arm. The first thing they wanted to look at were my LPs. I think that stack of records got me the job in Fairport more than my vocal abilities."

2. Per Jacqui McShee: "John, Bert and myself along with a drummer and bass player I can't remember started rehearsing during 1966. It didn't quite work out. John had already established that the band would be called Pentangle. It wasn't until January 1967 that we started rehearsing with Danny Thompson (upright bass) and Terry Cox (drums) at the Horseshoe Pub in Tottenham Court Road on Sunday afternoons to then perform in the evening. Therefore, to be absolutely correct, you can say that the idea of the band began in 1966 but didn't perform with the final lineup till 1967."

3. The cottage still exists, and apparently someone lives there. He says he doesn't care if people take pictures of the house, but it annoys him to no end when obnoxious tourists invite themselves in to take interior shots.

LIST OF SOURCES

INTRODUCTION

Interviews

Peter Frampton, Greg Lake

Book

Daltrey, Roger. *Thanks a Lot Mr. Kibblewhite: My Story*. New York: Henry Holt, 2018.

Other

Led Zeppelin interview by David Letterman, *Late Show with David Letterman*, December 3, 2012, https://www.youtube.com/watch?v=huztn5XHKO8.

CHAPTER 1

Interviews

Keith Altham, Ian Anderson, Rod Argent, Chris Barber, Arthur Brown, Bill Bruford, Mike Cotton, Spencer Davis, Ramblin' Jack

Elliott, Ray Everitt, Peter Frampton, Roger Glover, Steve Howe, Paul Jones, Wizz Jones, Terry Marshall, John Mayall, Jim McCarty, Ian McLagan, Mike Murphy, Mike Pinder, Jan Roberts, Hylda Sims, David Snelling, John Steel, Top Topham, Hilton Valentine, Rick Wakeman, Barrie Wentzell

Periodicals

Melody Maker, *New Musical Express*, *Record Mirror*

Books

Barber, Chris, with Alyn Shipton. *Jazz Me Blues: The Autobiography of Chris Barber*. Sheffield, South Yorkshire: Equinox Publishing, 2014.

Pointon, Mike, and Ray Smith. *Goin' Home: The Uncompromising Life and Music of Ken Colyer*. Great Britain: Ken Colyer Trust, 2010.

Richards, Keith, with James Fox. *Life*. New York: Back Bay Books / Little, Brown, 2010.

Stewart, Rod. *Rod: The Autobiography*. New York: Crown Archetype, 2012.

Van Der Vat, Dan, and Michele Whitby. *Eel Pie Island*. London: Frances Lincoln, 2009.

Websites

AllMusic.com; ChrisBarber.net; CyrilDavies.com; Discogs.com; Ealingclub.com; Eelpieislandmusic.com; Eelpiemuseum.co.uk; TheBeatles.com

Other

Giorgio Gomelsky interviewed by Joly MacFie, 2009, https://www.youtube.com/watch?v=DLwPcNVhinI; Hylda Sims's *On That Train and Gone: The Fifties* (unpublished work).

CHAPTER 2

Interviews

Rod Argent, Brian Auger, Chris Barber, Mike Cotton, Dave Davies, Spencer Davis, Peter Frape, Colin Green, Mike Hugg, Paul Jones, Greg Lake, Manfred Mann, Jim McCarty, Zoot Money, Mike Murphy, Peter Noone, Tony Norman, P. J. Proby, Keith Skues, John Steel, Dick Taylor, Top Topham, Hilton Valentine

Periodicals

Melody Maker, *New Musical Express*, *Record Mirror*

Books

Clapton, Eric. *Clapton: The Autobiography*. New York: Broadway Books, 2007.

Miles, Barry. *London Calling: A Countercultural History of London since 1945*. London: Atlantic Books, 2010.

Oldham, Andrew Loog. *Rolling Stoned*. Vancouver: Because Entertainment, 2013.

Richards, Keith, with James Fox. *Life*. New York: Back Bay Books / Little, Brown, 2010.

Websites

Allmusic.com; BBC.com/culture/story/20140515-when-two-tribes-went-to-war; offringfa.nl/radioluxembourg.htm; Offshoreradio.co.uk; RadioCaroline.co.uk; RadioLondon.co.uk; Radiosoundsfamiliar.com; Rockhall.com; Sixtiescity.net

Other

The Beatles Anthology (DVD), directed by Bob Smeaton, Geoff Wonfor, and Kevin Godley, released 2003; John Steel diary; John

Steel letter; *Quadrophenia* film by the Who, directed by Franc Roddam, released 1979.

CHAPTER 3

Interviews

Barry Allchin, Keith Altham, Ian A. Anderson, J. P. Bean, Joe Boyd, Dave Cousins, Terry Cox, Dave Davies, Kenney Jones, Manfred Mann, Terry Marshall, Jim McCarty, Ian McLagan, Jacqui McShee, Mike Rivers, Peggy Seeger, John Steel, Al Stewart, Mick Underwood, Stan Webb, Barrie Wentzell

Periodicals

Melody Maker, *New Musical Express*, *Record Mirror*

Books

Bean, J. P. *Singing from the Floor: A History of British Folk Clubs*. London: Faber & Faber, 2014.

Cousins, Dave. *Exorcising Ghosts: Strawbs and Other Lives*. Kent, UK: Witchwood Media, 2014.

Jones, Kenney. *Let the Good Times Roll: My Life in Small Faces, Faces, and the Who*. New York: Thomas Dunne Books, 2018.

McLagan, Ian. *All the Rage: My High Life with Small Faces, Faces, the Rolling Stones and Many More*. London: Pan Books, 2013.

Townshend, Pete. *Who I Am*. New York: HarperCollins, 2012.

Websites

guitar-bass.net/features/marshall-amp-history; Ianaanderson.com/les-cousins; jimmarshall.co.uk/biography; marshall.com; MickUnderwood.com; Modyourspace.com; TheWho.com

CHAPTER 4

Interviews

John Alder aka Twink, Ian Anderson, Jon Anderson, Rod Argent, Arthur Brown, Bill Bruford, Judy Dyble, Roger Glover, Steve Howe, Neil Innes, Greg Lake, Phil May, David O'List, Peter Noone, Carl Palmer, Mike Pinder, Dick Taylor

Periodicals

Evening Standard, Melody Maker, New Musical Express, Record Mirror

Books

Jones, Kenney. *Let the Good Times Roll: My Life in Small Faces, Faces, and the Who*. New York: Thomas Dunne Books, 2018.
McLagan, Ian. *All the Rage: My High Life with Small Faces, Faces, the Rolling Stones and Many More*. London: Pan Books, 2013.

Websites

AllMusic.com; CarlPalmer.com; JethroTull.com; MikePinder.com; PinkFloyd.com; TheWho.com; Ultimateclassicrock.com

Other

Deep Purple in concert with the Royal Philharmonic Orchestra, 1969, https://www.youtube.com/watch?v=gnA1IMnLZr4.

CHAPTER 5

Interviews

Ian Anderson, Martin Barre, Joe Boyd, Dave Cousins, Terry Cox, Spencer Davis, Judy Dyble, Dave Mason, Iain Matthews, Jacqui McShee, Simon Nicol, Richard Thompson, Rick Wakeman

Periodicals

Melody Maker, *New Musical Express*, *Rolling Stone*

Book

Cousins, Dave. *Exorcising Ghosts*. Kent: Witchwood Media, 2014.

Websites

AllMusic.com; FairportConvention.com; JohnRenbourn.co.uk

CHAPTER 6

Interviews

Judy Dyble, Peter Frampton, Andy Fraser, Roger Glover, Simon Kirke, Greg Lake, Jim McCarty, Tony McPhee, Peter Noone, P. J. Proby, Paul Rodgers, Jeremy Spencer

Periodicals

Guardian, *Melody Maker*, *New Musical Express*, *Record Mirror*

Books

Cross, Charles R. *Room Full of Mirrors: A Biography of Jimi Hendrix*. New York: Hyperion, 2005.

Fleetwood, Mick, with Stephen Davis. *Fleetwood: My Life and Adventures in Fleetwood Mac*. New York: William Morrow, 1990.

Hanson, Martyn. *Hoggin' the Page: Groundhogs, the Classic Years*. Bordon, Hants: Northdown, 2005.

Richards, Keith, with Richard Fox. *Life*. New York: Back Bay Books / Little, Brown, 2010.

Websites

AllMusic.com; AndyFraser.com; AZlyrics.com; Discogs.com; JeremySpencer.com; LedZeppelin.com; Rockhall.com; SimonKirkeofficial.com; ukblues.org

Other

Ritchie Blackmore interview, 2007, https://www.youtube.com/watch?v=YzJJgSls5-U; Eric Clapton interview, *Standing at the Crossroads*, TLC special, aired 1999, https://www.youtube.com/watch?v=yYLRXo6dMa4; Mick Fleetwood interview conducted by Anthony DeCurtis, 2017, https://www.youtube.com/watch?v=8WCnszn4zTU.

EPILOGUE

Interviews

Geno Washington, Stan Webb

Other

Ram Jam Band drummer Herb Prestidge interview, https://www.youtube.com/watch?v=cvX115kR8VI.

INDEX

outside of the blues, 100–101; Jethro Tull, 153–155; King Crimson, 130–131, 132; Move, 116–118; New Vaudeville Band, 127–128; Nice, 120–124, 126–123; Pentangle, 148–152; Pink Floyd, 115–116; presentation productions, 110–112, 113; Pretty Things, 104–105; psychedelia, 112–119, 120; rock music arriving from, 137–138; *Sgt. Pepper's Lonely Hearts Club Band*, 98–99; Spencer Davis Group, 152–153; *Tommy*, 108–109; Traffic, 152–153; Underground bands, 114–115; various paths to, 99–100; Who and, 81–82; Yes, 131–132; Zombies, 119–120. *See also* folk club scene
psychedelia, 112–119, 120, 163–164

Quay, Russell, 6–7
A Quick One, 81–82
"A Quick One While He's Away," 98

radio stations, 188; Radio Caroline, 54–55, 56; Radio London, 55; Radio Luxembourg, 20, 34, 56
Ram Jam Band, 189–190
Ready Steady Go! television show, 56–58
Really the Blues (Mezzrow), 2
Redding, Noel, 158
Relf, Keith, 38, 39, 180
Renbourn, John, 147, 149–151
Rhodes, Emitt, 141
rhythm and blues: Animals, 41–46; crossroads in 1965, 61–63; debate about, 52–54; Mod movement and, 58–61; Pretty Things, 47–48; radio stations broadcasting, 54–55; *Ready Steady Go!* television show, 56–58; Rockers, 60–61; Spencer Davis Group, 48; Williamson, Sonny Boy, 49–52; Yardbirds, 37–41, 50; Zoot Money, 47. *See also* blues; Rolling Stones
Rich, Buddy, xv, 125, 135, 176
Richards, Keith, 12, 20, 27–28, 31, 35, 53, 163–164
Ridley, Greg, 169–170
Roberts, Chris, 58
Roberts, Jan, 12, 22

Rockers, 60–61
"Rock Island Line," 4–5
rock operas, 105, 106. *See also specific rock operas*
Rod (Stewart), 13
Rodgers, Paul, 165, 172–175
Rolling Stones: Beatles and, 35–37; early accessibility of, 11–12; finding rhythm section, 28–31; "(I Can't Get No) Satisfaction," 77–78; R&B and, 26–32; on *Ready Steady Go!* television show, 57; rejection of psychedelia, 163–164; sitar used by, 80; as support band, 26; writing pop songs, 61; Yardbirds compared to, 37–39. *See also* Jagger, Mick; Richards, Keith
Roundhouse club, 114–115, 116, 117, 174
Rowland, Steve, 181
Royal Philharmonic Orchestra, 132, 135

S. F. Sorrow, 106
Samwell-Smith, Paul, 38, 41
Scrugg, Earl, 88
Secunda, Tony, 117, 118
Seeger, Peggy, 84–85, 149
Sgt. Pepper's Lonely Hearts Club Band, 81, 98–99, 103
"She's Not There," 46
Shirley, Jerry, 169–170
Sims, Hylda, 6–7
Singing from the Floor (Bean), 83
sitars, 78–79, 80
skiffle, 3–7
Slater, Rodney, 127
Small Faces, 72–75, 107–108, 169–170
Smith, Norman, 105
"Smoke on the Water," 177–179
Snelling, David, 11–12, 16
"Song of a Sad Little Girl," 146
Spencer, Jeremy, 165–166
Spencer Davis Group, 48, 152–153
Stamp, Chris, 68
Stanshall, Vivian, 129
Starr, Ringo, 34
Steam Packet, 148
Steel, John, 11, 14, 18, 22, 41–43, 51
Stevens, Geoff, 127
Stewart, Al, 85, 87, 139
Stewart, Ian, 28

ABOUT THE AUTHOR

Stephen Tow is a rock 'n' roll historian and has been teaching popular music history and general American history at Delaware Valley University since 1999. His classes have featured guest speakers such as Yes's Steve Howe, Jethro Tull's Ian Anderson, Nirvana's Chad Channing, the Go-Go's' Kathy Valentine, the Kinks' Dave Davies, the Byrds' Roger McGuinn, the Patti Smith Group's Lenny Kaye, and Blind Melon's Rogers Stevens. Stephen is the author of *The Strangest Tribe: How a Group of Seattle Rock Bands Invented Grunge*. An avid guitar player, he evaluates his playing by saying, "People who don't know anything about guitar think I'm good." He lives near Philadelphia with his wife, daughter, and two dogs.